Exquisite Rebel

Voltairine de Cleyre, Philadelphia, 1901.

Exquisite Rebel

The Essays of Voltairine de Cleyre—
Feminist, Anarchist, Genius

Voltairine de Cleyre

Sharon Presley and Crispin Sartwell, editors

State University of New York Press

Published by
State University of New York Press, Albany

Printed in the United States of America

For information, address State University of New York Press,
90 State Street, Suite 700, Albany, NY 12207

Production by Michael Haggett
Marketing by Michael Campochiaro

Library of Congress Cataloging-in-Publication Data

De Cleyre, Voltairine, 1866–1912.
    Exquisite rebel : essays of Voltairine de Cleyre : American feminist,
anarchist, genius / Voltairine de Cleyre ; Sharon Presley and Crispin
Sartwell, editors.
        p. cm.
    Includes bibliographical references and index.
    ISBN 0-7914-6093-2 (alk. paper) — ISBN 0-7914-6094-0
(pbk. : alk. paper)
        1. Anarchism—United States. 2. Feminism—United States.
    3. De Cleyre, Voltairine, 1866–1912—Criticism and interpretation.
    I. Presley, Sharon. II. Sartwell, Crispin, 1958– III. Title.

HX843.D43 2005
335'.83'092—dc22   2004059138

10 9 8 7 6 5 4 3 2 1

Crispin Sartwell dedicates his work on this volume to his daughters Emma and Jane. May they live freely.

Sharon Presley dedicates her work on this volume to the memories of her mother Geneva Presley and her friend Arlen Riley Wilson, each remarkable women in their own way.

Voltairine de Cleyre, Chicago, 1910.

Contents

Foreword

The winds of turmoil and labor strife that ushered in twentieth century America were countered by extraordinary visionaries—women and men for whom the concept of complete freedom held the alluring promise of social harmony. Anarchism, a philosophy often considered on the outermost edge of possibility and conflated with chaos, attracted many remarkably eloquent and lucid thinkers. Voltairine de Cleyre (1866–1912), recognized in her circles as "the most thoughtful woman anarchist of this century,"[1] on a par with Emma Goldman, her more florid Russian immigrant counterpart, has yet to be given an appropriate place in the permanent record. A long standing prejudice among American historians against a serious study of anarchism, combined with a frequent dismissal of women as an intellectual and political force consigned de Cleyre's legacy almost exclusively under the guardianship of subsequent generations of anarchist followers, with few 'non-believers' among them. This, coupled with her untimely death at the age of forty-five, obscured her memory and threatened to diminish her importance. According to Paul Avrich, de Cleyre's dazzling biographer, traces of the life and work of one of "the movement's most respected and devoted representatives" left "the glow of legend"—"a brief comet in the anarchist firmament."

The publication of this new volume of Voltairine de Cleyre's selected writings allows for the permanent historical record to stand corrected with an elegance and clarity fitting to its subject. The editors, Sharon Presley and Crispin Sartwell, chose representative essays that track the development of de Cleyre's thought against a backdrop of ideas central to anarchist theorists and activists. Set in an anarchist frame, the collection offers the reader an opportunity to sample and engage in the flavor and content of debates on a variety of issues including the political equality of women, the economy, the social order, violence, religion, criminal justice, education, and aesthetics—tracking the emergence of de Cleyre's ideas as they were influenced by the works of others. Pieced together, her writings and accompanying introductory notes present bold patterns and surprising tangents to the broad, vibrant social and intellectual fabric of her time.

Exquisite Rebel: The Essays of Voltairine de Cleyre—Feminist, Anarchist, Genius, is in itself an exquisite contribution.

De Cleyre, who considered herself "more of a lecturer than an orator, and more of a writer than either"[2] left coherent tracks explaining her understanding of and attraction to anarchism, the reasons for her skepticism about religion and enthusiasm for the free thought movement, a philosophical analysis of the link between internal and external forces, between emotion and reason especially with regard to the habits of mind and accompanying behavior toward women and of women themselves. Practical templates for modern educational and criminal reform, critical pleas for the defense of imprisoned cohorts, and commentary on the controversies within the anarchist movement of her day, ground her more philosophical writings in contemporary action. Dubbed the "rebel-poet" by Emma Goldman, de Cleyre's thrust to channel her emphatic concerns into a poetic cadence considered artful in her day, extended into an analysis of literary forms and particulars. Scientific, methodical, heartfelt and earnest—Voltairine de Cleyre's singular devotion to anarchism—"the Dominant Idea"—is woven throughout the intriguing and classic selections of *Exquisite Rebel.*

Not surprisingly, because Voltairine de Cleyre had few women contemporaries of her stature in the anarchist movement who combined her attributes as a thinker, writer, and lecturer, other than Emma Goldman; thus, they were, and continue to be, compared to each other. In spite of the underlying sexism of such an exercise, evident when one examines the manner in which male contemporaries are compared and contrasted—most often with relation to their ideas, rather than their earnestness to the cause or levels of physical attractiveness (which in the case of de Cleyre and Goldman often displayed less about aesthetic sensibility and more about stereotypical ethnic prejudice), it is nonetheless an entwinement important to unravel. Both were profoundly influenced by the works of European anarchists, but found threads of anarchist impulses and ideology woven through America's history and embodied in the ideology of the nation's founders who spurned tyranny and nurtured the spirit of individualism and cooperation. Yet, the relationship between the American anarchist Voltairine de Cleyre who spent more of her time devoted to the education and welfare of Eastern European Jews than the Russian-Jewish immigrant Emma Goldman ever did, was constantly scrutinized. For a movement that heralded independence and freedom of the spirit, the two women were locked in a strangle hold alternatively of competition and of caring, of withdrawal and of staunch support for each others efforts. Temperamentally and culturally worlds apart, they were united by their unwavering devotion to the cause of anarchism, and a forced accountability to each other as the designated women of stature. United also by shared horrors of the so-called "Gilded Age" and lingering persecution for their beliefs, they wrote for and about each other—often with great eloquence, and sometimes in a template of projected distortions. The light and the shadows of their lives flicker and intertwine. Goldman the outgoing, de Cleyre the introvert, each channeled inner darkness with an exquisite ability to perceive and articulate injustice and to move people toward the light of anarchism as the embodiment of freedom and harmony.

In the mid-1890s, Voltairine de Cleyre reached out to Alexander Berkman, anarchist theorist, organizer, and close comrade of Emma Goldman while he was in jail serving time for his attempted assassination of Henry Clay Frick, the man he held accountable for the shooting of striking workers at Carnegie Steel Plant in Homestead, Pennsylvania. She cheered him on in his darkest moments, linking her experience as one who also fought the demons of suicidal thoughts, urging him to believe that the feelings would pass and that he still had so much to give to the anarchist cause. Several years after his release, she continued to help him expunge that harrowing time from his mind by editing his book of *Prison Memoirs*. Then in 1914, two years after her death, Berkman was moved to return the favor, and edited and published a commemorative edition of *The Selected Works of Voltairine de Cleyre*, a volume of over four-hundred pages of poetry, essays, sketches, and short stories—described as "an arsenal of knowledge for the student and soldier of freedom." Now, ninety years later, a new mix of documents—primarily political in nature—spanning de Cleyre's life and work, enhanced by biographical and analytical essays, is a welcome and important addition to the study of the intellectual and social history of political movements, especially in America. De Cleyre, who championed anarchism without adjectives, hoping to minimize the factional barriers to unity even in her own political ranks, left a written legacy and a practical challenge. This fine volume offers the next wave of interested scholars and activists an opportunity to contemplate the pitfalls and the promise of the ideas of a nearly forgotten luminary, one of a small circle of visionary thinkers whose ideas can now gracefully ripple into the next century.

Candace Falk
Editor/Director, The Emma Goldman Papers Project

Notes

1. See Sharon Presley, introduction, re: Marcus Graham, editor of the anarchist journal *Man!*

2. Voltairine de Cleyre, autobiographical sketch, Wess Papers. From Paul Avrich, *An American Anarchist: The Life of Voltairine de Cleyre*, p. 41.

Acknowledgments

This book is the result of two different projects that were merged together in 2002. It blends two visions into one whole—to better present Voltairine de Cleyre in all her complexity, richness, and passion. For each of us it was a labor of love and admiration. We each wish to acknowledge those who helped make this tribute possible.

I (Crispin) gratefully acknowledge Bob Helms, for sharing his knowledge of Voltairine de Cleyre and for discovering the essay "The Political Equality of Women"; Elisa Gurule and Julie Herrada for research at the Labadie Collection at the University of Michigan, which turned up some new material; and Lynn Gorchov and Marion Winik for reading the biographical essay and commenting on it. Anyone working on Voltairine is indebted to the work of her biographer Paul Avrich.

I (Sharon) most of all want to thank the person who inspired me to begin working on an anthology of Voltairine, my old friend Geoff T. Not only did he urge me to do this project, he did much of the research tracking down and copying obscure articles of hers that were not in the *Selected Works of Voltairine de Cleyre*. His editing suggestions for the biographical essay and outline were invaluable. The name of the person who long ago donated an original 1914 copy of the *Selected Works of Voltairine de Cleyre* to the Association of Libertarian Feminists has been lost but I hope he reads this and knows how grateful we are to him. The essay on Voltairine by Emma Goldman I used was an exquisite original 1932 volume from Oriole Press that came from Laurance Labadie's library via his grandniece, Carlotta Anderson.

Others who sent me useful material about Voltairine include Bob Helms, Chris Dodge, Julie Herrada (Curator of the Labadie Collection at the University of Michigan), and Annie Laurie Gaylor of the Freedom From Religion Foundation. A copy of the article, "Secular Education," was provided by Geraldine Strey of the State Historical Society of Wisconsin. Candace Falk, of the Emma Goldman Papers at the University of California, Berkeley, allowed me to copy the letter written by Voltairine's son, Harry de Cleyre, commenting on the essay written about his mother by Goldman.

The book of Voltairine's poetry, *Written in Red*, with the beautiful essay by Franklin Rosemont that I quote was donated to the Association of Libertarian Feminists by Left Bank Books of Seattle.

Others who encouraged me and gave useful advice include Paul Avrich, Frank Brooks, Susan Love Brown, Morgan and Shoshana Edwards, Robert Kephart, Andrea Millen Rich, Art Smith, Sidney Solomon and Joan Kennedy Taylor. Natasha Shebeko heroically helped me proofread the galleys. The Roy Childs Fund for Independent Scholars provided a grant that allowed me to devote time to the writing of the essays on which the ones that accompany this book are based.

Harry de Cleyre.

Voltairine de Cleyre's tombstone, Waldheim Cemetery, Chicago.
Photo courtesy of Chris Dodge.

Part I

Biographical Essays

Three Views of Voltairine de Cleyre

Priestess of Pity and Vengeance

CRISPIN SARTWELL

If Joan of Arc were to be reincarnated as an American atheist, she would be Voltairine de Cleyre. De Cleyre is an almost forgotten figure, but she committed her life to a vision of human liberation, a vision which encompassed even the man who tried to kill her. She was an incandescent writer and an original thinker, though she also lived much of her life in despair to the point of suicide.

De Cleyre and Emma Goldman in their own time were often mentioned in the same breath as the two great women of American anarchism. They had much in common. Both were celebrated speakers and writers. Both mounted scathing critiques of sexual oppression and the institution of marriage. They were active in the same circles and on the same issues, though de Cleyre was centered in Philadelphia, Goldman in New York.

But Goldman and de Cleyre were opposite poles of the same world. Where Goldman was a communist anarchist, de Cleyre was an individualist, at least early in her career. Where Goldman was an immigrant, de Cleyre grew up in rural Michigan. Where Goldman drew on the work of European thinkers such as Kropotkin and Bakunin, de Cleyre associated her thought with Americans such as Paine, Jefferson, Emerson, and the individualist writer Benjamin Tucker. Where Goldman was given to the free expression of desire, de Cleyre spent much of her youth in a nunnery and even after she rejected organized religion she remained quite a severe ascetic. And where Goldman was almost pathologically social, de Cleyre was fundamentally solitary.

They knew each other and admired each other from the soapbox and in print, though their relationship was not untainted by rivalry. Each thought the other ugly, and said so. Goldman wrote that "physical beauty and feminine attraction were withheld from her, their lack made more apparent by ill-health and her abhorrence of artifice." This is rather an odd assessment since many of her contemporaries described Voltai (as she was known to friends and family) as pretty, a view that is borne out by pictures.

De Cleyre for her part called Emma a "fishwife," accused her of "billings-gate" (talking abusively) (*Avrich, p.135*) and thought her vulgar and deca-dent. They hated each other's lovers as well; De Cleyre despised Emma's notorious Ben Reitman, probably in part because of his continual sexual advances toward her and anyone else who got within range. And de Cleyre's lover Samuel Gordon was a follower of Johann Most and supported him in his condemnation of Emma's friend and associate Alexander Berkman's shooting and stabbing of the industrialist Henry Clay Frick. When Most repudiated Berkman, Emma horsewhipped Most in public, and you will understand why she refused to allow de Cleyre to visit her in jail if she brought Gordon.

But they also grudgingly admired and publicly defended one another. In 1894, Emma was arrested for telling a crowd "Ask for work; if they do not give you work ask for bread; if they do not give you bread then take bread." De Cleyre delivered a speech in her defense which is one of the most astonishing documents in American letters. And after de Cleyre's death in 1912, Emma published an extremely moving eulogy in *Mother Earth,* which, though it contains the quoted observations about Voltai's appearance, is full also of praise for her work and her personality.

Life

Voltairine de Cleyre was born in Leslie, Michigan on 17 November 1866. Her mother's father had been an active abolitionist. She was named by her father, who was a "freethinker" (i.e., an atheist) after Voltaire. The family was very poor and through most of Voltai's girlhood the de Claires (later Voltai changed the spelling of her name for unknown reasons) barely subsisted. Her sister Addie said that at Christmas, "We wanted, as all children do, to give our parents and each other something, but spending money was an unknown quantity with us." She recalls that one year Voltai made a little box for her mother and a case for Addie's crochet-hook out of cardboard (*A, p. 21*).

Paul Avrich, the great chronicler of American anarchism, wrote in his biography, *An American Anarchist*, that "Voltairine de Cleyre grew up to be an intelligent and pretty child, with long brown hair, blue eyes, and inter-esting, unusual features. She had a passionate love of nature and animals. But, already displaying the qualities that were to trouble her personal rela-tions in later life, she was headstrong and emotional. She was 'a very way-ward girl,' says Addie, 'often very rude to those who loved her best.' Her eyes could be warm or 'cold as ice.' When only four, her 'indignation was boundless' when she was refused admission to the primary school in St. Johns because she was under age.' She had already taught herself to read, says Addie, 'and could read a newspaper at four!' " (*A, p. 24*). She was admitted to the school the next year and continued until she was twelve.

Possibly because he could not afford to keep her and possibly because he was returning to his lapsed Catholicism, her father placed her in the Convent of Our Lady of Port Huron in Ontario when she was thirteen. She was there, omitting escape attempts, from September 1880 to December 1883. Though she received a decent education, particularly in music (which she loved and taught her whole life) and though she grew close to some of the nuns, it is obvious that her experience in the convent was part of her journey toward extreme anti-authoritarianism. But as well as rebelling against it, she also internalized the convent's modesty and asceticism. Most pictures of her in later life show her in plain, high-necked garb that could almost be a habit. And her life of extreme frugality and devotion to her calling mirrored that of the nuns who helped raise her. She was often referred to by her acquaintances in religious terms as a priestess (the journalist Leonard D. Abbott called her the "priestess of pity and vengeance" (*A, p. 245*) or as the bride of her cause.

She never attended college, but was thoroughly self-educated. After she left the convent, she embarked on the career that supported her, though in poverty, throughout the rest of her life: offering private lessons in English, music, penmanship, and other subjects. In immediate response, by her own account, to her treatment at the convent, where she was often punished for misbehavior and the frank statement of her opinions, she became a free-thinker and began to contribute to atheist periodicals and to lecture on Tom Paine and other subjects around the Midwest. In November 1887 she told a Michigan audience this: "I spent four years in a convent, and I have seen the watchwords of their machinations. I have seen bright intellects... loaded down with chains, made abject, prostrate nonentitites. I have seen frank, generous dispositions made morose, sullen, and deceitful, and I have seen rose-leaf cheeks turn to a sickly pallor, and glad eyes lose their brightness, and elastic youth lose its vitality and go down to an early grave murdered—murdered by the church" (*A, p. 40–41*). As a lecturer, despite the firmness of her words, she seemed very self-contained. Where Goldman, Most, and many others breathed fire, Voltai did a slow burn. One of her listeners said "The even delivery, the subdued enthusiasm of her voice, the abundance of information, thought and argument, and the logical sequence of the same made a deep impression on me" (*Jay Fox, quoted in A, p. 42*).

Like Goldman and so many others, she was converted from a vague socialism to anarchism by the execution of the Haymarket leaders in 1887. When, at 19, she read the news of the explosion that led to the executions— an explosion to which the anarchist leaders were never convincingly connected—she declared that the anarchists ought to be hanged. She berated herself for the rest of her life for that single thought, and spoke every year on the anniversary of the executions. But while Goldman gravitated toward Kropotkin's communist anarchism, de Cleyre moved toward the individualist anarchism associated with Josiah Warren, Thoreau, and Benjamin Tucker and began to contribute to the latter's journal, *Liberty*. The main practical disagreement between communist and individualist anarchists concerns the institution of property. Communists such as Goldman and Berkman held it to be antithetical to human freedom, whereas individualists such as Warren and Tucker considered it essential. Both, however, were critics of rapacious capitalism and shared a vision of voluntary social arrangements. Later, de Cleyre stepped up her critique of capitalism and called herself an "anarchist without adjectives." She held that any attempt to dictate the future development of politics or economy was itself incompatible with anarchism. As many voluntary systems ought to be tried as there were people who wanted to live in them. Goldman, to her credit, also realized that something like this was the only position consistent with anarchism. But for de Cleyre, the origin of a social liberation had to be a personal transformation: for her, ultimately, the liberation of a people had to proceed through a liberation of each person, and the primordial scene of enslavement and freedom was within the human self.

In 1889, Voltairine moved to Philadelphia, where she lived and taught and spoke and organized, largely in the Jewish immigrant community, until 1910. She had several lovers over the years, and in 1890 bore one of them, James Elliott, a son. She had no interest in raising the boy, whose name was Harry, and he was cared for by Elliott's family. As Avrich puts it, "Moody and irritable, in chronic illness, [poverty], and desperate need of privacy, she could not face the task of raising a child" (*A, p. 72*). Through this period, she was much in demand on the lecture circuit, and she toured the country and later England, though lecturing left her so exhausted and in so much pain that she had to take to her bed afterwards. (It is not clear what exactly her illnesses were, though it is apparent that they were extremely serious from a young age and caused her death at age 45.) And she contributed poems, stories and essays to many publications, notably Goldman and Berkman's *Mother Earth,* which in 1914 published her *Selected Works* under Berkman's editorship. That book is a bit hard to obtain, in part because the U.S. government seized it upon publication. Of all American anarchists, native born or immigrant, and with the exception of Thoreau, Voltairine de Cleyre is certainly the most distinguished writer; nevertheless, most of her writings are out of print.

In March 1902, in an expression of the anti-anarchist mania that followed President McKinley's assassination by a young European anarchist, Senator Joseph Hawley announced that he would give a thousand dollars to have a shot at an anarchist. De Cleyre's response: "You may by merely paying your carfare to my home (address below) shoot at me for nothing. I will not resist. I will stand straight before you at any distance you wish me to, and you may shoot, in the presence of witnesses. Does not your American commercial instinct seize upon this as a bargain? But if payment of the $1,000 is a necessary part of your proposition, then when I have given you the shot, I will give the money to the propaganda of the idea of a free society in which there shall be neither assassins nor presidents, beggars nor senators" (*A, p. 136*). Indeed, such flashes of humor, even in the context of extremely serious matters and de Cleyre's extremely depressive personality, are characteristic of her writing and in particular of her correspondence.

On 19 December of that same year, Voltairine de Cleyre was shot three times at point-blank range. The would-be assassin was not Senator Hawley, but a former student of hers named Herman Helcher, who declared to the police that he loved Voltairine and that she had broken his heart, despite the fact that it had been several years since they had seen one another. Helcher laid in wait for de Cleyre in a building that she passed daily on her way to give lessons. As she boarded a streetcar, he pulled at her sleeve. When she turned, he shot her in the chest. The bullet spun her around, and then he put two more bullets into her back. She managed to run a block before another of her pupils, a doctor, found her. She was expected to die, but as she wrote later to a friend, "I believe that outside of the actual physical pain of the first three days, my friends suffered more than I did. I don't know what kind of curious constitution I am blessed with, but some way I settled down to the coldest kind of mental attitude in which the chief characteristic was an unshakable determination not to die" (*V to Maggie Duff, A, p. 171*).

As we ponder de Cleyre's response to the shooting, we need to keep in mind that she had early on renounced violence, though she came late in her career to endorse "direct action," largely as a result of her support of revolutionary anarchists in Mexico. But she had also expressed sympathy with anarchist assassins such as Bresci and Czolgosz, saying (as had Goldman) that their actions, while regrettable, were understandable under the circumstances, and that poverty and oppression ever led to violence. And de Cleyre had criticized the legal and penal system in extreme terms on many occasions. So she refused to identify her assailant or participate in any way in his trial. In fact she sent an appeal on his behalf to the journal *Free Society*:

Dear Comrades,
   I write to appeal to you on behalf of the unfortunate child (for in intellect he has never been more than a child) who made the assault upon me.

He is friendless, he is in prison, he is sick—had he not been sick in the brain he never would have done this thing.

Nothing can be done to relieve him until a lawyer is secured, and for that money is needed. I know it is hard to ask, for our comrades are always giving more than they can afford. But I think this is a case where all Anarchists are concerned that the world may learn our ideas concerning the treatment of so-called "criminals," and that they will therefore be willing to make even unusual sacrifices.

What this poor half-crazed boy needs is not the silence and cruelty of a prison, but the kindness, care, and sympathy which heal.

These have all been given to me, in unstinted quantity. I can never express the heart of my gratitude for it all. Be as ready to help the other who is perhaps the greater sufferer.

With love to all,

Voltairine de Cleyre

Philadelphia, 807 Fairmount Avenue (*A, p.177*)

This letter puts into practice in the clearest way the thoughts contained in one of de Cleyre's strongest essays. Titled "Crime and Punishment," it is not an abstract treatment of issues in penology and jurisprudence, but a philosophy of life based in passionate empathy.

A great ethical teacher once wrote words like unto these: "I have within me the capacity of every crime."

Few, reading them, believe that he meant what he said. Most take it as the sententious utterance of one who, in an abandonment of generosity, wished to say something large and leveling. But I think he meant exactly what he said. I think that with all his purity Emerson had within him the turbid stream of passion and desire; for all his hard-cut granite features he knew the instincts of the weakling and the slave; and for all the sweetness, the tenderness, and the nobility of his nature, he had the tiger and the jackal in his soul. I think that within every bit of human flesh and spirit that has ever crossed the enigma bridge of life, from the prehistoric racial morning until now, all crime and all virtue were germinal. (*Selected Works, p. 177*)

Thus, de Cleyre came to a politics of punishment through empathy with transgressors, and to empathy with transgressors through self-scrutiny. Throughout her life, she subjected herself to withering self-examination (indeed too withering; it drove her to attempt suicide). But in a way that only great saints and exemplars ever have, she let her understanding of herself inform totally her understanding of others, even of those she most deeply despised. "Ask yourself, each of you, whether you are quite sure that you have feeling enough, understanding enough, and *have you suffered* enough, to be able to weigh and measure out another's man's life or liberty, no matter what he has done?" (*SW, p. 199*). That attitude led to great self-loathing and great charity. She was herself the poor she was trying to feed; she was the criminal she was trying to free. And just as truly, she was the industrialist she was trying to overthrow; she was the president or priest whose doctrine she was dedicated to refuting and whose power she was dedicated to destroying.

For de Cleyre, then, anarchism was more than a political doctrine; it was an approach to ethics and hence to jurisprudence. One was to leave others free not only to live as they liked but to believe and to be as they liked, and the limits of judgment and of justice were precisely fixed by the limits of empathy. Anarchism thus transcended any moral system: it opened the possibility of people inventing and living according to whatever values seemed right to them. On her view, one takes responsibility for oneself, and leaves the question of the responsibility of others for themselves to themselves. This view connects de Cleyre with the American libertarian tradition of Josiah Warren and Lysander Spooner, but she develops the thought much more directly out of her own continual charitable and teaching work with the poor, and out of her acute sensibility of suffering.

De Cleyre's ethics was not based upon abstract principles, though there is a metaphysics underlying it: an Emersonian metaphysics of the connection of all things. But the metaphysics itself is given in and articulated out of an extremely profound, life-transfiguring experience of that connection which has its origin in self-reflection. And this idea that together we are "rushing upon doom" tempers de Cleyre's politics with an existentialist sense of the finitude and even the futility of human life: she resolves to do good in the face of absurdity, to love even in the darkness, to love even the darkness itself.

Helcher's bullets were never removed from de Cleyre's body, and they contributed to a downward spiral in physical and emotional health, and an ever-darkening outlook on the world. Voltairine de Cleyre died on 20 June 1912.

DARKNESS AND LIBERATION

Emma Goldman and Voltairine de Cleyre were anarchists for different reasons and in different ways. For Emma, anarchism promised a flowering of life and creativity. She viewed life as a force which could fill all things if it were liberated. De Cleyre, on the other hand, found life a continual trial, and even toyed with the idea that its universal extinction was preferable to its continuation. Her anarchism was driven by her extremely intense experience of and empathy for suffering. To Alexander Berkman she wrote: "In the last analysis it is life itself I hate, not a fat bourgeois. Life, life this fiendish thing which brings millions of little creatures forth mercilessly, only to hunger, pain, madness. There is not a day when the sufferings of the little waif animals in the street does not create in one a bitter rage against life" (*A, p. 206*).

And thus where Goldman turned always toward life as experience— toward art, sexuality, liberation of human potential—de Cleyre turned away in pity and in disgust and in depression. But she also continuously returned. Despite immense physical and emotional problems, she devoted herself to the relief of suffering wherever it might be found. Where Emma imagined a beautiful ideal, and never stopped aspiring to it even in the most difficult circumstances, de Cleyre had a dark realism and little hope for anarchism or any other ideal. Of all things, she was most acutely aware of the suffering that surrounded her; she made of it her own suffering. She habitually rescued animals and human beings from the street. After a particularly brutal quarrel with Gordon in the 1890s, they both swallowed poison, though they both survived. And de Cleyre tried to commit suicide on at least one other occasion. By the end of her life she continued her political work by sheer force of will. "I am not sure of anything," she wrote to Berkman on 24 June 1910. "I am not sure that liberty is good. I am not sure that progress exists. I do not feel able to theorize or philosophize or preach at all. ... I can see no use in doing anything. Everything turns bitter in my mouth and ashes in my hands. ... All my tastes are dying" (*A, p. 215*). And to another correspondent around the same time: "I have nothing—*nothing* to say. I would like to finish my life in silence" (*A, p. 216*). She was continuously, grindingly ill in body and spirit, and in the last years of her life experienced terrible headaches and continual roaring noises in her ears.

This perhaps makes Voltairine de Cleyre out to be an unremittingly depressed and depressing figure. But against this infinitely dark background, Voltairine de Cleyre's writing and her commitment are incandescent. When she wrote of the suffering of others and the means to achieve its surcease, she wrote with total passion. And in dedicating her life to hope even in the face of overwhelming continual hopelessness, she displayed a heroic overcoming not only of the circumstances that surrounded her, but of herself. Many people who suffer suicidal depression of the sort she faced throughout her life turn inexorably inward; the sufferings of others and indeed the external world quite in general, come to seem unreal; action becomes impossible.

But Voltairine de Cleyre used her reflection on her own suffering and her intense desire for a liberation from it as a tool to understand all that suffers, as a connection to the world's suffering, as a motivation for its remediation.

So intense were her connections to all things that suffered that she lived much of her life in utter despair. But so intense was it, too, that in the face of that despair she made beautiful language and demonstrated amazing generosity. She died at age 45 and death must have come as a relief, something that in some sense she had sought all her life. But there is a kind of existential nobility that despairs and fights anyway, that defies God or indeed any authority even as it acknowledges that it can't win and even that it is impossible to know what victory means or whether it is desirable. But it pursues liberation anyway, acknowledges and shapes the absurdity of life. Voltairine de Cleyre acknowledged our finitude, our impotence, the inevitability of our failure, our pain, and our death. And even as she did so she kept fighting to alleviate these conditions. That resolution to hope in the face of hopelessness, that song on the edge of the abyss, marks a courage even greater than that of the idealist.

De Cleyre's prose is paradigmatically American. She is in many ways a florid romantic, but driving the poetical gesture there is muscle. It is hard to quote her briefly, in part because when she's pouring, her sentences are extremely long, and in part because her figures of speech take a very long time to unfold. But when you examine her rhetoric, you also find that she is remarkably plain-spoken, and even in at her most poetic and passionate she is utterly direct. Here is a passage from her essay on Goldman. Recall that Goldman had been arrested for urging the poor to "take bread."

My second reason for not repeating Emma Goldman's words is that I, as an anarchist, have no right to advise another to do anything involving a risk to himself; nor would I give a fillip for an action done by the advice of some one else, unless it is accompanied by a well-argued, well-settled conviction on the part of the person acting, that it really is the best thing to do. Anarchism, to me, means not only the denial of authority, not only a new economy, but a revision of the principles of morality. It means the development of the individual as well as the assertion of the individual. It means self-responsibility, and not leader worship. I say it is your business to decide whether you will starve and freeze in sight of food and clothing ... And in saying this I mean to cast no reflection whatever upon Miss Goldman for doing otherwise. She and I hold many differing views on both Economy and Morals; and that she is honest in hers she has proven better than I have proven mine. Miss Goldman is a communist; I am an individualist. She wishes to destroy the right of property; I wish to assert it. ... But whether she or I be right, or both of us be wrong, of one thing I am sure: the spirit which animates Emma Goldman is the only one which will emancipate the slave from his slavery, the tyrant from his tyranny—the spirit which is willing to dare and suffer. (7–10)

De Cleyre was certainly a spirit willing to dare and suffer, and though she lived in want and pain, she spoke and wrote with a courage that was total.

One interesting theme of this speech is de Cleyre's ambivalent relation to the idea of "leadership," whether Goldman's, her own, or anyone else's. She certainly could not, conformably to her own ethics, tell people what to do, even were they willing to follow her. Her leadership, then, was not rabble-rousing or even large-scale organizing. Rather, she reached people one at a time in a kind of ministry and when she spoke she took care that the autonomy of each member of her audience was respected in her words and in her delivery. She led, of course, by example, by her purity of purpose, by her deep dedication to helping specific people to survive and thrive. And she led by the inspiring vision given in her writings. But she refused to seize the sort of power that those writings were dedicated to critiquing. In that sense, she provides an alternative model of leadership that is highly personal and self-consciously respects the autonomy of those over whom it is exercised.

Her essay "Sex Slavery" is one of her most impassioned. And the feminism she puts forward in it is strikingly modern, though it also takes up and pushes forward an existing tradition. She compares marriage (as it stood in the late nineteenth century) to chattel slavery. And she traces its origin to God and the state. "[T]hat is rape, where a man forces himself sexually upon a woman whether he is licensed by the marriage law to do it or not. And that is the vilest tyranny where a man compels a woman he says he loves, to endure the agony of bearing children that she does not want, and for whom, as is the rule rather than the exception, they cannot properly provide. It is worse than any other human oppression; it is fairly *God*-like! To the sexual tyrant there is not parallel upon earth; one must go to the skies to find a fiend who thrusts life upon his children only to starve and curse and outcast and damn them!" (*SW, p. 345*). This is de Cleyre at her blasphemous best. "At Macon in the sixth century… the fathers of the Church met and proposed the decision of the question, 'Has woman a soul?' Having ascertained that the permission to own a nonentity wasn't going to injure any of their parsnips, a small majority vote decided this momentous question in our favor. … The question of souls is old—we demand our bodies, now" (*SW, p. 350*). And she goes on to assert that women's bodies are entrapped by restrictive and "modest" clothing, by limitations on such activities as team sports and horsemanship, and above all by the domination of their sexuality by men. And typically, she finishes by proposing liberty, and by saying that no one can see what sorts of relations might be possible in the future between the sexes, but that all the possibilities are permissible as long as they are voluntary.

YEARNING

Despite her extreme tendency toward heresy, there remained throughout de Cleyre's life a yearning toward transcendence. It would seem, indeed, to be a yearning for God, though of course we must acknowledge her self-declared atheism. This certainly is the key to understanding her asceticism, her apparent vow of poverty and dedication to self-sacrifice, self-abnegation, and perhaps self-destruction. De Cleyre wanted to erase herself into pure generosity and hence pure emptiness. There is a kind of an American Platonism lurking in her renunciation of the beyond and in her love of nature and its transcendence. Only one who is deep in soul-darkness and self-loathing seeks both immersion in pain and its overcoming through its intensification. And only someone with that power of self-overcoming really understands from inside the expressions of transcendence by which oppressed people transform pain into art. That was the origin of the blues that de Cleyre heard, and, more, celebrated and embodied.

Her philosophy is eclectic and finally quite original; she was the opposite of an ideologue, and it is to the credit of Alexander Berkman—an ideologue if ever there was one—that he could edit her writings and try to disseminate them. But her philosophy is also characteristically American. I would, again, call her metaphysics transcendental in the Emersonian vein. Whereas the philosophy of, let us say, Hegel, denigrates the physical world or sees it as a mere shadow of the Idea, Emerson and de Cleyre seek the transcendent in the immanent, and find it. And thus her ethics emerges directly from her metaphysics; it is an ethics that makes use of what Emerson would call the "oversoul," the sense in which or the level at which we are all connected in one cycle of life and suffering and death and transcendence. Here is how she begins her wonderful essay "The Dominant Idea":

> In everything that lives, if one looks searchingly, is limned the shadow line of an idea—an idea, dead or living, sometimes stronger when dead, with rigid, unswerving lines that mark the living embodiment with the stern, immobile cast of the non-living. Daily we move among these unyielding shadows, less pierceable, more enduring than granite, with the blackness of ages in them, dominating living, changing bodies, with dead, unchanging souls. And we meet, also, living souls dominating dying bodies—living ideas regnant over decay and death. Do not imagine that I speak of human life alone. The stamp of persistent or of shifting Will is visible in the grass-blade rooted in its clod of earth, as in the gossamer web of being that floats and swims far over our heads in the free world of air. (*SW, p. 81*)

In de Cleyre's metaphysics, then, the beauty and truth of the eternal, the will that is the source of the cosmos, is inside the world and indeed inside us: or indeed is the world and is us. If our suffering distances us from it by enclosing us within ourselves, it also issues a call for its own amelioration through connection, through concrete acts of charity. And so charity or the relief of suffering brings us to a kind of truth; it lets us see the modes of connection that constitute the human community and the world. And from this immanent transcendence, Voltairine rejects materialism and determinism, and holds that one can incorporate an idea in oneself, that one can live toward an ideal, that even in death one is free and connected to the ideas that animate all nature.

The philosophy that de Cleyre then articulates—both optimistic and intensely realistic—is an original version of the American pragmatism then being articulated by William James and soon to be elaborated in very much the way Voltai does, by John Dewey. De Cleyre:

> [A]gainst the accepted formula of modern Materialism, "Men are what circumstances make them," I set the opposing declaration, "Circumstances are what men make them"; and I contend that both these things are true to the point where the combating powers are equalized, or one is over-thrown. In other words, my conception of mind, or character, is not that of a powerless reflection of a momentary condition of stuff and form, but an active modifying agent, reacting on its environment and transforming circumstances, sometimes greatly, sometimes, though not often, entirely. (*SW, p. 82–83*)

Here and in many other places, de Cleyre's philosophy and her writing find a pitch of synthesis, originality, and lucidity which certainly no contemporary anarchist ever reached, and which indeed is rare in any context. Because of the relation of immanence and transcendence in her philosophy, this meliorism becomes a declaration that the world itself can become an arena of transcendence through concrete human action, in particular through a transformation of social conditions.

Compatibly with this philosophy, throughout de Cleyre's writing you will find the most prosaic and practical observations interrupted by flashes of poetry and radical intuition. I conclude with this long quotation from her essay "Anarchism," in which she pauses in her discussion of various economic models to deliver a sublime account of the human self in general and in particular of her self.

> Once and forever to realize that one is not a bundle of well-regulated lit-tle reasons bound up in the front room of the brain to be sermonized and held in order with copy-book maxims or moved and stopped by a syllo-gism, but a bottomless, bottomless depth of all strange sensations, a rock-ing sea of feeling wherever sweep strong storms of unaccountable hate

and rage, invisible contortions of disappointment, low ebbs of meanness, quakings and shudderings of love that drives to madness and will not be controlled, hungerings and moanings and sobbings that smite upon the inner ear, now first bent to listen. ... To look down upon that, to know the blackness, the midnight, the dead ages in oneself, to feel the jungle and the beast within,—and the swamp and the slime, and the desolate desert of the heart's despair—to see, to know, to feel to the uttermost,— and then to look at one's fellow, sitting across from one in the street-car, so decorous, so well got up, so nicely combed and brushed and oiled and to wonder what lies beneath that commonplace exterior,—to picture the cavern in him which somewhere far below has a narrow gallery running into your own—to imagine the pain that racks him to the finger-tips perhaps while he wears that placid ironed-shirt-front countenance ... to draw back respectfully from the Self-gate of the plainest, most unpromising creature, even from the most debased criminal in oneself—to spare all condemnation (how much more trial and sentence) because one knows the stuff of which man is made and recoils at nothing since all is in himself,—this is what Anarchism may mean to you. It means that to me.

And then, to turn cloudward, starward, skyward, and let the dreams rush over one—no longer awed by outside powers of any order— recognizing nothing superior to oneself—painting, painting endless pictures, creating unheard symphonies that sing dream sounds to you alone, extending sympathies to the dumb brutes as equal brothers, kissing the flowers as one did when a child, letting oneself go free, go free beyond the bounds of what fear and *custom* call the "possible,"—this too Anarchism may mean to you, if you dare apply it so. And if you do some day,—if sitting at your work-bench, you see a vision of surpassing glory, some picture of that golden time when there shall be no prisons on the earth, nor hunger, nor houselessness, nor accusation, nor judgment, and hearts open as printed leaves, and candid as fearlessness, if then you look across at your low-browed neighbor, who sweats and smells and curses at his toil,—remember that as you do not know his depth neither do you know his height. He too might dream if the yoke of custom and law and dogma were broken from him. Even now you know not what blind, bound, motionless chrysalis is working there to prepare its winged thing. (*SW, p. 113–15*)

SOURCES

Paul Avrich, *An American Anarchist: The Life of Voltairine de Cleyre* (Princeton NJ: Princeton University Press, 1978) (A).

Alexander Berkman, ed., *Selected Works of Voltairine de Cleyre* (New York: Mother Earth Publishing Association, 1914) (SW).

The Exquisite Rebel
The Anarchist Life of Voltairine de Cleyre

Sharon Presley

Emma Goldman called her "the most gifted and brilliant anarchist woman America ever produced." Yet today, Voltairine de Cleyre is virtually unknown even among libertarians and anarchists. Though her writings and speeches on the subject of what was then called "the woman question" were as radical, passionate, and popular as Goldman's, Voltairine de Cleyre is even less known among feminists today than among anarchists. Voltairine was, in the words of her biographer, Paul Avrich, "A brief comet in the anarchist firmament, blazing out quickly and soon forgotten by all but a small circle of comrades whose love and devotion persisted long after her death." But "her memory," continues Avrich, "possesses the glow of legend." (*Avrich, p. 6*)

VOLTAIRINE DE CLEYRE'S LEGACY:
WHY WE SHOULD CARE

This "legend" deserves to be more than merely a fond glow in the hearts of a handful of aficionados of anarchist history. Many of the issues that Voltairine struggled with are still being debated today. Her insights into political, social, religious, and feminist controversies are still fresh, and, especially in matters of religion and politics, very nearly as unconventional and challenging now as then:

- On the social origin of gender roles, she was as clear-sighted as any feminist social scientist today, and far more radical than mainstream feminists of her day.
- Her own bitter experience with being treated as a sex object by her lovers and her recognition of the difficulty of maintaining one's individuality in a close relationship are issues women still struggle with to this day. Her exhortation to maintain that individuality still speaks to the hearts and minds of modern women.

17

- Her elucidation of the concept of the "Dominant Idea" dealt with an earlier version of the contemporary debate on whether individuals have free will or are merely victims of the social environment. It not only offers still-relevant psychological insights but also stands as an inspiring anthem to the power of individual will to overcome obstacles and to find purpose and meaning in life.
- Her radical insistence on the inherently authoritarian nature of the Church and the State and their joint role in oppressing women challenges modern feminists to examine cherished but unquestioned assumptions more critically.
- Her call for tolerance among the different anarchist factions is still painfully relevant as numerous versions of the "Lenin-Trotsky syndrome" (more bitter in-fighting with those close in ideology than with the external real enemy) continue to play themselves out today among political activists of many stripes, including anarchist, libertarian, skeptic, and feminist.
- Her insistence that individuals in a free society would choose many diverse paths, not just the "one true way" favored by any given faction, demonstrates both common sense and insight into human nature.
- Her holistic balancing of reason and compassion challenges activists such as libertarians and individualist anarchists to be more caring and less abstract in their advocacy of individual rights, while it challenges activists such as liberals and communalist anarchists to be less emotionally sloppy and unconcerned about individual rights in their quest for justice.

Voltairine de Cleyre's Life and Work: Triumph Over Adversity

Born in a small village in Michigan in 1866, Voltairine, plagued all her life by poverty, pain, and ill health, died at the age of 45 in 1912. The short span of her life, ending before great events of the twentieth century, is, in Avrich's opinion, the major reason why Voltairine de Cleyre has been overlooked, unlike the longer-lived anarchist activists Emma Goldman and Alexander Berkman.

The strength of will and independence of mind that so strongly characterized this remarkable woman manifested themselves early in Voltairine's life. Forced into a Catholic convent school as a teenager, she chafed at the stifling, authoritarian atmosphere and later spoke of the "white scars on my soul" left by this painful experience. "She left the convent a doubter," writes Avrich, "if not yet an outright infidel, eager for ideas more congenial to her rebellious temperament. Her revulsion against religious dogma and the doctrine of absolute obedience, so deeply implanted by these years at [the convent] were to evolve into a generalized hatred of authority and obscurantism in all their manifestations." (*A, p. 37*)

Bruised but unbroken, Voltairine soon gravitated toward the flourishing freethinkers' movement. In 1886, she began writing for a small freethought weekly, *The Progressive Age,* and soon became its editor. Later she wrote numerous articles for prominent secularist publications, including *The Freethinkers' Magazine, Freethought,* and *The Truth Seeker.* During this time, she also began lecturing on the freethought circuit. As her reputation grew, her lectures, including frequent tours for the American Secular Union, a nationwide freethought organization, took her to many Midwestern and Eastern states.

"The Economic Tendency of Freethought," a lecture originally given before the Boston Secular Society, was later published in Benjamin Tucker's individualist anarchist periodical, *Liberty.* In this essay, Voltairine expounded the idea that the concept of God presented by the Church is a reflection of an authoritarian mentality. In her view, as soon as a supreme authority is set up, whether government or God, the individuals in this group are denied rights. "... upon that one idea of supreme authority," she wrote, "is based every tyranny that was ever formulated. Why? Because, if God is, then no human being, no thing that lives, ever had a *right!* He simply had a *privilege,* bestowed, granted, conferred, gifted to him, for such a length of time as God sees fit."

It was as an orator, according to Avrich, that Voltairine first made her mark in radical circles. Though not a flamboyant speaker like Emma Goldman, she was, by most accounts, compelling and eloquent. Emma herself considered Voltairine's speeches to be highly original and even brilliant. In noting the intensity of Voltairine's style, Emma wrote of "her pale face lit up with the inner fire of her ideal."

In 1887, impressed by a speech given by Clarence Darrow, Voltairine flirted briefly with socialism, but her deep-running anti-authoritarian spirit soon rejected it in favor of anarchism. After debating an anarchist, she began an extensive study of anarchist theory and practice. Influenced by Tucker's *Liberty,* the leading anarchist journal of the day, she soon dropped the socialist label. It was *Liberty,* she wrote, "which finally convinced me that 'Liberty is not the Daughter but the Mother of Order.'"

As with Emma Goldman, the hanging of the Haymarket martyrs, innocent victims of anti-anarchist hysteria convicted in a patently unfair trial, made a profound impression on Voltairine and was a major impetus in her turn toward anarchism. In 1888, she threw herself into the anarchist movement, dedicating herself unceasingly to the cause of liberty for the rest of her life.

Though seldom in the limelight—unlike Emma Goldman, she shrank from notoriety—Voltairine was a popular speaker and an untiring writer. In spite of financial circumstances that led her to work long hours, and despite a profoundly unhappy life, which included several near-suicides, an almost fatal assassin's bullet, and a number of ill-fated love affairs, she wrote hundreds of poems, essays, stories, and sketches in her all too brief life. Highly praised by her colleagues for the elegance and stylistic beauty of her writing, Voltairine possessed, in Avrich's opinion, "a greater literary talent than any other American anarchist," surpassing even Berkman, Goldman, and Tucker. Goldman herself believed Voltairine's prose to be distinguished by an "extreme clarity of thought and originality of expression." (*A, p. 7*)

Unfortunately, only one collection of her writings—*Selected Works of Voltairine de Cleyre,* edited by Alexander Berkman and published by Goldman's *Mother Earth* in 1914—was ever put together, leaving much fine material buried in obscure journals. Of this collection, Leonard Abbott, writing in the journal *Mother Earth,* said: "There are few, if any, books in the literature of Anarchism as lofty as these. ... 'Selected Writings.' I have read Kropotkin and Elisée Reclus, and I know something of the writings of Stirner and Nietzsche and Tolstoy and Benjamin Tucker. But Voltairine de Cleyre stands alone. She has the individuality that only very great writers possess."

Abbott also commented on Voltairine's unhappy life. "Her character," he observed, "became great through suffering and in spite of suffering. Voltairine de Cleyre failed to win happiness. But she won something that may be more precious—the satisfaction that comes from honest self-expression and from the exercise of rare intellectual gifts. Her writings will be an inspiration to humanity for generations to come."

Both Voltairine's life and her writings reflect, in Avrich's words, "an extremely complicated individual." Though an atheist, Voltairine had, according to Goldman, a "religious zeal which stamped everything she did ... Her whole nature was that of an ascetic." "By living a life of religious-like austerity," says Avrich, "she became a secular nun in the Order of Anarchy." (*A, p. 12*) In describing that persistence of will which inspired her, the anarchist poet Sadikichi Hartmann declared, "Her whole life seemed to center upon the exaltation over, what she so aptly called, the Dominant Idea. Like an anchorite, she flayed her body to utter more and more lucid and convincing arguments in favor of direct action."

"The Dominant Idea," wrote Emma Goldman in her commemorative essay "Voltairine de Cleyre" (reproduced below), "was the *Leitmotif* throughout Voltairine de Cleyre's remarkable life. Though she was constantly harassed by ill-health, which held her body captive and killed her at the end, the Dominant Idea energized Voltairine to ever greater intellectual efforts, raised her to the supreme heights of an exalted ideal and steeled her will to conquer every handicap in her tortured life." The Dominant Idea, was, in Voltairine's view, the force of individual will and purpose that inspires one's actions, of "intent *within* holding its purpose against obstacles *without.*"

In her essay, "The Dominant Idea," Voltairine foreshadowed a debate on free will versus environmental determinism that still rages today among social scientists and policy makers. "And first, against the accepted formula of modern Materialism," she wrote, " 'Men are what circumstances make them,' I set the opposing declaration, 'Circumstances are what men make them' ... In other words, my conception of mind, or character, is not that it is a powerless reflection of a momentary condition of stuff and form, but an active modifying agent, reacting on its environment and transforming circumstances, sometimes greatly, sometimes, though not often, entirely." Her own life was a living testimony to the truth of this assertion.

"At the end of your life," she exhorts us, "you may close your eyes saying: I have not been dominated by the Dominant Idea of my Age; I have chosen my own allegiance, and served it. I have proved by a lifetime that there is in man that which saves him from the absolute tyranny of Circumstance, which in the end conquers and remoulds Circumstance,— the immortal fire of Individual Will, which is the salvation of the Future."

The ascetic also had the soul of a poet. In her poetry and even in her prose, Voltairine eloquently expressed a passionate love of music, of nature, and of beauty. "With all her devotion to her social ideals," said Emma, "she had another god—the god of Beauty. Her life was a ceaseless struggle between the two: the ascetic determinedly stifling her longing for beauty, but the poet in her determinedly yearning for it, worshipping it in utter abandonment. . . ."

HOLISTIC BALANCE: REASON, COMPASSION AND TOLERANCE

Another manifestation of Voltairine's complex nature was her ability to balance both reason and compassion, a combination that Benjamin Tucker, like some modern-day individualist anarchists, thought led to inconsistency and ambivalence. Voltairine didn't see it that way. "I think it has been the great mistake of our people, especially our American Anarchists represented by Benjamin R. Tucker, to disclaim sentiment," she declared. In her essay, "Why I am an Anarchist," she wrote, "It is to men and women of feeling that I speak ... Not to the shallow egotist who holds himself apart, and with the phariseeism of intellectuality, exclaims, 'I am more just than thou'; but to those whose every fiber of being is vibrating with emotion as aspen leaves quiver in the breath of Storm! To those whose hearts swell with a great pity at the pitiful toil of women, the weariness of young children, the handcuffed helplessness of strong men!"

But Voltairine was no emotional sentimentalist, lacking in serious arguments. Though Tucker became increasingly skeptical of her talents, most of her associates considered her a brilliant thinker. Marcus Graham, editor of the anarchist journal *Man!*, called her "the most thoughtful woman anarchist of this century," while George Brown, the anarchist orator, declared her "the most intellectual woman I ever met." (*A, p. 101*) Joseph Kucera, her last lover, praised her logical, analytic mind. Avrich himself, a careful historian not given to undue praise, concludes that she was a "first-rate intellect."

Voltairine's political-economic stance within the anarchist spectrum was no less complicated than her other views and even less well understood. Avrich dispels the myth created by erroneous claims of Rudolph Rocker and Emma Goldman that Voltairine became a communist anarchist. In 1907, points out Avrich, Voltairine replied to Emma's claim, saying, "I am not now and never have been at any time a Communist." Beginning as a Tuckerite individualist, Voltairine turned in the 1890s to the mutualism of Dyer Lum. But she eventually grew to the conclusion that neither individualism nor collectivism nor even mutualism was entirely satisfactory. "I am an Anarchist, simply, without economic labels attached," she was finally to declare.

Unhyphenated anarchism, or "anarchism without adjectives" had other adherents as well—Errico Malatesta, Max Nettlau, and Dyer Lum among them. These advocates of non-sectarian anarchism tried to promote tolerance for different economic views within the movement, believing that economic preferences would vary according to individual tastes and that no one person or group had the only correct solution. "There is nothing un-Anarchistic about any of [these systems]," declared Voltairine "until the element of compulsion enters and obliges unwilling persons to remain in a community whose economic arrangements they do not agree to."

Voltairine's plea for tolerance and cooperation among the anarchist schools strikes a contemporary note, making us realize how little things have changed. Factionalism rages yet, with fervent apostles still all too eager to read other tendencies (whether "anarcho-capitalist" or "anarcho-communist" or "green") out of the anarchist fold. The notion that the pluralistic anarchist societies envisioned by people like Voltairine de Cleyre might in fact be the most realistic expectation about human nature seems even more lost on anarchists today than in her time.

Probably Voltairine's best-known work is the often-reprinted essay "Anarchism and American Traditions," in which she shows how the ideas of anarchism follow naturally from the premises on which the American Revolution was based. The revolutionary republicans, she says, "took their starting point for deriving a minimum of government upon the same sociological ground that the modern Anarchist derives the no-government theory; viz., that equal liberty is the political ideal." But the anarchist, unlike the revolutionary republicans, she goes on to point out, cannot accept the premise of majority rule. All governments, regardless of their form, say the anarchists, will always be manipulated by a small minority. She then goes on to cite other similarities between the ideas of the anarchists and the republicans, including the belief in local initiative and independent action. "This then was the American Tradition," she writes, "that private enterprise manages better all that to which it is equal. Anarchism declares that private enterprise, whether individual or cooperative, is equal to all the undertakings of society."

Passionate Feminist: Revolt Against Patriarchal Tyranny

Another of Voltairine's special concerns was what was then called "women's emancipation." In a time when the law treated women like chattel, "Voltairine de Cleyre's whole life," asserts Avrich, "was a revolt against this system of male domination which, like every other form of tyranny and exploitation, ran contrary to her anarchistic spirit." These themes of gender equality provided the subjects of frequent lectures and speeches in Voltairine's years of activity, including topics such as "Sex Slavery," "Love and Freedom," "The Case of Woman vs. Orthodoxy," and "Those Who Marry Do Ill."

That such a brilliant, unusual woman would be a feminist is no surprise. "Let every woman ask herself," cried Voltairine, "Why am I the slave of Man? Why is my brain said not to be the equal of his brain? Why is my work not paid equally with his? Why must my body be controlled by my husband? Why may he take my children away from me? Will them away while yet unborn? Let every woman ask." "There are two reasons why," Voltairine answered in her essay, "Sex Slavery," "and these ultimately reducible to a single principle—the authoritarian supreme power GOD-idea, and its two instruments—the Church—that is, the priests—the State—that is, the legislators ... These two things, the mind domination of the Church and the body domination of the State, are the causes of Sex Slavery." Her belief that the Church was one of the main instruments of oppression against women led Voltairine in 1890 to become one of the founding members of the Woman's National Liberal Union which, according to historian Margaret Marsh, was a short-lived "freethought" feminist organization under the direction of the prominent women's rights activist,

Matilda Joslyn Gage. Voltairine was also a principal organizer of the
Philadelphia Ladies Liberal League, a forum for public discussion of different political viewpoints.

Marriage was one of Voltairine's favorite topics. Though she valued
love, she totally rejected formal marriage, considering it "the sanction for all
manner of bestialities" and the married woman, "a bonded slave." Marriage,
in the context of 19th century society and law, was a prison that precluded
the possibility of what she considered the prerequisite for sex-equality: *freedom to control her own person*" (italics in the original). Her own unfortunate
experiences with most of her lovers, who even without the ties of formal
marriage, treated her as a sex object and servant, convinced Voltairine that
even living with a man was to be avoided. When she learned that William
Godwin and Mary Wollstonecraft (her heroine) had lived in separate apart-
ments even though they were lovers, she was delighted. Foreshadowing
Virginia Woolf's classic essay "A Room of One's Own," as well as French
existentialist Simone de Beauvoir's relationship with philosopher Jean-Paul
Sartre (in which she insisted on separate residences), Voltairine wrote to her
mother, "Every individual should have a room or rooms for *himself exclusively,*
never subject to the intrusive familiarities of our present 'family life'... To
me, any dependence, anything which destroys the complete selfhood of the
individual, is in the line of slavery and destroys the pure spontaneity of
love." Voltairine, writes Marsh, "argued that once a man and a woman
became bound together, they lost the freedom to follow their own ideals,
their own paths to intellectual as well as emotional self-fulfillment."

Voltairine took her anarchist feminist views beyond the realm of politics
and into the realm of individual behavior as well. Insisting on a direct link
between anarchism and feminism, she called for a new code of ethics that
would recognize the "complete individuality of woman." Women must free
themselves through individual acts of rebellion against prevailing attitudes
and behaviors. But this individualistic attitude did not mean she was insen-
sitive to the social conditions that restrained women. To those who, in
response to Voltairine's protests against the outrages women suffered in marriage, asked "Why don't the wives leave?" she replied eloquently, "Why don't
you run when your feet are chained together? Why don't you cry out when
a gag is on your lips? ... Will you tell one where they will go and what they
shall do? ... there is not refuge upon earth for the enslaved sex." "Material
conditions," she recognized, "determine the social relations of men and
women." Yet ultimately, she stressed individual rebellion. "Right where we
are," she believed, "there we must dig our trenches, and win or die."

The complete individuality of woman, in Voltairine's view, also required
the rejection of gender role stereotyping. Recognizing that psychological
differences in adult men and women stem from childhood conditioning,

not from their inherent natures, she wrote " 'Women can't rough it like men.' Train any animal, or any plant, as you train your girls, and it won't be able to rough it either." She also decried the restrictions put on women, the "subordinate cramped circle, prescribed for women in daily life," that made her into "an irresponsible doll or a creature not to be trusted outside a 'doll's house.' "

VOLTAIRINE AND EMMA: POETRY AND PROSE

Not surprisingly for that day, Voltairine's experiences with the traditionalism of her lovers was a misfortune she shared with Emma Goldman. Though extremely different in personality—"Voltairine differed from Emma as poetry from prose," says Avrich—the lives of the two women had curious parallels. Most of their lovers turned out to be disappointingly conventional in matters of gender roles but there was in each woman's life at least one lover who was not of this traditionalist stripe. Each loved a man who was her intellectual equal and who treated *her* as an equal—for Voltairine, it was Dyer Lum; for Emma, Alexander Berkman. But sadly, both women lost these men as lovers. Lum committed suicide in 1893 and Berkman's fourteen years in prison left psychological scars that ended his sexual relationship with Emma, though not their emotional one.

In other matters, Voltairine and Emma had little in common and, in fact, often criticized each other personally. Yet, in spite of their personal differences, Emma and Voltairine respected each other intellectually. For her part, Voltairine publicly defended Emma on several occasions, including a passionate speech given when Emma was arrested, which Emma in turn noted in her commemoration of Voltairine (reprinted below). She was, wrote Emma, "the wonderful spirit ... born in some obscure town in the state of Michigan, and who lived in poverty all her life, but who by sheer force of will pulled herself out of a living grave [the cloister], cleared her mind from the darkness of superstition—turned her face to the sun, perceived a great ideal and determinedly carried it to every corner of her native land ... The American soil sometimes does bring forth exquisite plants."

SOURCES

Paul Avrich. *An American Anarchist: The Life of Voltairine de Cleyre*. Princeton, (NJ: Princeton University Press, 1978), (A).

Margaret S. Marsh. *Anarchist Women: 1870–1920*, Philadelphia: Temple University Press, 1981.

Emma Goldman's "Voltairine de Cleyre"

A Moving but Flawed Tribute

Sharon Presley

Unquestionably the best known American anarchist, Emma Goldman was a Russian Jewish émigré, atheist, birth control activist, and feminist as well, four strikes against her in turn-of-the-nineteenth century America. Like Voltairine de Cleyre, she was an untiring activist for the cause of liberty and individual freedom all of her adult life. "Voltairine de Cleyre and Emma Goldman," wrote Harry Kelly, a friend to them both, "will always stand out in my mind as the two most notable women it was ever my good fortune to meet."

The memorial to Voltairine included in the present volume was privately published by Joseph Ishill through his anarchist Oriole Press in an edition of 200 in 1932. Emma considered this essay "among the best things I have done." To my knowledge, it has not been in print in a paper version since.

However, there are some inaccuracies in this essay. In a letter to the essay's publisher Joseph Ishill, dated October 15, 1934, Voltairine's son Harry de Cleyre pointed out some of the mistakes. The essay states the time of her death as June 6 but it was June 20, 1912. Emma claims that Voltairine's father wanted her to become a nun, an assertion that Harry denied as did Voltairine's sister Addie. Though not noted by Harry, Emma also erroneously called the father August de Cleyre but his name was Hector de Claire (Voltairine changed the spelling of her last name when she became an adult for reasons that are not entirely clear).

Though he did not consider them important, Harry also pointed out several other minor discrepancies. Emma says that Voltairine was "a teacher of languages" in Philadelphia, New York and Chicago but she taught English to immigrants and did so only in Philadelphia and Chicago. Nor did she die among dreary and wretched surroundings, according to Harry, who was present at her deathbed. In spite of the errors, he did, however, consider the essay a "glowing tribute" and "flattering."

Another inaccuracy in Emma's essay was her portrayal of Harry de Cleyre. Emma's claim that Harry "was overawed by [Voltairine's] intellect, repelled by her austere mode of living," and that "[he] went his way" make it sound as if Harry did care not for his mother. Quite the contrary, according to Avrich. Though she did not raise him, says Avrich, "Harry loved his mother with an intensity that never abated. It was her name, not his father's that he took; and he called his first daughter Voltairine." Emma's speculation that Harry "is today probably one of the 100% Americans, commonplace and dull," is also quite unfair, according to Avrich. Though he did not become an anarchist, Harry was a devotee of Thomas Paine, and, writes Avrich, "his letters reflect more than a little of her intelligence and independent spirit." He worshiped her memory, was proud of her defense of the oppressed, and wanted to talk about her "all the time." Emma, however, to her credit, later apologized for her remarks about Harry.

Emma's remarks that "physical beauty and feminine attraction were withheld from her" is belied by the many photos of Voltairine showing a delicate, mysterious beauty that contrasts favorably with Emma's plainness. "Emma was jealous of all the pretty women, including Voltairine," remarked a friend. Nor is Emma's suggestion that Voltairine was unattractive to men accurate. In spite of her austere ways, Voltairine had many friends and many lovers in her life.

Though flawed by these errors, Emma's essay remains, nonetheless, an intimate and cogent testimony to a remarkable woman. "The American soil sometimes does bring forth exquisite plants."

Sources

Paul Avrich. *An American Anarchist: The Life of Voltairine de Cleyre.* Princeton, NJ: Princeton University Press, 1978.

Harry de Cleyre to Joseph Ishill, Oct. 15, 1934, Emma Goldman Papers.

Voltairine De Cleyre

Emma Goldman

WRITTEN IN RED
Bear it aloft, O roaring flame!
Skyward aloft, where all may see.
Slaves of the world! our cause is the same;
One is the immemorial shame;
One is the struggle, and in One name—
MANHOOD—we battle to set men free.
VOLTAIRINE DE CLEYRE

THE FIRST TIME I MET HER—THIS MOST GIFTED AND BRIL-
LIANT ANARCHIST WOMAN AMERICA EVER PRODUCED—was
in Philadelphia, in August 1893. I had come to that city to address the
unemployed during the great crisis of that year, and I was eager to visit
Voltairine, of whose exceptional ability as a lecturer I had heard while in
New York. I found her ill in bed, her head packed in ice, her face drawn with
pain. I learned that this experience repeated itself with Voltairine after her
every public appearance: she would be bed-ridden for days, in constant
agony from some disease of the nervous system which she had developed in
early childhood and which continued to grow worse with the years. I did not
remain long on this first visit, owing to the evident suffering of my hostess,
though she was bravely trying to hide her pain from me. But fate plays
strange pranks. In the evening of the same day, Voltairine de Cleyre was
called upon to drag her frail, suffering body to a densely packed, stuffy hall,
to speak in my stead. At the request of the New York authorities, the protec-
tors of law and disorder in Philadelphia captured me as I was about to enter
the Hall and led me off to the Police Station of the City of Brotherly Love.

The next time I saw Voltairine was at Blackwell's Island Penitentiary. She
had come to New York to deliver her masterly address, IN DEFENSE OF
EMMA GOLDMAN AND FREE SPEECH, and she visited me in prison.
From that time until her end our lives and work were frequently thrown

together, often meeting harmoniously and sometimes drifting apart, but always with Voltairine standing out in my eyes as a forceful personality, a brilliant mind, a fervent idealist, an unflinching fighter, a devoted and loyal comrade. But her strongest characteristic was her extraordinary capacity to conquer physical disability—a trait which won for her the respect even of her enemies and the love and admiration of her friends. A key to this power in so frail a body is to be found in Voltairine's illuminating essay, THE DOMINANT IDEA.

> "In everything that lives," she writes there, "if one looks searchingly, is limned to the shadow-line of an idea—an idea, dead or living, sometimes stronger when dead, with rigid, unswerving lines that mark the living embodiment with stern, immobile, cast of the non-living. Daily we move among these unyielding shadows, less pierceable, more enduring than granite, with the blackness of ages in them, dominating living, changing bodies, with dead, unchanging souls. And we meet also, living souls dominating dying bodies—living ideas regnant over decay and death. Do not imagine that I speak of human life alone. The stamp of persistent or of shifting Will is visible in the grass-blade rooted in its clod of earth, as in the gossamer web of being that floats and swims far over our heads in the free world of air."

As an illustration of persistent Will, Voltairine relates the story of the morning-glory vines that trellised over the window of her room, and "everyday they blew and curled in the wind, their white, purple-dashed faces winking at the sun, radiant with climbing life. Then, all at once, some mischance happened,—some cut-worm or some mischievous child tore one vine off below, the finest and most ambitious one, of course. In a few hours, the leaves hung limp, the sappy stem wilted and began to wither, in a day it was dead,— all but the top, which still clung longingly to its support, with bright head lifted. I mourned a little for the buds that could never open now, and pitied that proud vine whose work in the world was lost. But the next night there was a storm, a heavy, driving storm, with beating rain and blinding lightning. I rose to watch the flashes, and lo! the wonder of the world! In the blackness of the mid-night, in the fury of wind and rain, the dead vine had flowered. Five white, moon-faced blossoms blew gayly round the skeleton vine, shining back triumphant at the red lightning ... But every day, for three days, the dead vine bloomed; and even a week after, when every leaf was dry and brown ... one last bud, dwarfed, weak, a very baby of a blossom, but still white and delicate, with five purple flecks, like those on the live vine beside it, opened and waved at the stars, and waited for the early sun. Over death and decay, the Dominant Idea smiled; the vine was in the world to bloom, to bear white trumpet blossoms, dashed with purple; and it held its will beyond death."

The Dominant Idea was the *Leitmotif* throughout Voltairine de Cleyre's remarkable life. Though she was constantly harassed by ill-health, which held her body captive and killed her at the end, the Dominant Idea energized Voltairine to ever greater intellectual efforts, raised her to the supreme heights of an exalted ideal, and steeled her Will to conquer every handicap and obstacle in her tortured life. Again and again, in days of excruciating physical torment, in periods of despair and spiritual doubt, the Dominant Idea gave wings to the spirit of this woman—wings to rise above the immediate, to behold a radiant vision of humanity and to dedicate herself to it with all the fervor of her intense soul. The suffering and misery that were hers during the whole of her life we can glimpse from her writings, particularly in her haunting story, THE SORROWS OF THE BODY [*Selected Works*, p.451, *ed.*]:

I have never wanted anything more than the wild creatures have," she relates, "a broad waft of clean air, a day to lie on the grass at times, with nothing to do but to slip the blades through my fingers, and look as long as I pleased at the whole blue arch, and the screens of green and white between; leave for a month to float and float along the salt crests and among the foam, or roll with my naked skin over a clean long stretch of sunshiny sand; food that I liked, straight from the cool ground, and time to taste its sweetness, and time to rest after tasting; sleep when it came, and stillness, that the sleep might leave me when it would, not sooner ... This is what I wanted,—this, and free contact with my fellows ... not to love and lie, and be ashamed, but to love and say I love, and be glad of it; to feel the currents of ten thousand years of passion flooding me, body to body, as the wild things meet. I have asked no more.

But I have not received. Over me there sits that pitiless tyrant, the Soul; and I am nothing. It has driven me to the city, where the air is fever and fire, and said, 'breathe this';—I would learn; I cannot learn in the empty fields; temples are here,—stay.' And when my poor, stifled lungs have panted till it seemed my chest must burst, the soul has said, 'I will allow you then, an hour or two; we will ride, and I will take my book and read meanwhile.'

And when my eyes have cried out the tears of pain for the brief vision of freedom drifting by, only for leave to look at the great green [and] blue an hour, after the long, dull-red horror of walls, the soul has said, 'I cannot waste the time altogether; I must know! read.' And when my ears have plead for the singing of the crickets and the music of the night, the soul has answered, 'No, gongs and whistles and shrieks are unpleasant if you listen; but school yourself to hearken to the spiritual voice, and it will not matter ...'

When I have looked upon my kind, and longed to embrace them, hungered wildly for the press of arms and lips, the soul has commanded

sternly, 'cease, [vile] creature of fleshly lusts! Eternal reproach! Will you
forever shame me with your beastliness?'
    And I have always yielded, mute, joyless, fettered, I have trod the
world of the soul's choosing ... Now I am broken before my time, bloodless, sleepless, breathless,—half blind, racked at every joint, trembling
with every leaf."

    Yet though racked and wrecked, her life empty of the music, the glory
of sky and sun, and her body rose in daily revolt against the tyrannical
master, it was Voltairine's soul that conquered—the Dominant Idea which
gave her strength to go on and on to the last.
    Voltairine de Cleyre was born in Nov. 17, 1866, in the town of Leslie,
Michigan. Her ancestry on her father's side was French-American, on her
mother's Puritan stock. She came to her revolutionary tendencies by inheritance, both her grand-father and father having been imbued with the
ideas of the Revolution of 1848. But while her grand-father remained true
to the early influences, even in late life helping in the underground railroad
for fugitive slaves, her father, August de Cleyre, who had begun as a freethinker and Communist, in later life, returned to the fold of the Catholic
Church and became as passionate a devotee of it, as he had been against it
in his younger days. So great had been his free thought zeal that when his
daughter was born he named her Voltairine, in honor of the revered
Voltaire. But when he recanted, he became obsessed by the notion that his
daughter must become a nun. A contributory factor may also have been
the poverty of the de Cleyres, as the result of which the early years of little
Voltairine were anything but happy. But even in her childhood she showed
little concern in external things, being almost entirely absorbed in her own
fancies. School held a great fascination for her and when refused admission
because of her extreme youth, she wept bitter tears.
    However, she soon had her way, and at the age of twelve she graduated
from the Grammar School with honors and would very likely have out-
stripped most women of her time in scholarship and learning, had not the
first great tragedy come into her life, a tragedy which broke her body and left
a lasting scar upon her soul. She was placed in a monastery, much against the
will of her mother who, as a member of the Presbyterian Church, fought—
in vain—against her husband's decision. At the Convent of Our Lady of
Lake Huron, at Sarnia, Ontario, Canada, began the four-years' calvary of the
future rebel against religious superstition. In her essay on THE MAKING
OF AN ANARCHIST she vividly describes the terrible ordeal of those years:

    How I pity myself now, when I remember it, poor lonesome little soul,
    battling solitary in the murk of religious superstition, unable to believe

and yet in hourly fear of damnation, hot, savage, and eternal, if I do not instantly confess and profess; how well I recall the bitter energy with which I repelled my teacher's enjoinder, when I told her I did not wish to apologize for an adjudged fault as I could not see that I had been wrong and would not feel my words. 'It is not necessary,' said she, 'that we should feel what we say, but it is always necessary that we obey our superiors.' 'I will not lie,' I answered hotly, and at the same time trembled, lest my disobedience had finally consigned me to torment ... it had been like the Valley of the Shadow of Death, and there are white scars on my soul, where ignorance and superstition burnt me with their hell fire in those stifling days. Am I blasphemous? It is their word, not mine. Beside that battle of my young days all others have been easy, for whatever was without, within my own Will was supreme. It has owed no allegiance, and never shall; it has moved steadily in one direction, the knowledge and the assertion of its own liberty, with all the responsibility falling thereon.

Her endurance at an end, Voltairine made an attempt to escape from the hateful place. She crossed the river to Port Huron and tramped seventeen miles, but her home was still far away. Hungry and exhausted, she had to turn back to seek refuge in a house of an acquaintance of the family. These sent for her father who took the girl back to the Convent.

Voltairine never spoke of the penance meted out to her, but it must have been harrowing, because as a result of her monastic life her health broke down completely when she had hardly reached the age of sixteen. But she remained in the Convent school to finish her studies: rigid self-discipline and perseverance, which so strongly characterised her personality, were already dominant in Voltairine's girlhood. But when she finally graduated from her ghastly prison, she was changed not only physically, but spiritually as well. "I struggled my way out at last," she writes, "and was a free-thinker when I left the institution, though I had never seen a book or heard a word to help me in my loneliness."

Once out of her living tomb she buried her false god. In her fine poem, THE BURIAL OF MY DEAD PAST, she sings:

"And now, Humanity, I turn to you;
I consecrate my service to the world!
Perish the old love, welcome to the new—
Broad as the space-aisles where the stars are whirled!"

Hungrily she devoted herself to the study of free-thought literature, her alert mind absorbing everything with ease. Presently she joined the secular movement and became one of its outstanding figures. Her lectures, always carefully prepared, (Voltairine scorned extemporaneous speaking) were richly studded with original thought and were brilliant in form and presentation. Her address on Thomas Paine, for instance, excelled similar efforts of Robert Ingersoll in all his flowery oratory.

During a Paine memorial convention, in some town in Pennsylvania, Voltairine de Cleyre chanced to hear Clarence Darrow on Socialism. It was the first time the economic side of life and the Socialist scheme of a future society were presented to her. That there is injustice in the world she knew, of course, from her own experience. But here was one who could analyse in such masterly manner the causes of economic slavery, with all its degrading effects upon the masses; moreover, one who could also clearly delineate a definite plan of reconstruction. Darrow's lecture was manna to the spiritually famished young girl. "I ran to it" she wrote later, "as one who has been turning about in darkness runs to the light, I smile now at how quickly I adopted the label 'Socialism' and how quickly I casted aside."

She cast it aside, because she realised how little she knew of the historic and economic back-ground of Socialism. Her intellectual integrity led her to stop lecturing on the subject and to begin delving into the mysteries of sociology and political economy. But, as the earnest study of Socialism inevitably brings one to the more advanced ideas of Anarchism, Voltairine's inherent love of liberty could not make peace with State-ridden notions of Socialism. She discovered, she wrote at this time, that "Liberty is not the daughter but the mother of order" [quotation from Proudhon, ed.].

During a period of several years she believed to have found an answer to her quest for liberty in the Individualist-Anarchist school represented by Benjamin R. Tucker's publication *Liberty*, and the works of Proudhon, Herbert Spencer, and other social thinkers. But later she dropped all economic labels, calling herself simply an Anarchist, because she felt that "Liberty and experiment alone can determine the best economic forms of Society."

The first impulse towards Anarchism was awakened in Voltairine de Cleyre by the tragic event in Chicago, on the 11th of November, 1887. In sending the Anarchists to the gallows, the State of Illinois stupidly boasted that it had also killed the ideal for which the men died. What a senseless mistake, constantly repeated by those who sit on the thrones of the mighty! The bodies of Parsons, Spies, Fisher, Engel and Lingg were barely cold when already new life was born to proclaim their ideals.

Voltairine, like the majority of the people of America, poisoned by the perversion of facts in the press of the time, at first joined in the cry, "They ought to be hanged!" But hers was a searching mind, not of the kind that could long be content with mere surface appearances. She soon came to regret her haste. In her first address, on the occasion of the anniversary of the 11th of November 1887, Voltairine, always scrupulously honest with herself, publicly declared how deeply she regretted having joined in the cry of "They ought to be hanged!" which, coming from one who at that time no longer believed in capital punishment, seemed doubly cruel.

> For that ignorant, outrageous, blood-thirsty sentence I shall never forgive myself," she said, "though I know the dead men would have forgiven me. But my own voice, as it sounded that night, will sound so in my ears till I die,—a bitter reproach and shame.

Out of the heroic death in Chicago a heroic life emerged, a life consecrated to the ideas for which the men were put to death. From that day until her end, Voltairine de Cleyre used her powerful pen and her great mastery of speech in behalf of the ideal which had come to mean to her the only raison d'etre of her life.

Voltairine de Cleyre was unusually gifted: as poet, writer, lecturer and linguist, she could have easily gained for herself a high position in her country and the renown it implies. But she was not one to market her talents for the flesh-pots of Egypt. She would not even accept the simplest comforts from her activities in the various social movements she had devoted herself to during her life. She insisted on arranging her life consistently with her ideas, on living among the people whom she sought to teach and inspire with human worth, with a passionate longing for freedom and a strength to strive for it. This revolutionary vestal lived as the poorest of the poor, amongst dreary and wretched surroundings, taxing her body to the utmost, ignoring externals, sustained only by the Dominant Idea which led her on.

As a teacher of languages in the ghettoes of Philadelphia, New York and Chicago, Voltairine eked out a miserable existence, yet out of her meagre earnings she supported her mother, managed to buy a piano on the installment plan (she loved music passionately and was an artist of no small measure) and to help others more able physically than she was. How she ever did it not even her nearest friends could explain. Neither could anyone fathom the miracle of energy which enabled her, in spite of a weakened condition and constant physical torture, to give lessons for 14 hours, seven days of the week, contribute to numerous magazines and papers, write poetry and sketches, prepare and deliver lectures which for lucidity and beauty were master-pieces. A short tour through England and Scotland in 1897, was the only relief from her daily drudgery. It is certain that she could not have survived such an ordeal for so many years but for the Dominant Idea that steeled her persistent Will.

In 1902, a demented youth who had once been Voltairine's pupil and who somehow developed the peculiar aberration that she was an anti-Semite (she who had devoted most of her life to the education of Jews!)

waylaid her while she was returning from a music lesson. As she approached him, unaware of impending danger, he fired several bullets into her body. Voltairine's life was saved, but the effects of the shock and her wounds marked the beginning of a frightful physical purgatory. She became afflicted with a maddening, ever-present din in her ears. She used to say that the most awful noises in New York were harmony compared to the deafening pounding in her ears. Advised by her physicians that a change of climate might help her, she went to Norway. She returned apparently improved, but not for long. Illness led her from hospital to hospital, involving several operations, without bringing relief. It must have been in one of these moments of despair that Voltairine de Cleyre contemplated suicide. Among her letters, a young friend of hers in Chicago found, long after her death, a short note in Voltairine's hand-writing, addressed to no one in particular, containing the desperate resolve:

I am going to do tonight that which I have always intended to do should those circumstances arise which have now arisen in my life. I grieve only that in my spiritual weakness I failed to act on my personal convictions long ago, and allowed myself to be advised, and misadvised by others. It would have saved me a year of unintermittant suffering and my friends a burden which, however kindly they have borne it, was still a useless one.

In accordance with my beliefs concerning life and its objects, I hold it to be the simple duty of anyone afflicted with an incurable disease to cut his agonies short. Had any of my physicians told me when I asked them the truth of the matter, a long and hopeless tragedy might have been saved. But, obeying what they call 'medical ethics,' they chose to promise the impossible (recovery), in order to keep me on the rack of life. Such action let them account for themselves, for I hold it to be one of the chief crimes of the medical profession that they tell these lies.

That no one be unjustly charged, I wish it understood that my disease is chronic catarrh of the head, afflicting my ears with incessant sound for a year past. It has nothing whatever to do with the shooting of two years ago, and no one is in any way to blame.

I wish my body to be given to the Hahnemann College to be used for dissection; I hope Dr. H. L. Northrop will take it in charge. I want no ceremonies, nor speeches over it. I die, as I have lived, a free spirit, an Anarchist, owing no allegiance to rulers, heavenly or earthly. Though I sorrow for the work I wished to do, which time and loss of health prevented, I am glad I lived no useless life (save this one last year) and hope that the work I did will live and grow with my pupils' lives and by them be passed on to others, even as I passed on what I had received. If my comrades wish to do aught for my memory, let them print my poems, the MSS. of which is in possession of N. N., to whom I leave this last task of carrying out my few wishes.

My dying thoughts are on the vision of a free world, without poverty
and its pain, ever ascending to sublimer knowledge.

VOLTAIRINE DE CLEYRE

There is no indication anywhere, why Voltairine, usually so determined, failed to carry out her intention. No doubt it was again the
Dominant Idea; her Will to life was too strong.

In the note revealing her decision of ending her life, Voltairine asserts
that her malady had nothing to do with the shooting which occurred two
years prior. She was moved to exonerate her assailant by her boundless
human compassion, as she was moved by it, when she appealed to her comrades for funds to help the youth and when she refused to have him prose-
cuted by "due process of law." She knew better than the judges the cause
and effect of crime and punishment. And she knew that in any event the
boy was irresponsible. But the chariot of law rolled on. The assailant was
sentenced to seven years prison, where soon he lost his mind altogether,
dying in an insane asylum two years later. Voltairine's attitude towards criminals and her view of the barbarous futility of punishment are incorporated
in her brilliant treatise on CRIME AND PUNISHMENT. After a pene-
trating analysis of the causes of crime, she asked:

> Have you ever watched it coming in,—the sea? When the wind comes
> roaring out of the mist and a great bellowing thunders up from the
> water? Have you watched the white lions chasing each other towards the
> walls, and leaping up with foaming anger, as they strike, and turn and
> chase each other along the black bars of their cage in rage to devour each
> other? And tear back? And leap in again? Have you ever wondered in the
> midst of it all, *which particular drops of water would strike the wall?* If one
> could know all the facts one might calculate even that. But who can
> know them all? Of one thing only we are sure; some must strike it.
>
> They are the criminals, those drops of water pitching against that
> silly wall and broken. Just why it was those particular ones we cannot
> know; but some had to go. Do not curse them; you have cursed them
> enough ..."

She closes her wonderful expose, of criminology with this appeal: "Let
us have done with this savage idea of punishment, which is without wisdom. Let us work for the freedom of man from the oppression which
makes criminals, and for the enlightened treatment of the sick."

Voltairine de Cleyre began her public career as a pacifist, and for many
years she sternly set her face against revolutionary methods. But the events in
Europe during the latter years of her life, the Russian Revolution of 1905, the
rapid development of Capitalism in her own country, with all its resultant

cruelty, violence and injustice, and particularly the Mexican Revolution changed her view of methods. As always when, after an inner struggle, Voltairine saw cause for change, her large nature would compel her to admit error freely and bravely stand up for the new. She did so in her able essays on DIRECT ACTION and THE MEXICAN REVOLUTION. She did more; she fervently took up the fight of the Mexican people who threw off their yoke; she wrote, she lectured, she collected funds for the Mexican cause. She even grew impatient with some of her comrades because they saw in the events across the American border only one phase of the social struggle and not the all-absorbing issue to which everything else should be subordinated. I was among the severely criticised and so was *Mother Earth,* a magazine I published. But I had often been censured by Voltairine for my "waste" of effort to reach the American intelligentsia rather than to consecrate all my efforts to the workers, as she did so ardently. But, knowing her deep sincerity, the religious zeal which stamped everything she did, no one minded her censorship: we went on loving and admiring her just the same. How deeply she felt the wrongs of Mexico can best be seen from the fact that she began to study Spanish and had actually planned to go to Mexico to live and work among the Yaqui Indians and to become an active force in the Revolution. In 1910, Voltairine de Cleyre moved from Philadelphia to Chicago, where she again took up teaching of immigrants; at the same time she lectured, worked on a history of the so-called Haymarket Riot, translated from French the life of Louise Michel, the priestess of pity and vengeance, as W. T. Stead had named the French Anarchist, and other works dealing with Anarchism by foreign writers. Constantly in the throes of her terrible affliction, she knew but too well that the disease would speedily bring her to the grave. But she endured her pain stoically, without letting her friends know the inroads her illness was making upon her constitution. Bravely she fought for life with infinite patience and pains, but in vain. The infection gradually penetrated deeper and, finally, there developed a mastoid which necessitated an immediate operation. She might have recovered from it had not the poison spread to the brain. The first operation impaired her memory; she could recollect no names, even of the closest friends who watched over her. It was reasonably certain that a second operation, if she could have survived it, would have left her without the capacity for speech. Soon grim Death made all scientific experiment on the much-tortured body of Voltairine de Cleyre unnecessary. She died on June 6th, 1912. In Waldheim cemetery, near the grave of the Chicago Anarchists, lies at rest Voltairine de Cleyre, and every year large masses journey there to pay homage to the memory of America's first Anarchist martyrs, and they lovingly remember Voltairine de Cleyre.

The bare physical facts in the life of this unique woman are not difficult to record. But they are not enough to clarify the traits that combined in her character, the contradictions in her soul, the emotional tragedies in her life. For, unlike other great social rebels, Voltairine's public career was not very rich in events. True, she had some conflicts with the powers that be, she was forcibly removed from the platform on several occasions, she was arrested and tried on others, but never convicted. On the whole, her activities went on comparatively smoothly and undisturbed. Her struggles were of psychologic nature, her bitter disappointments having their roots in her own strange being. To understand the tragedy of her life, one must try to trace its inherent causes. Voltairine herself has given us the key to her nature and inner conflicts. In several of her essays and, specifically, in her autobiographical sketches. In THE MAKING OF AN ANARCHIST we learn, for instance, that if she were to attempt to explain her Anarchism by the ancestral vein of rebellion, she would be, even though at bottom convictions are temperamental, "a bewildering error in logic; for, by early influences and education I should have been a nun, and spent my life glorifying Authority in its most concentrated form."

There is no doubt that the years in the Convent had not only undermined her physique but had also a lasting effect upon her spirit; they killed the mainsprings of joy and of gaiety in her. Yet there must have been an inherent tendency to asceticism, because even four years in the living tomb could not have laid such a crushing hand upon her entire life. Her whole nature was that of an ascetic. Her approach to life and ideals was that of the old-time saints who flagellated their bodies and tortured their souls for the glory of God. Figuratively speaking, Voltairine also flagellated herself, as if in penance for our Social Sins; her poor body was covered with ungainly clothes and she denied herself even the simplest joys, not only because of lack of means, but because to do otherwise would have been against her principles.

Every social and ethical movement had had its ascetics, of course, the difference between them and Voltairine was that they worshipped no other gods and had no need of any, excepting their particular ideal. Not so Voltairine. With all her devotion to her social ideals, she had another god—the god of Beauty. Her life was a ceaseless struggle between the two; the ascetic determinedly stifling her longing for beauty, but the poet in her as determinedly yearning for it, worshipping it in utter abandonment, only to be dragged back by the ascetic to the other deity, her social ideal, her devotion to humanity. It was not given to Voltairine to combine them both; hence the inner lacerating struggle.

Nature has been very generous towards Voltairine, endowing her with a singularly brilliant mind, with a rich and sensitive soul. But physical beauty and feminine attraction were witheld from her, their lack made more apparent by ill-health and her abhorrence of artifice. No one felt this more poignantly than she did herself. Anguish over her lack of physical charm speak in her hauntingly autobiographic sketch, THE REWARD OF AN APOSTATE [*Selected Writings*, p.433, *ed.*]:

> Oh, that my god will none of me! That is an old sorrow! My god was Beauty, and I am all unbeautiful, and ever was. There is no grace in these harsh limbs of mine, nor was at any time. I, to whom the glory of a lit eye was as the shining of stars in a deep well, have only dull and faded eyes, and always had; the chiselled lip and chin whereover runs the radiance of life in bubbling gleams, the cup of living wine was never mine to taste or kiss. I am earth-colored and for my own ugliness sit in the shadows, that the sunlight may not see me, nor the beloved of my god. But, once, in my hidden corner, behind a curtain of shadows, I blinked at the glory of the world, and had such joy of it as only the ugly know, sitting silent and worshipping, forgetting themselves and forgotten. Here in my brain it glowed, the shimmering of the dying sun upon the shore, the long [gold] line between the sand and sea, where the sliding foam caught fire and burned to death ...
>
> Here in my brain, my silent unrevealing brain, were the eyes I loved, the lips I dared not kiss, the sculptured head and tendrilled hair. They were here always in my wonder-house, my house of Beauty. The temple of my god. I shut the door on common life and worshipped here. And no bright, living, flying thing in whose body beauty dwells as guest can guess the ecstatic joy of a brown, silent creature, a toad-thing, squatting on the shadowed ground, self-blotted, motionless, thrilling with the presence of All-Beauty, though it has no part therein.

This is complemented by a description of her other god, the god of physical strength, the maker and breaker of things, the re-moulder of the world. Now she followed him and would have run abreast because she loved him so,—

> not with that still ecstacy of [flooding] joy wherewith my own god filled me of old, but with impetuous, eager fires, that burned and beat through all the blood-threads of me. 'I love you, love me back,' I cried, and would have flung myself upon his neck. Then he turned on me with a ruthless blow; and fled away over the world, leaving me crippled, stricken, powerless, a fierce pain driving through my veins—gusts of pain!—and I crept back into my [old] cavern, stumbling, blind and deaf, only for the haunting vision of my shame and the rushing sound of fevered blood.

I quoted at length because this sketch is symbolic of Voltairine's emotional tragedies and singularly self-revealing of the struggles silently fought against the fates that gave her so little of what she craved most. Yet,

Voltairine had her own peculiar charm which showed itself most pleasingly when she was roused over some wrong, or when her pale face lit up with the inner fire of her ideal. But the men who came into her life rarely felt it; they were too overawed by her intellectual superiority, which held them for a time. But the famished soul of Voltairine de Cleyre craved for more than mere admiration which the men had either not the capacity or the grace to give. Each in his own way "turned on her with a ruthless blow," and left her desolate, solitary, heart-hungry.

Voltairine's emotional defeat is not an exceptional case; it is the tragedy of many intellectual women. Physical attraction always has been, and no doubt always will be, a decisive factor in the love-life of two persons. Sex-relationship among modern peoples has certainly lost much of its former crudeness and vulgarity. Yet it remains a fact today, as it has been for ages, that men are chiefly attracted not by a woman's brain or talents, but by her physical charm. That does not necessarily imply that they prefer woman to be stupid. It does imply, however, most men prefer beauty to brains, perhaps because in true male fashion they flatter themselves that they have no need of the former in their own physical make-up and that they have sufficient of the latter not to seek for it in their wives. At any rate, therein has been the tragedy of many intellectual women.

There was one man in Voltairine's life who cherished her for the beauty of her spirit and the quality of her mind, and who remained a vital force in her life until his own sad end. This man was Dyer D. Lum, the comrade of Albert Parsons and his co-editor on *The Alarm*—the Anarchist paper published in Chicago before the death of Parsons. How much their friendship meant to Voltairine we learn from her beautiful tribute to Dyer D. Lum in her poem IN MEMORIAM from which I quote the last stanza:

Oh, Life, I love you for the love of him
Who showed me all your glory and your pain!
'Into Nirvana'—so the deep tones sing—
And there—and there—we shall—be—one—again."

Measured by the ordinary yard-stick, Voltairine de Cleyre was anything but normal in her feelings and reactions. Fortunately, the great of the world cannot be weighed in numbers and scales; their worth lies in the meaning and purpose they give to existence, and Voltairine has undoubtedly enriched life with meaning and given sublime idealism as its purpose. But, as a study of human complexities she offers rich material. The woman who consecrated herself to the service of the submerged, actually experiencing poignant agony at the sight of suffering, whether of children or dumb animals (she was obsessed by love for the latter and would give shelter and nourishment to every stray cat and dog, even to the extent of breaking with a friend because she objected to her cats invading every corner of the house), the woman who loved her mother devotedly, maintaining her at the cost of her own needs,—this generous comrade whose heart went out to all who were in pain or sorrow, was almost entirely lacking in the mother instinct. Perhaps it never had a chance to assert itself in an atmosphere of freedom and harmony. The one child she brought into the world had not been wanted. Voltairine was deathly ill the whole period of pregnancy, the birth of her child nearly costing the mother's life. Her situation was aggravated by the serious rift that took place at this time in her relationship with the father of this child. The stifling Puritan atmosphere in which the two lived did not serve to improve matters. All of it resulted in the little one being frequently changed from place to place and later even used by the father as a bait to compel Voltairine to return to him. Subsequently, deprived of opportunity to see her child, kept in ignorance even of its whereabouts, she gradually grew away from him. Many years passed before she saw the boy again and he was then seventeen years of age. Her efforts to improve his much-neglected education met with failure. They were strangers to each other. Quite naturally perhaps, her male child felt like most men in her life; he, too, was overawed by her intellect, repelled by her austere mode of living. He went his way. He is today probably, one of the 100% Americans, commonplace and dull.

Yet Voltairine de Cleyre loved youth and understood it as few grown people do. Characteristically, she wrote to a young friend who was deaf and with whom it was difficult to converse orally:

> Why do you say you are drifting farther and farther from those dear to you? I do not think your experience in that respect is due to your deafness; but to the swell of life in you. All young creatures feel the time come when a new surge of life overcomes them, drives them onward, they know not where. And they lose hold on the cradles of life, and parental love, and they almost suffocate with the pressure of forces in themselves. And even if they hear they feel so vague, restless, looking for some definite thing to come.
>
> It seems to you it is your deafness; but while that is a terrible thing, you mustn't think it would solve the problem of loneliness if you could hear. I know how your soul must fight against the inevitability of your depriva-tion; I, too, could never be satisfied and resigned to the 'inevitable.' I fought it when there was no use and no hope. But the main cause of loneliness is, as I say, the surge of life, which in time will find its own expression.

Full well she knew "the surge of life," and the tragedy of vain seeking for an outlet, for in her it had been suppressed so long that she was rarely able to give vent to it, except in her writings. She dreaded "company" and crowds, though she was at home on the platform; proximity she shrank from. Her reserve and isolation, her inability to break through the wall raised by years of silence in the Convent and years of illness are disclosed in a letter to her young correspondent:

> Most of the time I shrink away from people and talk—especially talk. With the exception of a few—a very few people, I hate to sit in people's company. You see I have (for a number of reasons I cannot explain to anybody) had to go away from the home and friends where I lived for twenty years. And no matter how good other people are to me, I never feel at home anywhere. I feel like a lost or wandering creature that has no place, and cannot find anything to be at home with. And that's why I don't talk much to you, nor to others (excepting the two or three that I knew in the east). I am always far away. I cannot help it. I am too old to learn to like new corners. Even at home I never talked much, with but one or two persons. I'm sorry. It's not because I want to be morose, but I can't bear company. Haven't you noticed that I never like to sit at table when there are strangers? And it gets worse all the time. Don't mind it.

Only on rare occasions could Voltairine de Cleyre freely communicate herself, give out of her rich soul to those who loved and understood her. She was a keen observer of man and his ways, quickly detecting sham and able to separate the wheat from the chaff. Her comments on such occasions were full of penetration, interspersed with a quiet, rippling humor. She used to tell an interesting anecdote about some detectives who had come to arrest her. It was in 1907, in Philadelphia, when the guardians of law descended upon her home. They were much surprised to find that Voltairine did not look like the traditional newspaper Anarchist. They seemed sorry to arrest her, but "them's orders," they apologetically declared. They made a search of her apartment, scattering her papers and books and, finally, discovering a copy of her revolutionary poems entitled: THE WORM TURNS. With contempt they threw it aside. "Hell, it's only about worms," they remarked.

They were rare moments when Voltairine could overcome her shyness and reserve, and really feel at home with a few selected friends. Ordinarily, her natural disposition, aggravated by constant physical pain, and the deafening roar in her ears, made her taciturn and extremely uncommunicative. She was sombre, the woes of the world weighing heavily upon her. She saw life mostly in greys and blacks and painted it accordingly. It is this which prevented Voltairine from becoming one of the greatest writers of her time.

But no one who can appreciate literary quality and musical prose will deny Voltairine de Cleyre's greatness after reading the stories and sketches already mentioned and the others contained in her collected works.

Particularly, her "Chain Gang" [*Selected Works*, p. 414, *ed.*], picturing the negro convicts slaving on the highways of the south, is for beauty of style, feeling and descriptive power, a literary gem that has few equals in English literature. Her essays are most forceful, of extreme clarity of thought and original expression. And even her poems, though somewhat old-fashioned in form, rank higher than much that now passes for poetry.

However, Voltairine did not believe in "art for art's sake." To her art was the means and the vehicle to voice life in its ebb and flow, in all its stern aspects for those who toil and suffer, who dream of freedom and dedicate their lives to its achievement. Yet more significant than her art was Voltairine de Cleyre's life itself, a supreme heroism moved and urged on by her ever-present Dominant Idea.

The prophet is alien in his own land. Most alien is the American prophet. Ask any 100-percenter what he knows of the truly great men and women of his country, the superior souls that give life inspiration and beauty, the teachers of new values. He will not be able to name them. How, then, should he know of the wonderful spirit that was born in some obscure town in the State of Michigan, and who lived in poverty all her life, but who by sheer force of will pulled herself out of a living grave, cleared her mind from the darkness of superstition,—turned her face to the sun, perceived a great ideal and determinedly carried it to every corner of her native land? The 100-percenters feel more comfortable when there is no one to disturb their drabness. But the few who themselves are souls in pain, who long for breadth and vision—they need to know about Voltairine de Cleyre. They need to know that American soil sometimes does bring forth exquisite plants. Such consciousness will be encouraging. It is for them that this sketch is written, for them that Voltairine de Cleyre, whose body lies in Waldheim, is being spiritually resurrected—as it were—as the poet-rebel, the liberty-loving artist, the greatest woman-Anarchist of America. But more graphically than any description of mine, her own words in the closing chapter of THE MAKING OF AN ANARCHIST express the true personality of Voltairine de Cleyre:—

> Good-natured satirists often remark that 'the best way to cure an Anarchist is to give him a fortune.' Substituting 'corrupt' for 'cure,' I would subscribe to this; and believing myself to be no better than the rest of mortals, I earnestly hope that as so far it has been my [lot] to work, and work hard, and for no fortune, so I may continue to the end; for let me keep the integrity of my soul, with all the limitations of my material conditions, rather than become the spine-less and ideal-less creation of material needs. My reward is that I live with the young; I keep step with my comrades; I shall die in the harness with my face to the east—the East and the Light.

Part II

Loving Freedom

Anarchism without Adjectives

Introduction

Voltairine de Cleyre loved freedom unreservedly. Fierce in her hatred of unjust authority, fervent in her love of individual liberty, she was born to be an anarchist. Even her teenage years trapped in a rigid Catholic convent could not quell her spirit. "Her revulsion against religious dogma and the doctrine of absolute obedience, so deeply implanted by these years at [the convent]," writes her biographer Paul Avrich, "were to evolve into a generalized hatred of authority and obscurantism in all their manifestations." She was later to say, in her essay, "Why I am an Anarchist," that her answer to this question of why was "because I cannot help it."

Inclined already by character to resist authority, Voltairine also acknowledged two specific influences that led her to the anarchist philosophy. One was an event, the famous Haymarket affair. Eight innocent anarchist men, (four were later hanged and one committed suicide), were convicted on flimsy and trumped up evidence for planting a bomb that killed seven policemen in the Chicago Haymarket Square on May 3, 1886. When four were finally executed, in spite of the pleas of many, she was bitterly disappointed. This gross miscarriage of justice had a profound effect on her, as it also did with Emma Goldman. "Till then," she wrote in this essay, "I believed in the essential justice of the American law and trial by jury. After that I never could."

The other major influence that propelled Voltairine toward anarchism was Benjamin Tucker's individualist anarchist journal *Liberty*. The heady doctrine of individual liberty and personal autonomy preached by the individualists was a natural for Voltairine's rebellious, anti-authoritarian spirit. She had dallied briefly with socialism, but quickly found it too authoritarian for her tastes. Her "inherent love of liberty," wrote Emma Goldman, "could not make peace with State-ridden notions of Socialism." Nor was she comfortable with the conventional standards of behavior of most socialists. Within anarchism, there was room for her iconoclastic temperament and her nonconformity. Though she did not continue to label herself an individualist anarchist, she was never to become a communist anarchist (as claimed by Goldman and others), as her short piece, "A Correction," shows. She remained distinctly individualistic in her outlook, even if not in her economic views, passionately espousing a belief in personal autonomy and individual freedom, most especially in her feminist works, the rest of her all too brief life.

Though Voltairine did not espouse one particular economic theory, she did think dire economic conditions were at the heart of social problems of the day. The State, she believed, contributed to the problem of poverty rather than to the solution. The uselessness of government in dealing with crimes against property, let alone in dealing with poverty itself, is a major reason she cites for becoming an anarchist in "Why I am an Anarchist."

Voltairine begins the essay, "Anarchism," with a declaration that there are two spirits abroad in the world—the spirit of Caution and the spirit of Dare; the spirit of Immobility, the spirit of change. Voltairine, the rebel, was on the side of change and dare: the side of anarchism. She discusses what were then four major branches of American anarchism: individualist, communist, mutualist, and socialist. What she sees in all of them is the denial of authority over the individual. All of them seek a change in the structure of society, a chance to try freedom. This change, she believed, would result both in more freedom and more plenty for all. But, she confesses in explaining her objections to each, none of these systems satisfy her.

"I am an Anarchist, simply," she declared in "A Correction," "without economic label attached." She was more interested in social issues such as women's rights and injustice than economics (the main, though not only, dividing line between anarchist factions). Instead she thought it likely that, given a chance, people would experiment with a wide range of economic systems in different locales, choosing the one that suited each.

The notion of unhyphenated anarchism or "anarchism without adjectives" had been developed by two Spanish anarchists, Ricardo Mella and Fernando Tarrida del Mármol. Troubled by bitter debates between mutualists, individualists and communists in 1880s, they called for greater tolerance. "We are anarchists and we proclaim anarchy without adjectives. Anarchy is an axiom; the economic question is secondary." During the next few years many prominent European anarchists adopted similar positions, including Errico Malatesta, Elisée Reclus, and Max Nettlau. Nettlau, one of the great historians of anarchism, echoing a sentiment expressed earlier by Voltairine, declared in two anarchist publications in 1914 that anarchists must "never permit themselves to become fossilized upholders of a given system," for "neither Communism nor Individualism, if it became the sole form, would realize freedom, which always demand a choice of ways, a plurality of possibilities." Similar sentiments were also expressed by Voltairine's colleagues, Dyer Lum and Jo Labadie.

In "Events are the True Schoolmaster," Voltairine takes a swipe at overinflated anarchist egos by pointing out that the society of the future will not fall neatly into any anarchist's forecast. Since there is no perfect method, fighting over which method is best is a little like a "Christian Inquisitor protecting the Almighty against heretics." In this essay, she also belies the notion that all anarchists are violent by declaring that forcible physical resistance is neither logical nor desirable. Her idea of a peaceful anarchism was very much in keeping with the American revolutionary tradition, a theme she developed in "Anarchism and American Traditions."

"Anarchism and American Traditions" is perhaps Voltairine's best known and certainly her most reprinted essay, appearing in several collections in the 1970s, with various small anarchist press editions since then. Considered one of her best essays as well as one of her most original, it was an attempt to dispel the frightening image that anarchism conjured up in the minds of many Americans. Fueled by sensationalistic reports of assassinations and attempted assassinations by alleged anarchists, anarchism was seen, in Hippolyte Havel's words, as a "foreign poison imported into the States from decadent Europe by criminal paranoiacs." The truth about anarchism, as Voltairine attempted to show, is very different. The essay traces the roots of the anarchist ideas of local self-rule, individual conscience, and decentralization of power as far back as the pre-Revolutionary War traditions of religious rebellion and small, self-sustaining communities.

What does this argument say to modern Americans? Most Americans pay lip service to the American political tradition but few really understand what it is and what its implications are. This essay can serve as an invitation to explore American libertarian roots, to ask ourselves what are the real lessons of the American Revolution, what are its ideals, how far have we strayed from these ideals? A century ago Voltairine railed against the growing gap between the early ideals of the revolutionary republicans and the actual practice of an increasingly oppressive government. What would she say now if she could see what the American government now has the power to do to its people? What has happened to the American ideal of local self-rule, the concept of decentralization of power? How have we become inured to oppressive rules and excessive taxation that make the complaints that precipitated the pre-Revolutionary War Boston Tea Party look trivial in comparison?

—Sharon Presley

Sources

All American Anarchist: Joseph A. Labadie and the Labor Movement by Carlotta Anderson. Detroit: Wayne State University Press,1998.

An American Anarchist: The Life of Voltairine de Cleyre by Paul Avrich. Princeton, NJ: Princeton University Press, 1978.

Voltairine de Cleyre by Emma Goldman. Berkeley Heights, NJ: Oriole Press, 1932.

Why I Am An Anarchist

This is something of a credo for Voltairine as she entered her last, most radical, period (it was originally delivered as a lecture in Indiana, and was published in *Mother Earth* in March 1908). It is a combination of autobiography and theory that has Voltairine describing the aspects of her own character that drove her toward anarchism, and then describing the anarchism her character drove her toward. It is revolutionary in its extraction of truth from emotion and politics from personality.

"Elisée and Elie and Paul Reclus": Elisée (1830–1905), Elie (1827–1904) were French anarchists and brothers. Paul Reclus (d. 1941) was Elie's son.

Peter Kropotkin (1842–1921) was a Russian prince and scientist. The pre-eminent figure of communist anarchism, he provided the theoretical underpinnings of the agitation of Emma Goldman and others.

Daniel Garrison Brinton of Philadelphia (1837–1899) began his career as a battlefield doctor during the Civil War. He then turned to Ethnology, authoring some twenty volumes on American Indian languages and religion. His radical side is revealed in his long essay on Giordano Bruno.

"Story of an African Farm": autobiographical novel by Olive Schreiner (1855–1920).

"Enemy of the People": play by Henrik Ibsen.

"Ghosts": play by Ibsen.

"History of the People of England": by John Richard Green (1837–1883).

"Single Tax": reformist proposal of the late nineteenth century, associated with Henry George (1839–1897), that envisioned the nationalization of all land and operation of the government exclusively by 100% tax on rents.

"Wm. Morris' 'News From Nowhere'": Utopian novel published in 1890 by the British designer and moralist William Morris (1834–1896).

"Channing" is William Ellery Channing (1780–1842), Unitarian minister and abolitionist.

Why I Am An Anarchist

IT was suggested to me by those who were the means of securing me this opportunity of addressing you, that probably the most easy and natural way for me to explain Anarchism would be for me to give the reasons why I myself am an Anarchist. I am not sure that they were altogether right in the matter, because in giving the reasons why I am an Anarchist, I may perhaps infuse too much of my own personality into the subject, giving reasons sufficient unto myself, but which cool reflection might convince me were not particularly striking as reasons why other people should be Anarchists, which is, after all, the object of public speaking on the question.

Nevertheless, I have been guided by their judgment, thinking they are perhaps right in this, that one is apt to put much more feeling and freedom into personal reasons than in pure generalizations.

The question "Why I am an Anarchist" I could very summarily answer with "because I cannot help it," I cannot be dishonest with myself; the conditions of life press upon me; I must do something with my brain. I cannot be content to regard the world as a mere jumble of happenings for me to wander my way through, as I would through the mazes of a department store, with no other thought than getting through it and getting out. Neither can I be contented to take anybody's dictum on the subject; the thinking machine will not be quiet. It will not be satisfied with century-old repetitions; it perceives that new occasions bring new duties; that things have changed, and an answer that fitted a question asked four thousand, two thousand, even one thousand years ago, will not fit any more. It wants something for today.

People of the mentally satisfied order, who are able to roost on one intellectual perch all their days, have never understood this characteristic of the mentally active. It was said of the Anarchists that they were peace-disturbers, wild, violent ignoramuses, who were jealous of the successful in life and fit only for prison or an asylum. They did not understand, for their sluggish temperaments did not assist them to perceive, that the peace was disturbed by certain elements, which men of greater mental activity had sought to seize and analyze. With habitual mental phlegm they took cause for effect, and mistook Anarchists, Socialists and economic reformers in general for the creators of that by which they were created.

The assumption that Anarchists were one and all ignoramuses was quite as gratuitously made. For years it was not considered worth while to find out whether they might not be mistaken. We who have been some years in the movement have watched the gradual change of impression in this respect, not over-patiently it is true; we are not in general a patient sort—till we have at length seen the public recognition of the fact that while many professed Anarchists are uneducated, some even unintelligent (though their number is few), the major portion are people of fair education and intense mental activity, going around setting interrogation points after things; and some, even, such as Elisée and Elie and Paul Reclus, Peter Kropotkin, Edward Carpenter, or the late Prof. Daniel G. Brinton, of the University of Pennsylvania, men of scientific pre-eminence.

Mental activity alone, however, would not be sufficient; for minds may be active in many directions, and the course of the activity depends upon other elements in their composition.

The second reason, therefore, why I am an Anarchist, is because of the possession of a very large proportion of sentiment.

In this statement I may very likely not be recommending myself to my fellow Anarchists, who would perhaps prefer that I proceeded immediately to reasons. I am willing, however, to court their censure, because I think it has been the great mistake of our people, especially of our American Anarchists represented by Benj. R. Tucker, to disclaim sentiment. Humanity in the mass is nine parts feeling to one part thought; the so-called "philosophic Anarchists" have prided themselves on the exaggeration of the little tenth, and have chosen to speak rather contemptuously of the "submerged" nine parts. Those who have studied the psychology of man, however, realize this: that our feelings are the filtered and tested results of past efforts on the part of the intellect to compass the adaptation of the individual to its surroundings. The unconscious man is the vast reservoir which receives the final product of the efforts of the conscious—that brilliant, gleaming, illuminate point at which mental activity centers, but which, after all, is so small a part of the human being. So that if we are to despise feeling we must equally despise logical conviction, since the former is but the preservation of past struggles of the latter.

Now my feelings have ever revolted against repression in all forms, even when my intellect, instructed by my conservative teachers, told me repression was right. Even when my thinking part declared it was nobody's fault that one man had so much he could neither swallow it down nor wear it out, while another had so little he must die of cold and hunger, my feelings would not be satisfied. They raised an unending protest against the heavenly administration that managed earth so badly. They could never be reconciled to the idea that any human being could be in existence merely through the benevolent toleration of another human being. The feeling always was that society ought to be in such a form that any one who was willing to work ought to be able to live in plenty, and nobody ought to have such "an awful lot" more than anybody else. Moreover, the instinct of liberty naturally revolted not only at economic servitude, but at the outcome of it, class-lines. Born of working parents (I am glad to be able to say it), brought up in one of those small villages where class differences are less felt than in cities, there was, nevertheless, a very keen perception that certain persons were considered better worth attentions, distinctions, and rewards than others, and that these certain persons were the daughters and sons of the well-to-do. Without any belief whatever that the possession of wealth to the exclusion of others was wrong, there was yet an instinctive decision that there was much injustice in educational opportunities being given to those who could scarcely make use of them, simply because their parents were wealthy; to quote the language of a little friend of mine, there was an inward protest against "the people with five hundred dollar brains getting five thousand dollar educations," while the bright children of the poor had to be taken out of school and put to work. And so with other material concerns.

Beyond these, there was a wild craving after freedom from conventional dress, speech, and custom; an indignation at the repression of one's real sentiments and the repetition of formal hypocrisies, which constitute the bulk of ordinary social intercourse; a consciousness that what are termed "the amenities" were for the most part gone through with as irksome forms, representing no real heartiness. Dress, too,—there was such an ever-present feeling that these ugly shapes with which we distort our bodies were forced upon us by a stupid notion that we must conform to the anonymous everybody who wears a stock-collar in mid-summer and goes dé-colleté at Christmas, puts a bunch on its sleeves to-day and a hump on its back to-morrow, dresses its slim tall gentlemen in claw-hammers this season, and its little fat gentlemen in Prince Alberts the next,—in short, affords no opportunity for the individuality of the person to express itself in outward taste or selection of forms.

An eager wish, too, for something better in education than the set program of the grade-work, every child's head measured by every other child's head, regimentation, rule, arithmetic, forever and ever; nothing to develop originality of work among teachers; the perpetual dead level; the eternal average. Parallel with all these, there was a constant seeking for something new and fresh in literature, and unspeakable ennui at the presentation and re-presentation of the same old ideal in the novel, the play, the narrative, the history. A general disgust for the poor but virtuous fair-haired lady with blue eyes, who adored a dark-haired gentleman with black eyes and much money, and to whom, after many struggles with the jealous rival, she was happily married; a desire that there should be persons who should have some other purpose in appearing before us than to exhibit their love-sickness, people with some other motive in walking through a book than to get married at the end. A similar feeling in taking up an account of travels; a desire that the narrator would find something better worth recounting than his own astonishment at some particular form of dress he had never happened to see before, or a dish he had never eaten in his own country; a desire that he would tell us of the conditions, the aspirations, the activities of those strange peoples. Again the same unrest in reading a history, an overpowering sentiment of revolt at the spun-out details of the actions of generals, the movements of armies, the thronement and dethronement of kings, the intrigues of courtiers, the gracing or disgracing of favorites, the place-hunting of republics, the count of elections, the numbering of administrations! A never-ending query, "What were the common people doing all this time? What did they do who did not go to war? How did they associate, how did they feel, how did they dream? What had they, who paid for all these things, to say, to sing, to act?"

And when I found a novel like the "Story of An African Farm," a drama like the "Enemy of the People" or "Ghosts," a history like Green's "History of the People of England," I experienced a sensation of exaltation at leaping out from the old forms, the old prohibitions, the old narrowness of models and schools, at coming into the presence of something broad and growing.

So it was with contemplation of sculpture or drawing,—a steady dissatisfaction with the conventional poses, the conventional subjects, the fig-leafed embodiments of artistic cowardice; underneath was always the demand for freedom of movement, fertility of subject, and ease and *non-shame*. Above all, a disgust with the subordinated cramped circle prescribed for women in daily life, whether in the field of material production, or in domestic arrangement, or in educational work; or in the ideals held up to her on all these various screens whereon the ideal reflects itself; a bitter, passionate sense of personal injustice in this respect; an anger at the institutions set up by men, ostensibly to preserve female purity, really working out to make her a baby, an irresponsible doll of a creature not to be trusted outside her "doll's house." A sense of burning disgust that a mere legal form should be considered as the sanction for all manner of bestialities; that a woman should have no right to escape from the coarseness of a husband, or conversely, without calling down the attention, the scandal, the scorn of society. That in spite of all the hardship and torture of existence men and women should go on obeying the old Israelitish command, "Increase and multiply," merely because they have society's permission to do so, without regard to the slaveries to be inflicted upon the unfortunate creatures of their passions.

All these feelings, these intense sympathies with suffering, these cravings for something earnest, purposeful, these longings to break away from old standards, jumbled about in the ego, produced a shocking war; they determined the bent to which mental activity turned; they demanded an answer,—an answer that should co-ordinate them all, give them direction, be the silver cord running through this mass of disorderly, half-articulate contentions of the soul.

The province for the operation of conscious reasoning was now outlined; all the mental energies were set to the finding of an ideal which would justify these clamors, allay these bitternesses. And first for the great question which over-rides all others, the question of bread. It was easy to see that any proposition to remedy the sorrows of poverty along old lines could only be successful for a locality or a season, since they must depend upon the personal good-nature of individual employers, or the leniency of a creditor. The power to labor at will would be forever locked within the hands of a limited number.

The problem is not how to find a way to relieve temporary distress, not to make people dependent upon the kindness of others, but to allow every one to be able to stand upon his own feet.

A study into history,—that is a history of the movements of peoples,—revealed that, while the struggless of the past have chiefly been political in their formulated objects, and have resulted principally in the disestablishment of one form of political administration by another, the causes of discontent have chiefly been economic—too great disparity in possessions between class and class. Even those uprisings centred around some religious leader were, in the last analysis, a revolt of the peasant against an oppressive landlord and tithe-taker—the Church.

It is extremely hard for an American, who has been nursed in the traditions of the revolution, to realize the fact that that revolution must be classed precisely with others, and its value weighed and measured by its results, just as they are. I am an American myself, and was at one time as firmly attached to those traditions as any one can be; I believed that if there were any way to remedy the question of poverty the Constitution must necessarily afford the means to do it. It required long thought and many a dubious struggle between prejudice and reason before I was able to arrive at the conclusion that the political victory of America had been a barren thing: that a declaration of equal rights on paper, while an advance in human evolution in so far that at least it crystallized a vague ideal, was after all but an irony in the face of facts; that what people wanted to make them really free was the *right to things;* that a "free country" in which all the productive tenures were already appropriated was not free at all; that any man who must wait the complicated working of a mass of unseen powers before he may engage in the productive labor necessary to get his food is the last thing but a free man; that those who do command these various resources and powers, and therefore the motions of their fellow-men, command likewise the manner of their voting, and that hence the reputed great safeguard of individual liberties, the ballot box, becomes but an added instrument of oppression in the hands of the possessor; finally, that the principle of majority rule itself, even granting it could ever be practicalized—which it could not on any large scale: it is always a real minority that governs in place of the nominal majority—but even granting it realizable, the thing itself is essentially pernicious; that the only desirable condition of society is one in which no one is compelled to accept an arrangement to which he has not consented.

Since it was a settled thing that to be free one must have liberty of access to the sources and means of production, the question arose, just what are those sources and means, and how shall the common man, whose right to them is now denied, come at them. And here I found a mass of propositions, by one school or another; all however agreed upon one point, viz.: that the land and all that was in it was the natural heritage of all, and none had a right to pre-empt it, and parcel it out to their heirs, administrators, executors, and assigns. But the practical question of how the land could be worked, how homes could be built upon it, factories, etc., brought out a number of conflicting propositions. First, there were the Socialists (that is the branch of Socialism dominant in this country) claiming that the land should become the property of the State, its apportionment to be decided by committees representing the majority of any particular community directly concerned in such apportionment, the right to reapportion, however, remaining perpetually under the control of the State, and no one to receive any more advantage from an extra-fine locality than others, since the surplus in production of one spot over another would accrue to the State, and be expended in public benefits. To accomplish this, the Socialist proposed to use the political machinery now in existence—a machinery which he assures us is in every respect the political reflex of the economics of capitalism; his plan is the old, familiar one of voting your own men in; and when a sufficient number are in, then by legal enactment to dispossess the possessors, confiscate estates, and declare them the property of all.

Examination of this program, however, satisfied me that neither in the end nor the accomplishment was it desirable. For as to the end, it appeared perfectly clear that the individual would still be under the necessity of getting somebody's permission to go to work; that he would be subject to the decisions of a mass of managers, to regulations and regimentations without end. That while, indeed, it was possible he might have more of material comforts, still he would be getting them from a bountiful dispenser, who assumed the knowledge of how to deal them out, and when, and where. He would still be working, not at what he chose himself, but at what others decided was the most necessary labor for society. And as to the manner of bringing into power this new dispenser of opportunities, the apparent ease of it disappeared upon examination. It sounds exceedingly simple—and Socialists are considered practical people because of that apparent simplicity—to say vote your men in and let them legalize expropriation. But ignoring the fact of the long process of securing a legislative majority, and the precarious holding when it is secured; ignoring the fact that meanwhile your men must either remain honest figure-heads or become compromising dealers with other politicians; ignoring the fact that officials once in office are exceedingly liable to insensible conversions (being like the boy, "anything to get that 'ere pup"); supposing all this overcome, Socialists and all legislative reformers are bound to be brought face to face with this,—that in accepting the present constitutional methods, they will sooner or later come against the judicial power, as reforms of a far less sweeping character have very often done in the past. Now the judges, if they act strictly according to their constitutional powers, have no right to say on the bench whether in their personal opinion the enactment is good or bad; they have only to pass upon its constitutionality; and certainly a general enactment for the confiscation of land-holdings to the State would without doubt be pronounced unconstitutional. Then what is the end of all the practical, legal, constitutional effort? That you are left precisely where you were.

Another school of land reformers presented itself; an ingenious affair, by which property in land is to be preserved in name, and abolished in reality. It is based on the theory of economic rent;—not the ordinary, everyday rent we are all uncomfortably conscious of, once a month or so, but a rent arising from the diverse nature of localities. Starting with the proposition that land values are created by the community, not by the individual, the logic goes as follows. The advantages created by all must not be monopolized by one; but as one certain spot can be devoted to one use only at a given time, then the person or business thereon located should pay to the State the difference between what he can get out of a good locality and a poor locality, the amount to be expended in public improvements. This plan of taxation, it was claimed, would compel speculators in land either to allow their idle lands to fall into the hands of the

State, which would then be put up at public auction and knocked down to the highest bidder, or they would fall to and improve them, which would mean employment to the idle, enlivening of the market, stimulation of trade, etc. Out of much discussion among themselves, it resulted that they were convinced that the great unoccupied agricultural lands would become comparatively free, the scramble coming in over the rental of mines, water-powers, and—above all—corner lots in cities.

I did some considerable thinking over this proposition, and came to the conclusion it wouldn't do. First, because it did not offer any chance to the man who could actually bid nothing for the land, which was the very man I was after helping. Second, because the theory of economic rent itself seemed to me full of holes; for, while it is undeniable that some locations are superior to others for one purpose or another, still the discovery of the superiority of that location has generally been due to an individual. The location unfit for a brickyard may be very suitable for a celery plantation; but it takes the man with the discerning eye to see it; therefore this economic rent appeared to me to be a very fluctuating affair, dependent quite as much on the individual as on the presence of the community; and for a fluctuating thing of that sort it appeared quite plain that the community would lose more by maintaining all the officials and offices of a State to collect it, than it would to let the economic rent go. Third, this public disposing of the land was still in the hands of officials, and I failed to understand why officials would be any less apt to favor their friends and cheat the general public then than now.

Lastly and mostly, the consideration of the statement that those who possessed large landholdings would be compelled to relinquish or improve them; and that this improvement would stimulate business and give employment to the idle, brought me to the realization that the land question could never be settled by itself; that it involved the settling of the problem of how the man who did not work directly upon the earth, but who transformed the raw material into the manufactured product, should get the fruit of his toil. There was nothing in this Single Tax arrangement for him but the same old program of selling himself to an employer. This was to be the relief afforded to the fellow who had no money to bid for the land. New factories would open, men would be in demand, wages would rise! Beautiful program. But the stubborn fact always came up that no man would employ another to work for him unless he could get more for his product than he had to pay for it, and that being the case, the inevitable course of exchange and re-exchange would be that the man *having received less than the full amount,* could buy back less than the full amount, so that eventually the unsold products must again accumulate in the capitalist's hands; again the period of non-employment arrives, and my landless worker is no better off than he was before the Single Tax went into operation. I perceived, therefore, that some settlement of the whole labor question was needed which would not split up the people again into land possessors and employed wage-earners. Furthermore, my soul was infinitely sickened by the everlasting discussion about the rent of the corner lot. I conceived that the reason there was such a scramble over the corner lot was because the people were jammed together in the cities, for want of the power to spread out over the country. It does not lie in me to believe that millions of people pack themselves like sardines, worry themselves into dens out of which they must emerge "walking backward," so to speak, for want of space to turn around, poison themselves with foul, smoke-laden, fever-impregnated air, condemn themselves to stone and brick above and below and around, if they just didn't *have* to.

How, then, to make it possible for the man who has nothing but his hands to get back upon the earth and make use of his opportunity? There came a class of reformers who said, "Lo, now, the thing all lies in the money question! The land being free wouldn't make a grain of difference to the worker, unless he had the power to capitalize his credit and thus get the where-with to make use of the land. See, the trouble lies here: the possessors of one particular form of wealth, gold and silver, have the sole power to furnish the money used to effect exchanges. Let us abolish this gold and silver notion; let all forms of wealth be offered as security, and notes issued on such as are accepted, by a mutual bank, and then we shall have money enough to transact all our business without paying interest for the borrowed use of an expensive medium which had far better be used in the arts. And then the man who goes upon the land can buy the tools to work it."

This sounded pretty plausible; but still I came back to the old question, how will the man who has nothing but his individual credit to offer, who has no wealth of any kind, how is he to be benefited by this bank?

And again about the tools: it is well enough to talk of his buying hand tools, or small machinery which can be moved about; but what about the gigantic machinery necessary to the operation of a mine, or a mill? It requires many to work it. If one owns it, will he not make the others pay tribute for using it?

And so, at last, after many years of looking to this remedy and to that, I came to these conclusions:—

That the way to get freedom to use the land is by no tampering and indirection, but plainly by the going out and settling thereon, and using it; remembering always that every newcomer has as good a right to come and labor upon it, become one of the working community, as the first initiators of the movement. That in the arrangement and determination of the uses of locations, each community should be absolutely free to make its own regulations. That there should be no such nonsensical thing as an imaginary line drawn along the ground, within which boundary persons having no interests whatever in common and living hundreds of miles apart, occupied in different pursuits, living according to different customs, should be obliged to conform to interfering regulations made by one another; and while this stupid division binds together those in no way helped but troubled thereby, on the other hand cuts right through the middle of a community united by proximity, occupation, home, and social sympathies.

Second:—I concluded that as to the question of exchange and money, it was so exceedingly bewildering, so impossible of settlement among the professors themselves, as to the nature of value, and the representation of value, and the unit of value, and the numberless multiplications and divisions of the subject, that the best thing ordinary workingmen or women could do was to organize their industry so as to get rid of money altogether. I figured it this way: I'm not any more a fool than the rest of ordinary humanity; I've figured and figured away on this thing for years, and directly I thought myself middling straight, there came another money reformer and showed me the hole in that scheme, till, at last, it appears that between "bills of credit," and "labor notes" and "time checks," and "mutual bank issues," and "the invariable unit of value," none of them have any sense. How many thousands of years is it going to take to get this sort of thing into people's heads by mere preaching of theories? Let it be this way: Let there be an end of the special monopoly on securities for money issues. Let every community go ahead and try some member's money scheme if it wants;—let every individual try it if he pleases. But better for the working people let them all go. Let them produce together, co-operatively rather than as employer and employed; let them fraternize group by group, let each use what he needs of his own product, and deposit the rest in the storage-houses, and let those others who need goods have them as occasion arises.

With our present crippled production, with less than half the people working, with all the conservatism of vested interest operating to prevent improvements in methods being adopted, we have more than enough to supply all the wants of the people if we could only get it distributed. There is, then, no fixed estimate to be put upon possibilities. If one man working now can produce ten times as much as he can by the most generous use dispose of for himself, what shall be said of the capacities of the free worker of the future? And why, then, all this calculating worry about the exact exchange of equivalents? If there is enough and to waste, why fret for fear some one will get a little more than he gives? We do not worry for fear some one will drink a little more water than we do, except it is in a case of shipwreck; because we know there is quite enough to go around. And since all these measures for adjusting equivalent values have only resulted in establishing a perpetual means whereby the furnisher of money succeeds in abstracting a percentage of the product, would it not be better to risk the occasional loss in exchange of things, rather than to have this false adjuster of differences perpetually paying itself for a very doubtful service?

Third:—On the question of machinery I stopped for some time; it was easy enough to reason that the land which was produced by nobody belonged to nobody; comparatively easy to conclude that with abundance of product no money was needed. But the problem of the machinery required a great deal of pro-ing and con-ing; it finally settled itself down so: Every machine of any complexity is the accumulation of the inventive genius of the ages; no one man conceived it; no one man can make it; no one man therefore has a right to the exclusive possession of the social inheritance from the dead; that which requires social genius to conceive and social action to operate, should be free of access to all those desiring to use it.

Fourth:—In the contemplation of the results to follow from the freeing of the land, the conclusion was inevitable that many small communities would grow out of the breaking up of the large communities; that people would realize then that the vast mass of this dragging products up and down the world, which is the great triumph of commercialism, is economic insanity; illustration: Paris butter carted to London, and London butter to Paris! A friend of mine in Philadelphia makes shoes; the factory adjoins the home property of a certain Senator whose wife orders her shoes off a Chicago firm; this firm orders of the self-same factory, which ships the order to Chicago. Chicago ships them back to the Senator's wife; while any workman in the factory might have thrown them over her backyard fence! That, therefore, all this complicated system of freight transportation would disappear, and a far greater approach to simplicity be attained; and hence all the international bureaus of regulation, aimed at by Socialists, would become as unnecessary as they are obnoxious. I conceived, in short, that, instead of the workingman's planting his feet in the mud of the bottomless abyss of poverty, and seeing the trains of the earth go past his tantalized eyes, he carrying the whole thing as Atlas did the world, would calmly set his world down, climb up on it, and go gleefully spinning around it himself, becoming world-citizens indeed. Man, the emperor of products, not products the enslaver of man, became my dream.

At this point I broke off to inquire how much government was left; land titles all gone, stocks and bonds and guarantees of ownership in means of production gone too, what was left of the State? Nothing of its existence in relation to the worker: nothing but its regulation of morals.

I had meanwhile come to the conclusion that the assumptions as to woman's inferiority were all humbug; that given freedom of opportunity, women were just as responsive as men, just as capable of making their own way, producing as much for the social good as men. I observed that women who were financially independent at present, took very little to the notion that a marriage ceremony was sacred, unless it symbolized the inward reality of psychological and physiological mateship; that most of them who were unfortunate enough to make an original mistake, or to grow apart later, were quite able to take their freedom from a mischievous bond without appealing to the law. Hence, I concluded that the State had nothing left to do here; for it has never attempted to do more than solve the material difficulties, in a miserable, brutal way; and these economic independence would solve for itself. As to the heartaches and bitterness attendant upon disappointments of this nature in themselves, apart from third-party considerations,—they are entirely a matter of individual temperament and ethical development, not to be assuaged by any State or social system.

The offices of the State were now reduced to the disposition of criminals. An inquiry into the criminal question made plain that the great mass of crimes are crimes against property; even those crimes arising from jealousy are property crimes resulting from the notion of a right of property in flesh. Allowing property to be eradicated, both in practice and spirit, no crimes are left but such as are the acts of the mentally sick—cases of atavism, which might well be expected occasionally, for centuries to come, as the result of all the repression poor humanity has experienced these thousands of years. An enlightened people, a people living in something like sane and healthy conditions, would consider these criminals as subjects for scientific study and treatment; would not retaliate and exhibit themselves as more brutal than the criminal, as is the custom to-day, but would "use all gently."

The State had now disappeared from my conception of society; there remained only the application of Anarchism to those vague yearnings for the outpouring of new ideals in education, in literature, in art, in customs, social converse, and in ethical concepts. And now the way became easy; for all this talking up and down the question of wealth was foreign to my taste. But education! As long ago as I could remember I had dreamed of an education which should be a getting at the secrets of nature, not as reported through another's eyes, but just the thing itself; I had dreamed of a teacher who should go out and attract his pupils around him as the Greeks did of old, and then go trooping out into the world, free monarchs, learning everywhere—learning nature, learning man, learning to know life in all its forms, and not to hug one little narrow spot and declare it the finest one on earth for the patriotic reason that they live there. And here I picked up Wm. Morris' "News from Nowhere," and found the same thing. And there were the new school artists in France and Germany, the literateurs, the scientists, the inventors, the poets, all breaking way from ancient forms. And there were Emerson and Channing and Thoreau in ethics, preaching the supremacy of individual conscience over the law,—indeed, all that mighty trend of Protestantism and Democracy, which every once in a while lifts up its head above the judgments of the commonplace in some single powerful personality. That indeed is the triumphant word of Anarchism: it comes as the logical conclusion of three hundred years of revolt against external temporal and spiritual authority—the word which has no compromise to offer, which holds before us the unswerving ideal of the Free Man.

Anarchism

One contribution of "Anarchism" is a clarification of the variety of anarchist philosophies and Voltairine's notion that they can be united by the simple idea of human freedom. But another is a clear statement of Voltairine's view of the human self. I quote an extraordinary sentence: "Once and forever to realize that one is not a bundle of well-regulated little reasons bound up in the front room of the brain to be sermonized and held in order with copy-book maxims or moved and stopped by a syllogism, but a bottomless, bottomless depth of all strange sensations, a rocking sea of feeling wherever sweep strong storms of unaccountable hate and rage, invisible contortions of disappointment, low ebbs of meanness, quakings and shudderings of love that drives to madness and will not be controlled, hungerings and moanings and sobbing that smite upon the inner ear, now first bent to listen, as if in all the sadness of the sea and the wailing of the great pine forests of the North had met to weep together there in the silence audible to you alone." "Anarchism" was published in *Free Society*, 13 October 1901, and later appeared in Spanish and Russian.

The "Bresci" referred to late in the piece is Gaetano Bresci, the Italian-American man who assassinated King Humbert of Italy in 1900. Bresci was later found strangled to death in his prison cell.

Anarchism

There are two spirits abroad in the world,—the spirit of Caution, the spirit of Dare, the spirit of Quiescence, the spirit of Unrest; the spirit of Immobility, the spirit of Change; the spirit of Hold-fast-to-that-which-you-have, the spirit of Let-go-and-fly-to-that-which-you-have-not; the spirit of the slow and steady builder, careful of its labors, loath to part with any of its achievements, wishful to keep, and unable to discriminate between what is worth keeping and what is better cast aside, and the spirit of the inspirational destroyer, fertile in creative fancies, volatile, careless in its luxuriance of effort, inclined to cast away the good together with the bad.

Society is a quivering balance, eternally struck afresh, between these two. Those who look upon Man, as most Anarchists do, as a link in the chain of evolution, see in these two social tendencies the sum of the tendencies of individual men, which in common with the tendencies of all organic life are the result of the action and counter-action of inheritance and adaptation. Inheritance, continually tending to repeat what has been, long, long after it is outgrown; adaptation continually tending to break down forms. The same tendencies under other names are observed in the inorganic world as well, and anyone who is possessed by the modern scientific mania for Monism can easily follow out the line to the vanishing point of human knowledge.

There has been, in fact, a strong inclination to do this among a portion of the more educated Anarchists, who having been working men first and Anarchists by reason of their instinctive hatred to the boss, later became students and, swept away by their undigested science, immediately conceived that it was necessary to fit their Anarchism to the revelations of the microscope, else the theory might as well be given up. I remember with considerable amusement a heated discussion some five or six years since, wherein doctors and embryo doctors sought for a justification of Anarchism in the development of the amoeba, while a fledgling engineer searched for it in mathematical quantities.

Myself at one time asserted very stoutly that no one could be an Anarchist and believe in God at the same time. Others assert as stoutly that one cannot accept the spiritualist philosophy and be an Anarchist.

At present I hold with C. L. James, the most learned of American Anarchists, that one's metaphysical system has very little to do with the matter. The chain of reasoning which once appeared so conclusive to me, namely, that Anarchism being a denial of authority over the individual could not co-exist with a belief in a Supreme Ruler of the universe, is contradicted in the case of Leo Tolstoy, who comes to the conclusion that none has a right to rule another just because of his belief in God, just because he believes that all are equal children of one father, and therefore none has a right to rule the other. I speak of him because he is a familiar and notable personage, but there have frequently been instances where the same idea has been worked out by a whole sect of believers, especially in the earlier (and persecuted) stages of their development.

It no longer seems necessary to me, therefore, that one should base his Anarchism upon any particular world conception; it is a theory of the relations due to man and comes as an offered solution to the societary problems arising from the existence of these two tendencies of which I have spoken. No matter where those tendencies come from, all alike recognize them as existent; and however interesting the speculation, however fascinating to lose oneself back, back in the molecular storm-whirl wherein the figure of man is seen merely as a denser, fiercer group, a livelier storm centre, moving among others, impinging upon others, but nowhere separate, nowhere exempt from the same necessity that acts upon all other centers of force,— it is by no means necessary in order to reason oneself into Anarchism.

Sufficient are a good observant eye and a reasonably reflecting brain, for anyone, lettered or unlettered, to recognize the desirability of Anarchistic aims. This is not to say that increased knowledge will not confirm and expand one's application of this fundamental concept; (the beauty of truth is that at every new discovery of fact we find how much wider and deeper it is than we at first thought it). But it means that first of all Anarchism is concerned with present conditions, and with the very plain and common people; and is by no means a complex or difficult proposition.

Anarchism, alone, apart from any proposed economic reform, is just the latest reply out of many the past has given, to that daring, breakaway, volatile, changeful spirit which is never content. The society of which we are part puts certain oppressions upon us,—oppressions which have arisen out of the very changes accomplished by this same spirit, combined with the hard and fast lines of old habits acquired and fixed before the changes were thought of. Machinery, which as our Socialistic comrades continually emphasize, has wrought a revolution in Industry, is the creation of the Dare Spirit; it has fought its way against ancient customs, privilege, and cowardice at every step, as the history of any invention would show if traced backward through all its transformations. And what is the result of it? That a system of working, altogether appropriate to hand production and capable of generating no great oppressions while industry remained in that state, has been stretched, strained to fit production in mass, till we are reaching the bursting point; once more the spirit of Dare must assert itself—claim new freedoms, since the old ones are rendered null and void by the present methods of production.

To speak in detail: in the old days of Master and Man—not so old but what many of the older workingmen can recall the conditions, the workshop was a fairly easy-going place where employer and employed worked together, knew no class feelings, chummed it out of hours, as a rule were not obliged to rush, and when they were, relied upon the principle of common interest and friendship (not upon a slave-owner's power) for overtime assistance. The proportional profit on each man's labor may even have been in general higher, but the total amount possible to be undertaken by one employer was relatively so small that no tremendous aggregations of wealth could arise. To be an employer gave no man power over another's incomings and outgoings, neither upon his speech while at work, nor to force him beyond endurance when busy, nor to subject him to fines and tributes for undesired things, such as ice-water, dirty spittoons, cups of undrinkable tea and the like; nor to the unmentionable indecencies of the large factory. The individuality of the workman was a plainly recognized quantity: his life was his own; he could not be locked in and driven to death, like a street-car horse, for the good of the general public and the paramount importance of Society.

With the application of steam-power and the development of Machinery, came these large groupings of workers, this subdivision of work, which has made of the employer a man apart, having interests hostile to those of his employes, living in another circle altogether, knowing nothing of them but as so many units of power, to be reckoned with as he does his machines, for the most part despising them, at his very best regarding them as dependents whom he is bound in some respects to care for, as a humane man cares for an old horse he cannot use. Such is his relation to his employes; while to the general public he becomes simply an immense cuttle-fish with tentacles reaching everywhere,—each tiny profit-sucking mouth producing no great effect, but in aggregate drawing up such a body of wealth as makes any declaration of equality or freedom between him and the worker a thing to laugh at.

The time is come therefore when the spirit of Dare calls loud through every factory and work-shop for a change in the relations of master and man. There must be some arrangement possible which will preserve the benefits of the new production and at the same time restore the individual dignity of the worker,—give back the bold independence of the old master of his trade, together with such added freedoms as may properly accrue to him as his special advantage from society's material developments.

This is the particular message of Anarchism to the worker. It is not an economic system; it does not come to you with detailed plans of how you, the workers, are to conduct industry; nor systemized methods of exchange; nor careful paper organizations of "the administration of things." It simply calls upon the spirit of individuality to rise up from its abasement, and hold itself paramount in no matter what economic reorganization shall come about. Be men first of all, not held in slavery by the things you make; let your gospel be, "Things for men, not men for things."

Socialism, economically considered, is a positive proposition for such reorganization. It is an attempt, in the main, to grasp at those great new material gains which have been the special creation of the last forty or fifty years. It has not so much in view the reclamation and further assertion of the personality of the worker as it has a just distribution of products.

Now it is perfectly apparent that Anarchy, having to do almost entirely with the relations of men in their thoughts and feelings, and not with the positive organization of production and distribution, an Anarchist needs to supplement his Anarchism by some economic propositions, which may enable him to put in practical shape to himself and others this possibility of independent manhood. That will be his test in choosing any such proposition,—the measure in which individuality is secured. It is not enough for him that a comfortable ease, a pleasant and well-ordered routine, shall be secured; free play for the spirit of change—that is his first demand.

Every Anarchist has this in common with every other Anarchist, that the economic system must be subservient to this end; no system recommends itself to him by the mere beauty and smoothness of its working; jealous of the encroachments of the machine, he looks with fierce suspicion upon an arithmetic with men for units, a society running in slots and grooves, with the precision so beautiful to one in whom the love of order is first, but which only makes him sniff—"Pfaugh! it smells of machine oil."

There are, accordingly, several economic schools among Anarchists; there are Anarchist Individualists, Anarchist Mutualists, Anarchist Communists and Anarchist Socialists. In times past these several schools have bitterly denounced each other and mutually refused to recognize each other as Anarchists at all. The more narrow-minded on both sides still do so; true, they do not consider it is narrow-mindedness, but simply a firm and solid grasp of the truth, which does not permit of tolerance towards error. This has been the attitude of the bigot in all ages, and Anarchism no more than any other new doctrine has escaped its bigots. Each of these fanatical adherents of either collectivism or individualism believes that no Anarchism is possible without that particular economic system as its guarantee, and is of course thoroughly justified from his own standpoint. With the extension of what Comrade Brown calls the New Spirit, however, this old narrowness is yielding to the broader, kindlier and far more reasonable idea, that all these economic conceptions may be experimented with, and there is nothing un-Anarchistic about any of them until the element of compulsion enters and obliges unwilling persons to remain in a community whose economic arrangements they do not agree to. (When I say "do not agree to" I do not mean that they have a mere distaste for, or that they think might well be altered for some other preferable arrangement, but with which, nevertheless, they quite easily put up, as two persons each living in the same house and having different tastes in decoration, will submit to some color of window shade or bit of bric-a-brac which he does not like so well, but which nevertheless, he cheerfully puts up with for the satisfaction of being with his friend. I mean serious differences which in their opinion threaten their essential liberties. I make this explanation about trifles, because the objections which are raised to the doctrine that men may live in society freely, almost always degenerate into trivialities,—such as, "what would you do if two ladies wanted the same hat?" etc. We do not advocate the abolition of common sense, and every person of sense is willing to surrender his preferences at times, provided he is not *compelled* to at all costs.)

Therefore I say that each group of persons acting socially in freedom may choose any of the proposed systems, and be just as thorough-going Anarchists as those who select another. If this standpoint be accepted, we are rid of those outrageous excommunications which belong properly to the Church of Rome, and which serve no purpose but to bring us into deserved contempt with outsiders.

Furthermore, having accepted it from a purely theoretical process of reasoning, I believe one is then in an attitude of mind to perceive certain material factors in the problem which account for these differences in proposed systems, and which even demand such differences, so long as production is in its present state.

I shall now dwell briefly upon these various propositions, and explain, as I go along, what the material factors are to which I have just alluded. Taking the last first, namely, Anarchist Socialism,—its economic program is the same as that of political Socialism, in its entirety;—I mean before the working of practical politics has frittered the Socialism away into a mere list of governmental ameliorations. Such Anarchist Socialists hold that the State, the Centralized Government, has been and ever will be the business agent of the property-owning class; that it is an expression of a certain material condition purely, and with the passing of that condition the State must also pass; that Socialism, meaning the complete taking over of all forms of property from the hands of men as the indivisible possession of Man, brings with it as a logical, inevitable result the dissolution of the State. They believe that every individual having an equal claim upon the social production, the incentive to grabbing and holding being gone, crimes (which are in nearly all cases the instinctive answer to some antecedent denial of that claim to one's share) will vanish, and with them the last excuse for the existence of the State. They do not, as a rule, look forward to any such transformations in the material aspect of society, as some of the rest of us do. A Londoner once said to me that he believed London would keep on growing, the flux and reflux of nations keep on pouring through its serpentine streets, its hundred thousand 'buses keep on jaunting just the same, and all that tremendous traffic which fascinates and horrifies continue rolling like a great flood up and down, up and down, like the sea-sweep,—after the realization of Anarchism, as it does now. That Londoner's name was John Turner; he said, on the same occasion, that he believed thoroughly in the economics of Socialism.

Now this branch of the Anarchist party came out of the old Socialist party, and originally represented the revolutionary wing of that party, as opposed to those who took up the notion of using politics. And I believe the material reason which accounts for their acceptance of that particular economic scheme is this (of course it applies to all European Socialists) that the social development of Europe is a thing of long-continued history; that almost from time immemorial there has been a recognized class struggle; that no workman living, nor yet his father, nor his grandfather, nor his great-grandfather has seen the land of Europe pass in vast blocks from an unclaimed public inheritance into the hands of an ordinary individual like himself, without a title or any distinguishing mark above himself, as we in America have seen. The land and the land-holder have been to him always unapproachable quantities,—a recognized source of oppression, class, and class-possession.

Again, the industrial development in town and city—coming as a means of escape from feudal oppression, but again bringing with it its own oppressions, also with a long history of warfare behind it, has served to bind the sense of class fealty upon the common people of the manufacturing towns; so that blind, stupid, and Church-ridden as they no doubt are, there is a vague, dull, but very certainly existing feeling that they must look for help in association together, and regard with suspicion or indifference any proposition which proposes to help them by helping their employers. Moreover, Socialism has been an ever recurring dream through the long story of revolt in Europe; Anarchists, like others, are born into it. It is not until they pass over seas, and come in contact with other conditions, breathe the atmosphere of other thoughts, that they are able to see other possibilities as well.

If I may venture, at this point, a criticism of this position of the Anarchist Socialist, I would say that the great flaw in this conception of the

State is in supposing it to be of *simple* origin; the State is not merely the tool of the governing classes; it has its root far down in the religious development of human nature; and will not fall apart merely through the abolition of classes and property. There is other work to be done. As to the economic program, I shall criticise that, together with all the other propositions, when I sum up.

Anarchist Communism is a modification, rather an evolution, of Anarchist Socialism. Most Anarchist Communists, I believe, do look forward to great changes in the distribution of people upon the earth's surface through the realization of Anarchism. Most of them agree that the opening up of the land together with the free use of tools would lead to a breaking up of these vast communities called cities, and the formation of smaller groups or communes which shall be held together by a free recognition of common interests only.

While Socialism looks forward to a further extension of the modern triumph of Commerce—which is that it has brought the products of the entire earth to your door-step—free Communism looks upon such a fever of exportation and importation as an unhealthy development, and expects rather a more self-reliant development of home resources, doing away with the mass of supervision required for the systematic conduct of such world exchange. It appeals to the plain sense of the workers, by proposing that they who now consider themselves helpless dependents upon the boss's ability to give them a job, shall constitute themselves independent producing groups, take the materials, do the work (they do that now), deposit the products in the warehouses, taking what they want for themselves, and letting others take the balance. To do this no government, no employer, no money system is necessary. There is only necessary a decent regard for one's own and one's fellow-worker's self-hood. It is not likely, indeed it is devoutly to be hoped, that no such large aggregations of men as now assemble daily in mills and factories, will ever come together by mutual desire. (A factory is a hot-bed for all that is vicious in human nature, and largely because of its crowding only.)

The notion that men cannot work together unless they have a driving-master to take a percentage of their product, is contrary both to good sense and observed fact. As a rule bosses simply make confusion worse confounded when they attempt to mix in a workman's snarls, as every mechanic has had practical demonstration of; and as to social effort, why men worked in common while they were monkeys yet; if you don't believe it, go and watch the monkeys. They don't surrender their individual freedom, either.

In short, the real workmen will make their own regulations, decide when and where and how things shall be done. It is not necessary that the projector of an Anarchist Communist society shall say in what manner separate industries shall be conducted, nor do they presume to. He simply conjures the spirit of Dare and Do in the plainest workmen—says to them: "It is you who know how to mine, how to dig, how to cut; you will know how to organize your work without a dictator; we cannot tell you, but we have full faith that you will find the way yourselves. You will never be free men until you acquire that same self-faith."

As to the problem of the exact exchange of equivalents which so frets the reformers of other schools, to him it does not exist. So there is enough, who cares? The sources of wealth remain indivisible forever; who cares if one has a little more or less, so all have enough? Who cares if something goes to waste? Let it waste. The rotted apple fertilizes the ground as well as if it had comforted the animal economy first. And, indeed, you who worry so much about system and order and adjustment of production to consumption, you waste more human energy in making your account than the precious calculation is worth. Hence money with all its retinue of complications and trickeries is abolished.

Small, independent, self-resourceful, freely cooperating communes— this is the economic ideal which is accepted by most of the Anarchists of the Old World to-day.

As to the material factor which developed this ideal among Europeans, it is the recollection and even some still remaining vestiges of the mediæval village commune—those oases in the great Sahara of human degradation presented in the history of the Middle Ages, when the Catholic Church stood triumphant upon Man in the dust. Such is the ideal glamored with the dead gold of a sun which has set, which gleams through the pages of Morris and Kropotkin. We in America never knew the village commune. White Civilization struck our shores in a broad tide-sheet and swept over the country inclusively; among us was never seen the little commune growing up from a state of barbarism independently, out of primary industries, and maintaining itself within itself. There was no gradual change from the mode of life of the native people to our own; there was a wiping out and a complete transplantation of the latest form of European civilization. The idea of the little commune, therefore, comes instinctively to the Anarchists of Europe,—particularly the continental ones; with them it is merely the conscious development of a submerged instinct. With Americans it is an importation.

I believe that most Anarchist Communists avoid the blunder of the Socialists in regarding the State as the offspring of material conditions purely, though they lay great stress upon its being the tool of Property, and contend that in one form or another the State will exist so long as there is property at all.

I pass to the extreme Individualists,—those who hold to the tradition of political economy, and are firm in the idea that the system of employer and employed, buying and selling, banking, and all the other essential institutions of Commercialism, centering upon private property, are in themselves good, and are rendered vicious merely by the interference of the State. Their chief economic propositions are: land to be held by individuals or companies for such time and in such allotments as they use only; redistribution to take place as often as the members of the community shall agree; what constitutes use to be decided by each community, presumably in town meeting assembled; disputed cases to be settled by a so-called free jury to be chosen by lot out of the entire group; members not coinciding in the decisions of the group to betake themselves to outlying lands not occupied, without let or hindrance from any one.

Money to represent all staple commodities, to be issued by whomsoever pleases; naturally, it would come to individuals depositing their securities with banks and accepting bank notes in return; such bank notes representing the labor expended in production and being issued in sufficient quantity, (there being no limit upon any one's starting in the business, whenever interest began to rise more banks would be organized, and thus the rate per cent would be constantly checked by competition), exchange would take place freely, commodities would circulate, business of all kinds would be stimulated, and, the government privilege being taken away from inventions, industries would spring up at every turn, bosses would be hunting men rather than men bosses, wages would rise to the full measure of the individual production, and forever remain there. Property, real property, would at last exist, which it does not at the present day, because no man gets what he makes.

The charm in this program is that it proposes no sweeping changes in our daily retinue; it does not bewilder us as more revolutionary propositions do. Its remedies are self-acting ones; they do not depend upon conscious efforts of individuals to establish justice and build harmony; competition in freedom is the great automatic valve which opens or closes as demands increase or diminish, and all that is necessary is to let well enough alone and not attempt to assist it.

It is sure that nine Americans in ten who have never heard of any of these programs before, will listen with far more interest and approval to this than to the others. The material reason which explains this attitude of mind is very evident. In this country outside of the Negro question we have never had the historic division of classes; we are just making that history now; we have never felt the need of the associative spirit of workman with workman, because in our society it has been the individual that did things; the workman of to-day was the employer to-morrow; vast opportunities lying open to him in the undeveloped territory, he shouldered his tools and struck out single-handed for himself. Even now, fiercer and fiercer though the struggle is growing, tighter and tighter though the workman is getting cornered, the line of division between class and class is constantly being broken, and the first motto of the American is "the Lord helps him who helps himself." Consequently this economic program, whose key-note is "let alone", appeals strongly to the traditional sympathies and life habits of a people who have themselves seen an almost unbounded patrimony swept up, as a gambler sweeps his stakes, by men who played with them at school or worked with them in one shop a year or ten years before.

This particular branch of the Anarchist party does not accept the Communist position that Government arises from Property; on the contrary, they hold Government responsible for the denial of real property (viz.: to the producer the exclusive possession of what he has produced). They lay more stress upon its metaphysical origin in the authority-creating Fear in human nature. Their attack is directed centrally upon the idea of Authority; thus the material wrongs seem to flow from the spiritual error (if I may venture the word without fear of misconstruction), which is precisely the reverse of the Socialistic view.

Truth lies not "*between* the two," but in a synthesis of the two opinions.

Anarchist Mutualism is a modification of the program of Individualism, laying more emphasis upon organization, co-operation and free federation of the workers. To these the trade union is the nucleus of the free co-operative group, which will obviate the necessity of an employer, issue time-checks to its members, take charge of the finished product, exchange with different trade groups for their mutual advantage through the central federation, enable its members to utilize their credit, and likewise insure them against loss. The mutualist position on the land question is identical with that of the Individualists, as well as their understanding of the State.

The material factor which accounts for such differences as there are between Individualists and Mutualists, is, I think, the fact that the first originated in the brains of those who, whether workmen or business men, lived by so-called independent exertion. Josiah Warren, though a poor man, lived in an Individualist way and made his free-life social experiment in small country settlements, far removed from the great organized industries. Tucker also, though a city man, has never had personal association with such industries. They had never known directly the oppressions of the large factory, nor mingled with workers' associations. The Mutualists had; consequently their leaning towards a greater Communism. Dyer D. Lum spent the greater part of his life in building up workmen's unions, himself being a hand worker, a book-binder by trade.

I have now presented the rough skeleton of four different economic schemes entertained by Anarchists. Remember that the point of agreement in all is: *no compulsion*. Those who favor one method have no intention of forcing it upon those who favor another, so long as equal tolerance is exercised toward themselves.

Remember, also, that none of these schemes is proposed for its own sake, but because through it, its projectors believe, liberty may be best secured. Every Anarchist, *as* an Anarchist, would be perfectly willing to surrender his own scheme directly, if he saw that another worked better.

For myself, I believe that all these and many more could be advantageously tried in different localities; I would see the instincts and habits of the people express themselves in a free choice in every community; and I am sure that distinct environments would call out distinct adaptations.

Personally, while I recognize that liberty would be greatly extended under any of these economies, I frankly confess that none of them satisfies me.

Socialism and Communism both demand a degree of joint effort and administration which would beget more regulation than is wholly consistent with ideal Anarchism; Individualism and Mutualism, resting upon property, involve a development of the private policeman not at all compatible with my notions of freedom.

My ideal would be a condition in which all natural resources would be forever free to all, and the worker individually able to produce for himself sufficient for all his vital needs, if he so chose, so that he need not govern his working or not working by the times and seasons of his fellows. I think that time may come; but it will only be through the development of the modes of production and the taste of the people. Meanwhile we all cry with one voice for the freedom *to try*.

Are these all the aims of Anarchism? They are just the beginning. They are an outline of what is demanded for the material producer. If as a worker, you think no further than how to free yourself from the horrible bondage of capitalism, then that is the measure of Anarchism for you. But you yourself put the limit there, if there it is put. Immeasurably deeper, immeasurably higher, dips and soars the soul which has come out of its casement of custom and cowardice, and dared to claim its Self.

Ah, once to stand unflinchingly on the brink of that dark gulf of passions and desires, once at last to send a bold, straight-driven gaze down into the volcanic Me, *once,* and in that once, and in that once *forever,* to throw off the command to cover and flee from the knowledge of that abyss,—nay, to dare it to hiss and seethe if it will, and make us writhe and shiver with its force! Once and forever to realize that one is not a bundle of well-regulated little reasons bound up in the front room of the brain to be sermonized and held in order with copy-book maxims or moved and stopped by a syllogism, but a bottomless, bottomless depth of all strange sensations, a rocking sea of feeling wherever sweep strong storms of unaccountable hate and rage, invisible contortions of disappointment, low ebbs of meanness, quakings and shudderings of love that drives to madness and will not be controlled, hungerings and moanings and sobbing that smite upon the inner ear, now first bent to listen, as if all the sadness of the sea and the wailing of the great pine forests of the North had met to weep together there in that silence audible to you alone. To look down into that, to know the blackness, the midnight, the dead ages in oneself, to feel the jungle and the beast within,—and the swamp and the slime, and the desolate desert of the heart's despair—to see, to know, to feel to the uttermost,—and then to look at one's fellow, sitting across from one in the street-car, so decorous, so well got up, so nicely combed and brushed and oiled and to wonder what lies beneath that commonplace exterior,—to picture the cavern in him which somewhere far below has a narrow gallery running into your own—to imagine the pain that racks him to the finger-tips perhaps while he wears that placid ironed-shirt-front countenance—to conceive how he too shudders at himself and writhes and flees from the lava of his heart and aches in his prison-house not daring to see himself—to draw back respectfully from the Self-gate of the plainest, most unpromising creature, even from the most debased criminal, because one knows the nonentity and the criminal in oneself—to spare all condemnation (how much more trial and sentence) because one knows the stuff of which man is made and recoils at nothing since all is in himself,—this is what Anarchism may mean to you. It means that to me.

And then, to turn cloudward, starward, skyward, and let the dreams rush over one—no longer awed by outside powers of any order—recognizing nothing superior to oneself—painting, painting endless pictures, creating unheard symphonies that sing dream sounds to you alone, extending sympathies to the dumb brutes as equal brothers, kissing the flowers as one did when a child, letting oneself go free, go free beyond the bounds of what *fear* and *custom* call the "possible,"—this too Anarchism may mean to you, if you dare to apply it so. And if you do some day,—if sitting at your work-bench, you see a vision of surpassing glory, some picture of that golden time when there shall be no prisons on the earth, nor hunger, nor houselessness, nor accusation, nor judgment, and hearts open as printed leaves, and candid as fearlessness, if then you look across at your lowbrowed neighbor, who sweats and smells and curses at his toil,—remember that as you do not know his depth neither do you know his height. He too might dream if the yoke of custom and law and dogma were broken from him. Even now you know not what blind, bound, motionless chrysalis is working there to prepare its winged thing.

Anarchism means freedom to the soul as to the body,—in every aspiration, every growth.

A few words as to the methods. In times past Anarchists have excluded
each other on these grounds also; revolutionists contemptuously said
"Quaker" of peace men; "savage Communists" anathematized the Quakers
in return.

This too is passing. I say this: all methods are to the individual capacity and decision.

There is Tolstoy,—Christian, non-resistant, artist. His method is to
paint pictures of society as it is, to show the brutality of force and the uselessness of it; to preach the end of government through the repudiation of
all military force. Good! I accept it in its entirety. It fits his character, it fits
his ability. Let us be glad that he works so.

There is John Most—old, work-worn, with the weight of prison years
upon him,—yet fiercer, fiercer, bitterer in his denunciations of the ruling
class than would require the energy of a dozen younger men to utter—
going down the last hills of life, rousing the consciousness of wrong among
his fellows as he goes. Good! That consciousness must be awakened. Long
may that fiery tongue yet speak.

There is Benjamin Tucker—cool, self-contained, critical,—sending
his fine hard shafts among foes and friends with icy impartiality, hitting
swift and cutting keen,—and ever ready to nail a traitor. Holding to passive resistance as most effective, ready to change it whenever he deems it
wise. That suits him; in his field he is alone, invaluable.

And there is Peter Kropotkin appealing to the young, and looking
with sweet, warm, eager eyes into every colonizing effort, and hailing with
a child's enthusiasm the uprisings of the workers, and believing in revolution with his whole soul. Him too we thank.

And there is George Brown preaching peaceable expropriation
through the federated unions of the workers; and this is good. It is his best
place; he is at home there; he can accomplish most in his own chosen field.

And over there in his coffin cell in Italy, lies the man whose method was
to kill a king, and shock the nations into a sudden consciousness of the hol-
lowness of their law and order. Him too, him and his act, without reserve I
accept, and bend in silent acknowledgement of the strength of the man.

For there are some whose nature it is to think and plead, and yield and
yet return to the address, and so make headway in the minds of their fel-
lowmen; and there are others who are stern and still, resolute, implacable
as Judah's dream of God;—and those men strike—strike once and have
ended. But the blow resounds across the world. And as on a night when
the sky is heavy with storm, some sudden great white flare sheets across it,
and every object starts sharply out, so in the flash of Bresci's pistol shot the

whole world for a moment saw the tragic figure of the Italian people, starved, stunted, crippled, huddled, degraded, murdered; and at the same moment that their teeth chattered with fear, they came and asked the Anarchists to explain themselves. And hundreds of thousands of people read more in those few days than they had ever read of the idea before.

Ask a method? Do you ask Spring her method? Which is more necessary, the sunshine or the rain? They are contradictory—yes; they destroy each other—yes, but from this destruction the flowers result.

Each choose that method which expresses your selfhood best, and condemn no other man because he expresses his Self otherwise.

Events Are the True
Schoolmasters

This essay is a brief plea for keeping anarchism eclectic and open, and also for the legitimacy of emotion as a factor in political movements. Both of these are central themes of Voltairine's work. It begins with a brief remembrance of her lover and mentor, Dyer Lum, one of the most interesting figures in the history of American anarchism. Twenty-seven years Voltai's senior, Lum came from a prominent family of New England abolitionists and individualists (he was a Civil War veteran, and had run for Lieutenant Governor of Massachusetts on a ticket with Wendell Phillips in 1876). Lum was also at one point secretary to the labor leader Samuel Gompers, and a friend and associate of the Haymarket martyrs. In fact, Dyer Lum was the person who smuggled a dynamite cigar to Louis Lingg, by which the latter committed suicide in prison, cheating the hangman. Lum himself committed suicide in 1893.

"Laputa": land visited by Gulliver in Swift's *Gulliver's Travels*.

Events Are the True Schoolmasters

I count it as one of the best fortunes of my life that in my early days as an anarchist it was my privilege to know Dyer D. Lum. These thirteen years he is in his grave, and yet whenever editors and contributors of anarchist journals fall to denouncing the actions of the unwise, the ebullitions of the mass, I hear his voice, as yesterday, saying in his short, brusque way: "Events are the true schoolmasters."

There was in his day, as there is now, a certain percentage of propagandists who think that they possess the truth, the whole truth, and nothing but the truth (a perhaps enviable condition of mind, but certainly an intolerant one). They appear to think that by the application of certain abstract principles they have been able to chalk-line the course of progress, and that if it be strictly adhered to an unquestionable triumph of these principles lies straight ahead. They are essentially reasonable, cool persons, somewhat over-impressed with their lack of sentimentality, having definite "plans of campaign" in their heads. The trouble is that when the plan is put in action, it meets with the difficulties the mathematical builders of Laputa met when they put up a wall. The planners never look to right or left of the chalk-line to measure the quantities with which they are dealing, or get a relative estimate of their own forces compared with the forces they are endeavoring to guide so straightly. All at once some one of these unreckoned, undisciplined forces flies right across the well-laid-out path; helter-skelter, topsy-turvy goes all the patient work, and the "plan of campaign" is smitten in the house of its friends. Do the campaigners give a look around, now, and take in the situation? Do they begin to recognize that their little labored ant-track was just a bit of a groove bearing relation to the path of progress, about as the rut of a toy cart-wheel to the whole road; that the road is by no means straight, but full of hills and holes and curves and angles according to the obstacles met and the powers of the moving quantity? Not they! The plan is all right; so much the worse for the campaign if it disregards the chalk! The planners adjust their blinkers, give a look in their pocket-mirrors that they may behold "the face of Anarchy" undegenerate, lift up their voices, call for clean water, and wash their

85

hands, publicly, clean—very clean. They have nothing in common with these monsters of the depths which the Frankenstein of the State creates for its own undoing. Take notice, Frankenstein; if you lack epithets to vilify them we, the plumb-line anarchists, will supplement your stock. Nothing in common with these unregulated, undisciplined minds which are devoid of logic and filled only with unreasoning sentiments and the desire for foolish and inconsequent talk. Take notice, Prosecutor; if you lack condemnatory arguments we will furnish them. "Our ways are ways of pleasantness, and all our paths are paths of peace."

What a very pretty thing progress would be if all her ways were likewise; all will admit that unconditionally. However, progress has to do with all mankind, not alone with the calm, the wise, and the patient. There is youth in the world, and youth is generally neither calm nor patient; it does not like to sit in the rear rows and listen to mature considerations rendered in the tone of a stock-market quotation concerning questions that are burning up its heart, itself silent; if it did, it might learn to be wise and calm,—and also ashy and inert. There is feeling in the world, and a very great quantity of it; and those who do the suffering and the sympathizing may be expected to say and to do many things not within the limits of logic. Sometimes these deeds take violent forms, sometimes they take merely foolish forms; but "Events are the true schoolmasters," and in the twenty years that have elapsed since 1886, we have seen the wisdom of the wise confounded more than once, and the action of the resolute, the desperate and the foolish break the line of the opposition and make room for wider action and farther-reaching effort.

Through witnessing these unexpected acts and their still more unanticipated results, I have gradually worked my way to the conviction that, while I cannot see the logic of forcible physical resistance (entailing perpetual retaliations until one of the offended finally refuses to retaliate), there are others who have reached the opposite conclusions, who will act according to their convictions, and who are quite as much part and parcel of the movement towards human liberty as those who preach peace at all costs; that my part as a social student and lover of freedom is to get as wide an outlook as I can, endeavor to appreciate the relative values of contending and interplaying forces, try to detect among the counter-movements the net results, the general forward impulse cutting new barriers, and to move with it, quite confident that there is room and enough for me to hold my individual course within that broad sweep. If someone cuts my course, why, then, I suppose I am cutting his at the same time. No doubt the believers in forcible resistance feel that those of us who eschew force and preach peace are on the wrong track; no doubt the censorious among them think we are a nuisance, a drawback, a damage to the movement, in fact, no anarchists at all. But let us neither read out nor be read out. The ideal of society without government allures us all; we believe in its possibility and that makes us anarchists. But since its realization is in the future, and since the future holds unknown factors, it is nearly certain that the free society of the unborn will realize itself according to no man's present forecast, whether individualist, communist, mutualist, collectivist, or what-not. Such forecasts are useful as centerizing points of striving only. Vast and vague the ideal persists, and a great social drift is setting towards it; somewhat of conscious anarchism therein, but infinitely more of the unconscious anarchism which is in all men. As well "put a bit in the jaws of the sea," as try to control the movements of that great tide. Then why exercise ourselves because someone conceived a different plan of free association from ours? Why, since no one can know a perfect method, nor even act always according to the best method he himself conceives, why fly to the defense of progress and protect destiny? It is a little too much like a Christian Inquisitor protecting the Almighty against heretics.

I believe that if those who feel called upon to act as guardians of the anarchist movement once realized how little it is in need of their guardianship, what a trifle each individual contribution is, even theirs, they would be content to fight the battle with the enemy as it develops (not as they preconceive it ought to develop); and not think it necessary to turn about and add their stripes to those who will be quite sufficiently beaten by the State, merely because such have not waged war as per the cold-blood, wisdom and experience of the gray heads of others.

Anarchism and American
Traditions

"Anarchism and American Traditions" was perhaps the best-known of Voltairine's writings during her lifetime: it was published in *Mother Earth* in late 1908 and early 1909; it has also circulated several times as a pamphlet and received fairly wide attention. In it, she connects her anarchism to the spirit of the American Revolution. She criticizes, among other things, government-sponsored compulsory education, and she compares the anti-Anarchist legislation that followed the McKinley assassination to the Alien and Sedition Acts. One might wish that Voltairine had seen fit to extend this essay into discussions of transcendentalists such as Emerson, Thoreau, and Fuller, and to the abolitionist and American progressive movements of the nineteenth century, to figures such as Josiah Warren, Ezra Heywood, and Victoria Woodhull.

C. L. James, who Voltairine refers to here as "the most learned of American anarchists," was a frequent contributor to anarchist periodicals. He died in 1911 in Wisconsin.

Anarchism and American Traditions

American traditions, begotten of religious rebellion, small self-sustaining communities, isolated conditions, and hard pioneer life, grew during the colonization period of one hundred and seventy years from the settling of Jamestown to the outburst of the Revolution. This was in fact the great constitution-making epoch, the period of charters guaranteeing more or less of liberty, the general tendency of which is well described by Wm. Penn in speaking of the charter for Pennsylvania: "I want to put it out of my power, or that of my successors, to do mischief."

The revolution is the sudden and unified consciousness of these traditions, their loud assertion, the blow dealt by their indomitable will against the counter force of tyranny, which has never entirely recovered from the blow, but which from then till now has gone on remolding and regrappling the instruments of governmental power, that the Revolution sought to shape and hold as defenses of liberty.

To the average American of to-day, the Revolution means the series of battles fought by the patriot army with the armies of England. The millions of school children who attend our public schools are taught to draw maps of the siege of Boston and the siege of Yorktown, to know the general plan of the several campaigns, to quote the number of prisoners of war surrendered with Burgoyne; they are required to remember the date when Washington crossed the Delaware on the ice; they are told to "Remember Paoli," to repeat "Molly Stark's a widow," to call General Wayne "Mad Anthony Wayne," and to execrate Benedict Arnold; they know that the Declaration of Independence was signed on the Fourth of July, 1776, and the Treaty of Paris in 1783; and then they think they have learned the Revolution—blessed be George Washington! They have no idea why it should have been called a "revolution" instead of the "English war," or any similar title: it's the name of it, that's all. And name-worship, both in child and man, has acquired such mastery of them, that the name "American Revolution" is held sacred, though it means to them nothing more than successful force, while the name "Revolution" applied to a further possibility, is a spectre detested and abhorred. In neither case have they any idea of the content of the word, save that of armed force. That has already happened, and long happened, which Jefferson foresaw when he wrote:

> "The spirit of the times may alter, will alter. Our rulers will become corrupt, our people careless. A single zealot may become persecutor, and better men be his victims. It can never be too often repeated that the time for fixing every essential right, on a legal basis, is while our rulers are honest, ourselves united. *From the conclusion of this war we shall be going down hill.* It will not then be necessary to resort every moment to the people for support. They will be forgotten, therefore, and their rights disregarded. They will forget themselves in the sole faculty of making money, and will never think of uniting to effect a due respect for their rights. The shackles, therefore, which shall not be knocked off at the conclusion of this war, will be heavier and heavier, till our rights shall revive or expire in a convulsion."

To the men of that time, who voiced the spirit of that time, the battles that they fought were the least of the Revolution; they were the incidents of the hour, the things they met and faced as part of the game they were playing; but the stake they had in view, before, during, and after the war, the real Revolution, was a change in political institutions which should make of government not a thing apart, a superior power to stand over the people with a whip, but a serviceable agent, responsible, economical, and trustworthy (but never so much trusted as not to be continually watched), for the transaction of such business as was the common concern, and to set the limits of the common concern at the line where one man's liberty would encroach upon another's.

They thus took their starting point for deriving a minimum of government upon the same sociological ground that the modern Anarchist derives the no-government theory; viz., that equal liberty is the political ideal. The difference lies in the belief, on the one hand, that the closest approximation to equal liberty might be best secured by the rule of the majority in those matters involving united action of any kind (which rule of the majority they thought it possible to secure by a few simple arrangements for election), and, on the other hand, the belief that majority rule is both impossible and undesirable; that any government, no matter what its forms, will be manipulated by a very small minority, as the development of the State and United States governments has strikingly proved; that candidates will loudly profess allegiance to platforms before elections, which as officials in power they will openly disregard, to do as they please; and that even if the majority will could be imposed, it would also be subversive of equal liberty, which may be best secured by leaving to the voluntary association of those interested in the management of matters of common concern, without coercion of the uninterested or the opposed.

Among the fundamental likenesses between the Revolutionary Republicans and the Anarchists is the recognition that the little must precede the great; that the local must be the basis of the general; that there can be a free federation only when there are free communities to federate; that the spirit of the latter is carried into the councils of the former, and a local tyranny may thus become an instrument for general enslavement. Convinced of the supreme importance of ridding the municipalities of the institutions of tyranny, the most strenuous advocates of independence, instead of spending their efforts mainly in the general Congress, devoted themselves to their home localities, endeavoring to work out of the minds of their neighbors and fellow-colonists the institutions of entailed property, of a State-Church, of a class-divided people, even the institution of African slavery itself. Though largely unsuccessful, it is to the measure of success they did achieve that we are indebted for such liberties as we do retain, and not to the general government. They tried to inculcate local initiative and independent action. The author of the Declaration of Independence, who in the fall of '76 declined a re-election to Congress in order to return to Virginia and do his work in his own local assembly, in arranging there for public education which he justly considered a matter of "common concern," said his advocacy of public schools was not with any "view to take its ordinary branches out of the hands of private enterprise, which manages *so much better* the concerns to which it is equal"; and in endeavoring to make clear the restrictions of the Constitution upon the functions of the general government, he likewise said: "Let the general government be reduced to foreign concerns only, and let our affairs be disentangled from those of all other nations, except as to commerce, *which the merchants will manage the better the more they are left free to manage for themselves*, and the general government may be reduced to a very simple organization, and a very inexpensive one; a few plain duties to be performed by a few servants." This then was the American tradition, that private enterprise manages better all that to which it is equal. Anarchism declares that private enterprise, whether individual or co-operative, is equal to all the undertakings of society. And it quotes the particular two instances, Education and Commerce, which the governments of the States and of the United States have undertaken to manage and regulate, as the very two which in operation have done more to destroy American freedom and equality, to warp and distort American tradition, to make of government a mighty engine of tyranny, than any other cause, save the unforeseen developments of Manufacture.

It was the intention of the Revolutionists to establish a system of common education, which should make the teaching of history one of its principal branches; not with the intent of burdening the memories of our
youth with the dates of battles or the speeches of generals, nor to make of
the Boston Tea Party Indians the one sacrosanct mob in all history, to be
revered but never on any account to be imitated, but with the intent that
every American should know to what conditions the masses of people had
been brought by the operation of certain institutions, by what means they
had wrung out their liberties, and how those liberties had again and again
been filched from them by the use of governmental force, fraud, and privilege. Not to breed security, laudation, complacent indolence, passive acquiescence in the acts of a government protected by the label "home-made,"
but to beget a wakeful jealousy, a never-ending watchfulness of rulers, a
determination to squelch every attempt of those entrusted with power to
encroach upon the sphere of individual action—this was the prime motive
of the revolutionists in endeavoring to provide for common education.

"Confidence," said the revolutionists who adopted the Kentucky
Resolutions, "is everywhere the parent of despotism; free government is
founded in jealousy, not in confidence; it is jealousy, not confidence,
which prescribes limited constitutions to bind down those whom we are
obliged to trust with power; our Constitution has accordingly fixed the
limits to which, and no further, our confidence may go. * * * In questions
of power, let no more be heard of confidence in man, but bind him down
from mischief by the chains of the Constitution."

These resolutions were especially applied to the passage of the Alien
laws by the monarchist party during John Adams' administration, and were
an indignant call from the State of Kentucky to repudiate the right of the
general government to assume undelegated powers, for, said they, to accept
these laws would be "to be bound by laws made, not with our consent, but
by others against our consent—that is, to surrender the form of government we have chosen, and to live under one deriving its powers from its
own will, and not from our authority." Resolutions identical in spirit were
also passed by Virginia, the following month; in those days the States still
considered themselves supreme, the general government subordinate.

To inculcate this proud spirit of the supremacy of the people over their
governors was to be the purpose of public education! Pick up to-day any
common school history, and see how much of this spirit you will find
therein. On the contrary, from cover to cover you will find nothing but
the cheapest sort of patriotism, the inculcation of the most unquestion-
ing acquiescence in the deeds of government, a lullaby of rest, security,
confidence,—the doctrine that the Law can do no wrong, a Te Deum
in praise of the continuous encroachments of the powers of the general

government upon the reserved rights of the States, shameless falsification of all acts of rebellion, to put the government in the right and the rebels in the wrong, pyrotechnic glorifications of union, power, and force, and a complete ignoring of the essential liberties to maintain which was the purpose of the revolutionists. The anti-Anarchist law of post-McKinley passage, a much worse law than the Alien and Sedition acts which roused the wrath of Kentucky and Virginia to the point of threatened rebellion, is exalted as a wise provision of our All-Seeing Father in Washington.

Such is the spirit of government-provided schools. Ask any child what he knows about Shays's rebellion, and he will answer, "Oh, some of the farmers couldn't pay their taxes, and Shays led a rebellion against the court-house at Worcester, so they could burn up the deeds; and when Washington heard of it he sent over an army quick and taught 'em a good lesson"—" And what was the result of it?" "The result? Why—why—the result was—Oh yes, I remember—the result was they saw the need of a strong federal government to collect the taxes and pay the debts." Ask if he knows what was said on the other side of the story, ask if he knows that the men who had given their goods and their health and their strength for the freeing of the country now found themselves cast into prison for debt, sick, disabled, and poor, facing a new tyranny for the old; that their demand was that the land should become the free communal possession of those who wished to work it, not subject to tribute, and the child will answer "No." Ask him if he ever read Jefferson's letter to Madison about it, in which he says:

"Societies exist under three forms, sufficiently distinguishable. 1. Without government, as among our Indians. 2. Under government wherein the will of every one has a just influence; as is the case in England in a slight degree, and in our States in a great one. 3. Under government of force, as is the case in all other monarchies, and in most of the other republics. To have an idea of the curse of existence in these last, they must be seen. It is a government of wolves over sheep. It is a problem not clear in my mind that the first condition is not the best. But I believe it to be inconsistent with any great degree of population. The second state has a great deal of good in it. ... It has its evils, too, the principal of which is the turbulence to which it is subject. ... But even this evil is productive of good. It prevents the degeneracy of government, and nourishes a general attention to public affairs. I hold that a little rebellion now and then is a good thing."

Or to another correspondent: "God forbid that we should ever be twenty years without such a rebellion! ... What country can preserve its liberties if its rulers are not warned from time to time that the people preserve the spirit of resistance? Let them take up arms. ... The tree of liberty must be refreshed from time to time with the blood of patriots and tyrants. It is its natural manure." Ask any school child if he was ever taught that the

author of the Declaration of Independence, one of the great founders of
the common school, said these things, and he will look at you with open
mouth and unbelieving eyes. Ask him if he ever heard that the man who
sounded the bugle note in the darkest hour of the Crisis, who roused the
courage of the soldiers when Washington saw only mutiny and despair
ahead, ask him if he knows that this man also wrote, "Government at best
is a necessary evil, at worst an intolerable one," and if he is a little better
informed than the average he will answer, "Oh well, *he* was an infidel!"
Catechize him about the merits of the Constitution which he has learned
to repeat like a poll-parrot, and you will find his chief conception is not of
the powers withheld from Congress, but of the powers granted.

Such are the fruits of government schools. We, the Anarchists, point
to them and say: If the believers in liberty wish the principles of liberty
taught, let them never intrust that instruction to any government; for the
nature of government is to become a thing apart, an institution existing for
its own sake, preying upon the people, and teaching whatever will tend to
keep it secure in its seat. As the fathers said of the governments of Europe,
so say we of this government also after a century and a quarter of independence: "The blood of the people has become its inheritance, and those
who fatten on it will not relinquish it easily."

Public education, having to do with the intellect and spirit of a people,
is probably the most subtle and far-reaching engine for molding the course of
a nation; but commerce, dealing as it does with material things and producing immediate effects, was the force that bore down soonest upon the paper
barriers of constitutional restriction, and shaped the government to its
requirements. Here, indeed, we arrive at the point where we, looking over
the hundred and twenty-five years of independence, can see that the simple
government conceived by the revolutionary republicans was a foredoomed
failure. It was so because of (1) the essence of government itself; (2) the
essence of human nature; (3) the essence of Commerce and Manufacture.

Of the essence of government, I have already said, it is a thing apart,
developing its own interests at the expense of what opposes it; all attempts
to make it anything else fail. In this Anarchists agree with the traditional
enemies of the Revolution, the monarchists, federalists, strong government
believers, the Roosevelts of to-day, the Jays, Marshalls, and Hamiltons of
then,—that Hamilton, who, as Secretary of the Treasury, devised a financial system of which we are the unlucky heritors, and whose objects were
twofold: To puzzle the people and make public finance obscure to those
that paid for it; to serve as a machine for corrupting the legislatures; "for
he avowed the opinion that man could be governed by two motives only,
force or interest;" force being then out of the question, he laid hold of
interest, the greed of the legislators, to set going an association of persons

having an entirely separate welfare from the welfare of their electors, bound together by mutual corruption and mutual desire for plunder. The Anarchist agrees that Hamilton was logical, and understood the core of government; the difference is, that while strong governmentalists believe this is necessary and desirable, we choose the opposite conclusion, NO GOVERNMENT WHATEVER.

As to the essence of human nature, what our national experience has made plain is this, that to remain in a continually exalted moral condition is not human nature. That has happened which was prophesied: we have gone down hill from the Revolution until now; we are absorbed in "mere money-getting." The desire for material ease long ago vanquished the spirit of '76. What was that spirit? The spirit that animated the people of Virginia, of the Carolinas, of Massachusetts, of New York, when they refused to import goods from England; when they preferred (and stood by it) to wear coarse homespun cloth, to drink the brew of their own growths, to fit their appetites to the home supply, rather than submit to the taxation of the imperial ministry. Even within the lifetime of the revolutionists the spirit decayed, The love of material ease has been, in the mass of men and permanently speaking, always greater than the love of liberty. Nine hundred and ninety-nine women out of a thousand are more interested in the cut of a dress than in the independence of their sex; nine hundred and nine-nine men out of a thousand are more interested in drinking a glass of beer than in questioning the tax that is laid on it; how many children are not willing to trade the liberty to play for the promise of a new cap or a new dress? This it is which begets the complicated mechanism of society; this it is which, by multiplying the concerns of government, multiplies the strength of government and the corresponding weakness of the people; this it is which begets indifference to public concern, thus making the corruption of government easy.

As to the essence of Commerce and Manufacture, it is this: to establish bonds between every corner of the earth's surface and every other corner, to multiply the needs of mankind, and the desire for material possession and enjoyment.

The American tradition was the isolation of the States as far as possible. Said they: We have won our liberties by hard sacrifice and struggle unto death. We wish now to be let alone and to let others alone, that our principles may have time for trial; that we may become accustomed to the exercise of our rights; that we may be kept free from the contaminating influence of European gauds, pagents, distinctions. So richly did they esteem the absence of these that they could in all fervor write: "We shall see multiplied instances of Europeans coming to America, but no man living will ever see an instance of an American removing to settle in Europe, and continuing there." Alas! In less than a hundred years the highest aim of a

"Daughter of the Revolution" was, and is, to buy a castle, a title, and a rotten lord, with the money wrung from American servitude! And the commencial interests of America are seeking a world-empire!

In the earlier days of the revolt and subsequent independence, it appeared that the "manifest destiny" of America was to be an agricultural people, exchanging food stuffs and raw materials for manufactured articles. And in those days it was written: "We shall by virtuous as long as agriculture is our principal object, which will be the case as long as there remain vacant lands in any part of America. When we get piled upon one another in large cities, as in Europe, we shall become corrupt as in Europe, and go to eating one another as they do there." Which we are doing, because of the inevitable development of Commerce and Manufacture, and the concomitant development of strong government. And the parallel prophecy is likewise fulfilled: "If ever this vast country is brought under a single government, it will be one of the most extensive corruption, indifferent and incapable of a wholesome care over so wide a spread of surface." There is not upon the face of the earth to-day a government so utterly and shamelessly corrupt as that of the United States of America. There are others more cruel, more tyrannical, more devastating; there is none so utterly venal.

And yet even in the very days of the prophets, even with their own consent, the first concession to this later tyranny was made. It was made when the Constitution was made; and the Constitution was made chiefly because of the demands of Commerce. Thus it was at the outset a merchant's machine, which the other interests of the country, the land and labor interests, even then foreboded would destroy their liberties. In vain their jealousy of its central power made them enact the first twelve amendments. In vain they endeavored to set bounds over which the federal power dare not trench. In vain they enacted into general law the freedom of speech, of the press, of assemblage and petition. All of these things we see ridden rough-shod upon every day, and have so seen with more or less intermission since the beginning of the nineteenth century. At this day, every police lieutenant considers himself, and rightly so, as more powerful than the General Law of the Union; and that one who told Robert Hunter that he held in his fist something stronger than the Constitution, was perfectly correct. The right of assemblage is an American tradition which has gone out of fashion; the police club is now the mode. And it is so in virtue of the people's indifference to liberty, and the steady progress of constitutional interpretation towards the substance of imperial government.

It is an American tradition that a standing army is a standing menace to liberty; in Jefferson's presidency the army was reduced to 3,000 men. It is American tradition that we keep out of the affairs of other nations. It is American practice that we meddle with the affairs of everybody else from the West to the East Indies, from Russia to Japan; and to do it we have a standing army of 83,251 men.

It is American tradition that the financial affairs of a nation should be transacted on the same principles of simple honesty that an individual conducts his own business; viz., that debt is a bad thing, and a man's first surplus earnings should be applied to his debts; that offices and office-holders should be few. It is American practice that the general government should always have millions of debt, even if a panic or a war has to be forced to prevent its being paid off; and as to the application of its income, office-holders come first. And within the last administration it is reported that 99,000 offices have been created at an annual expense of $63,000,000. Shades of Jefferson! "How are vacancies to be obtained? Those by deaths are few; by resignation none." Roosevelt cuts the knot by making 99,000 new ones! And few will die,—and none resign. They will beget sons and daughters, and Taft will have to create 99,000 more! Verily, a simple and a serviceable thing is our general government.

It is American tradition that the Judiciary shall act as a check upon the impetuosity of Legislatures, should these attempt to pass the bounds of constitutional limitation. It is American practice that the Judiciary justifies every law which trenches on the liberties of the people and nullifies every act of the Legislature by which the people seek to regain some measure of their freedom. Again, in the words of Jefferson: "The Constitution is a mere thing of wax in the hands of the Judiciary, which they may twist and shape in any form they please." Truly, if the men who fought the good fight for the triumph of simple, honest, free life in that day, were now to look upon the scene of their labors, they would cry out together with him who said: "I regret that I am now to die in the belief that the useless sacrifice of themselves by the generation of '76 to acquire self-government and happiness to their country, is to be thrown away by the unwise and unworthy passions of their sons, and that my only consolation is to be that I shall not live to see it."

And now, what has Anarchism to say to all this, this bankruptcy of republicanism, this modern empire that has grown up on the ruins of our early freedom? We say this, that the sin our fathers sinned was that they did not trust liberty wholly. They thought it possible to compromise between liberty and government, believing the latter to be "a necessary evil", and the moment the compromise was made, the whole misbegotten monster of our present tyranny began to grow. Instruments which are set up to safeguard rights become the very whip with which the free are struck.

Anarchism says, Make no laws whatever concerning speech, and speech will be free; so soon as you make a declaration on paper that speech shall be free, you will have a hundred lawyers proving that "freedom does not mean abuse, nor liberty license"; and they will define and define freedom

out of existence. Let the guarantee of free speech be in every man's determination to use it, and we shall have no need of paper declarations. On the
other hand, so long as the people do not care to exercise their freedom, those
who wish to tyrannize will do so; for tyrants are active and ardent, and will
devote themselves in the name of any number of gods, religious and otherwise, to put shackles upon sleeping men.

The problem then becomes, Is it possible to stir men from their indifference? We have said that the spirit of liberty was nurtured by colonial
life; that the elements of colonial life were the desire for sectarian independence, and the jealous watchfulness incident thereto; the isolation of
pioneer communities which threw each individual strongly on his own
resources, and thus developed all-around men, yet at the same time made
very strong such social bonds as did exist; and, lastly, the comparative
simplicity of small communities.

All this has mostly disappeared. As to sectarianism, it is only by dint of
an occasional idiotic persecution that a sect becomes interesting; in the
absence of this, outlandish sects play the fool's role, are anything but
heroic, and have little to do with either the name or the substance of liberty. The old colonial religious parties have gradually become the "pillars of
society," their animosities have died out, their offensive peculiarities have
been effaced, they are as like one another as beans in a pod, they build
churches and—sleep in them.

As to our communities, they are hopelessly and helplessly interde-
pendent, as we ourselves are, save that continuously diminishing proportion
engaged in all around farming; and even these are slaves to mortgages. For our
cities, probably there is not one that is provisioned to last a week, and certainly
there is none which would not be bankrupt with despair at the proposition
that it produce its own food. In response to this condition and its correlative
political tyranny, Anarchism affirms the economy of self-sustenance, the
disintegration of the great communities, the use of the earth.

I am not ready to say that I see clearly that this *will* take place; but I see
clearly that this *must* take place if ever again men are to be free. I am so well
satisfied that the mass of mankind prefer material possessions to liberty, that
I have no hope that they will ever, by means of intellectual or moral stirrings
merely, throw off the yoke of oppression fastened on them by the present
economic system, to institute free societies. My only hope is in the blind
development of the economic system and political oppression itself. The
great characteristic looming factor in this gigantic power is Manufacture.
The tendency of each nation is to become more and more a manufacturing
one, an exporter of fabrics, not an importer. If this tendency follows its own
logic, is must eventually circle round to each community producing for

itself. What then will become of the surplus product when the manufacturer shall have no foreign market? Why, then mankind must face the dilemma of sitting down and dying in the midst of it, or confiscating the goods.

Indeed, we are partially facing this problem even now; and so far we are sitting down and dying. I opine, however, that men will not do it forever; and when once by an act of general expropriation they have overcome the reverence and fear of property, and their awe of government, they may waken to the consciousness that things are to be used, and therefore men are greater than things. This may rouse the spirit of liberty.

If, on the other hand, the tendency of invention to simplify, enabling the advantages of machinery to be combined with smaller aggregations of workers, shall also follow its own logic, the great manufacturing plants will break up, population will go after the fragments, and there will be seen not indeed the hard, self-sustaining, isolated pioneer communities of early America, but thousands of small communities stretching along the lines of transportation, each producing very largely for its own needs, able to rely upon itself, and therefore able to be independent. For the same rule holds good for societies as for individuals,—those may be free who are able to make their own living.

In regard to the breaking up of that vilest creation of tyranny, the standing army and navy, it is clear that so long as men desire to fight, they will have armed force in one form or another. Our fathers thought they had guarded against a standing army by providing for the voluntary militia. In our day we have lived to see this militia declared part of the regular military force of the United States, and subject to the same demands as the regulars. Within another generation we shall probably see its members in the regular pay of the general government. Since any embodiment of the fighting spirit, any military organization, inevitably follows the same line of centralization, the logic of Anarchism is that the least objectionable form of armed force is that which springs up voluntarily, like the minute-men of Massachusetts, and disbands as soon as the occasion which called it into existence is past: that the really desirable thing is that all men—not Americans only—should be at peace; and that to reach this, all peaceful persons should withdraw their support from the army, and require that all who make war shall do so at their own cost and risk; that neither pay nor pensions are to be provided for those who choose to make man-killing a trade.

As to the American tradition of non-meddling, Anarchism asks that it be carried down to the individual himself. It demands no jealous barrier of isolation; it knows that such isolation is undesirable and impossible; but it teaches that by all men's strictly minding their own business, a fluid society, freely adapting itself to mutual needs, wherein all the world shall belong to all men, as much as each has need or desire, will result.

And when Modern Revolution has thus been carried to the heart of the whole world—if it ever shall be, as I hope it will,—then may we hope to see a resurrection of that proud spirit of our fathers which put the simple dignity of Man above the gauds of wealth and class, and held that to be an American was greater than to be a king.

In that day there shall be neither kings nor Americans,—only Men; over the whole earth, MEN.

A Correction

This paragraph, published in *Mother Earth*, November 1907, is a brief statement of Voltairine's mature reflection of her own place in the taxonomy of anarchism. She was, as she said elsewhere, an "anarchist without adjectives." This was her way of negotiating the differences between home-grown American individualism and the communist anarchism associated with Peter Kropotkin and, in the States, with Emma Goldman.

A Correction

Owing to a perhaps natural misunderstanding, it was stated in the American report to the Amsterdam Congress that I am a worker in the cause of Anarchist Communism. The report should have said Anarchism, simply, as I am not now, and never have been at any time, a Communist. I was for several years an individualist, but becoming convinced that a number of the fundamental propositions of individualistic economy would result in the destruction of equal liberty, I relinquished those beliefs. In doing so, however, I did not accept the proposed economy of Communism, which in some respects would entail the same result, destruction of equal freedom; always, of course, in my opinion, which I very willingly admit should not be weighed by others as of equal value with the opinions of those who make economy a thorough study, but which must, nevertheless, remain supreme with me. I am an Anarchist, simply, without economic label attached.

Part III

Wild Freedom

A Passion for Liberty and Justice

Introduction

Voltairine de Cleyre's compassion for the downtrodden and her passionate belief in freedom for all were marked by the almost religious zeal and fervent intensity that characterized her entire life. Even in the last year of her life, when her always fragile health was failing, she was, in the words of Franklin Rosemont, "an impassioned defender of the Revolution in Mexico."[1]

No essay of Voltairine's more clearly shows her passion and intensity than "The Dominant Idea." Speaking of this essay, Emma Goldman wrote, "[It] was the *Leitmotif* throughout Voltairine de Cleyre's remarkable life."[2] It posits that each age has a dominant idea or "master-thought" to which most people adhere. Railing against her age's dominant idea, material possession, Voltairine asserts the principle of free will and moral responsibility. We need not, she believed, adhere to the dominant ideal of our age; we have the choice and responsibility to embrace our own ideal. "And now, to-day," she wrote, "though the Society about us is dominated by 'Thing-Worship,' ... there is no reason any single soul should be."

The Dominant Idea, was, in Voltairine's view, the force of individual will and purpose that inspires one's actions, of "intent *within* holding its purpose against obstacles *without*." In place of the Marxian formula, "Men are what circumstances make of them," she substitutes the opposite, "Circumstances are what men make of them."

In spite of her insistence on free will and individual choice, Voltairine did recognize the role of environmental conditions in influencing people toward crime. Though she held people individually responsible for their actions, she did not believe that harsh punishment was the solution to the problem of crime. In her essay, "Crime and Punishment," she emphasizes the role of material conditions in creating crime. Making a distinction between crimes that violate life and liberty and those that violate property, she argued that the final cause of much crime was not individual depravity but economic conditions. The solution to crimes of property is, therefore, for society to rectify the wrongs done that have led to such dire economic conditions.

It will not surprise anyone that Voltairine's commitment to liberty made her a fierce supporter of the right to free speech. In a time when avowing radical or unpopular thoughts was considerably more dangerous than now, Voltairine and her anarchist compatriots spoke out again and again against censorship. She asserted with many before and since that the Constitutional right to free speech means nothing unless it means freedom to declare unpopular ideas. Putting this idea to the test, she wrote several speeches and articles defending fellow anarchist Emma Goldman's right to say what she believed after Emma's lectures were suppressed by the police. These essays included "Our Police Censorship" and "In Defense of Emma Goldman and the Right of Expropriation," both published in *Mother Earth*.

In his short book of Voltairine's poetry, *Written in Red*, Franklin Rosemont writes, "what interested Voltairine almost to the exclusion of all else, was *wild freedom*."[3] Though he was speaking primarily of her poetry, it is no less a fitting phrase to describe Voltairine's commitment to liberty and justice. With zeal, with passion, with unswerving devotion, she made her Dominant Idea freedom in all its unrestrained glory.

—Sharon Presley

NOTES

1. Franklin Rosemont, *Written in Red*, Chicago: Charles H. Kerr Publishing, 1990, p. 9.

2. Emma Goldman, Voltairine de Cleyre, Baltimore: Oriole Press, 1932, p. 8.

3. Rosemont, *ibid.*, p. 11.

The Dominant Idea

This brilliant essay, surely one of Voltairine's best, is an attack, among other things, on materialism. One might think of this as a contribution to the internecine battles of the left; she was surely here thinking of Marx among others. But this essay is much more a testament to the human spirit and the deepest expression of Voltairine's own. It embodies her commitment to live an entire life devoted to an ideal. It also displays what we might think of as Voltairine's existentialism: at once a morbid fascination with death and a resolve to live with strength and truth in the midst of suffering. This essay is, for one thing, directly in the line of American transcendentalism, and she sounds more like Margaret Fuller than like Alexander Berkman. One hears in "The Dominant Idea" echoes of Plato and Emerson, and anticipations of Sartre, but one should also hear in it an original and indispensable contribution to philosophy and to American letters. It was originally issued as a pamphlet by the Mother Earth Publishing Association in 1910, and was later translated into French.

Ragnar Lodbrog is a Danish King of Norse legend, usually dated to the eighth century CE.

'Kaffirs' is a term that would then have been common to refer to native peoples of South Africa; it is now considered derogatory. This passage is about the Boer War, a conflict that pitted the British against Dutch immigrants (Boers) in South Africa.

St. Teresa of Avila was a sixteenth-century Spanish mystic and reformer.

Terence Powderly (1849–1924) was an American labor leader, later a government official.

The Dominant Idea

In everything that lives, if one looks searchingly, is limned the shadow line of an idea—an idea, dead or living, sometimes stronger when dead, with rigid, unswerving lines that mark the living embodiment with the stern immobile cast of the non-living. Daily we move among these unyielding shadows, less pierceable, more enduring than granite, with the blackness of ages in them, dominating living, changing bodies, with dead, unchanging souls. And we meet, also, living souls dominating dying bodies—living ideas regnant over decay and death. Do not imagine that I speak of human life alone. The stamp of persistent or of shifting Will is visible in the grass-blade rooted in its clod of earth, as in the gossamer web of being that floats and swims far over our heads in the free world of air.

Regnant ideas, everywhere! Did you ever see a dead vine bloom? I have seen it. Last summer I trained some morning-glory vines up over a second story balcony; and every day they blew and curled in the wind, their white, purple-dashed faces winking at the sun, radiant with climbing life. Higher every day the green heads crept, carrying their train of spreading fans waving before the sun-seeking blossoms. Then all at once some mischance happened, some cut worm or some mischievous child tore one vine off below, the finest and most ambitious one, of course. In a few hours the leaves hung limp, the sappy stem wilted and began to wither; in a day it was dead,—all but the top which still clung longingly to its support, with bright head lifted. I mourned a little for the buds that could never open now, and tied that proud vine whose work in the world was lost. But the next night there was a storm, a heavy, driving storm, with beating rain and blinding lightning. I rose to watch the flashes, and lo! the wonder of the world! In the blackness of the mid-NIGHT, in the fury of wind and rain, the dead vine had flowered. Five white, moon-faced blossoms blew gaily round the skeleton vine, shining back triumphant at the red lightning. I gazed at them in dumb wonder. Dear, dead vine, whose will had been so strong to bloom, that in the hour of its sudden cut-off from the feeding earth, it sent the last sap to its blossoms; and, not waiting for the morning, brought them forth in storm and flash, as white night-glories, which should have been the children of the sun.

In the daylight we all came to look at the wonder, marveling much, and saying, "Surely these must be the last." But every day for three days the dead vine bloomed; and even a week after, when every leaf was dry and brown, and so thin you could see through it, one last bud, dwarfed, weak, a very baby of a blossom, but still white and delicate, with five purple flecks, like those on the live vine beside it, opened and waved at the stars, and waited for the early sun. Over death and decay the Dominant Idea smiled: the vine was in the world to bloom, to bear white trumpet blossoms dashed with purple; and it held its will beyond death.

Our modern teaching is, that ideas are but attendant phenomena, impotent to determine the actions or relations of life, as the image in the glass which should say to the body it reflects: "*I* shall shape *thee*." In truth we know that directly the body goes from before the mirror, the transient image is nothingness; but the real body has its being to live, and will live it, heedless of vanished phantoms of itself, in response to the ever-shifting pressure of things without it.

It is thus that the so-called Materialist Conception of History, the modern Socialists, and a positive majority of Anarchists would have us look upon the world of ideas,—shifting, unreal reflections, having naught to do in the determination of Man's life, but so many mirror appearances of certain material relations, wholly powerless to act upon the course of material things. Mind to them is in itself a blank mirror, though in fact never wholly blank, because always facing the reality of the material and bound to reflect some shadow. To-day I am somebody, to-morrow somebody else, if the scenes have shifted; my Ego is a gibbering phantom, pirouetting in the glass, gesticulating, transforming, hourly or momentarily, gleaming with the phosphor light of a deceptive unreality, melting like the mist upon the hills. Rocks, fields, woods, streams, houses, goods, flesh, blood, bone, sinew,—these are realities, with definite parts to play, with essential characters that abide under all changes; but my Ego does not abide; it is manufactured afresh with every change of these.

I think this unqualified determinism of the material is a great and lamentable error in our modern progressive movement; and while I believe it was a wholesome antidote to the long-continued blunder of Middle Age theology, viz., that Mind was an utterly irresponsible entity making laws of its own after the manner of an Absolute Emperor, without logic, sequence, or relation, ruler over matter, and its own supreme determinant, not excepting God (who was himself the same sort of a mind writ large)—while I do believe that the modern re-conception of Materialism has done a wholesome thing in pricking the bubble of such conceit and restoring man and his "soul" to its "place in nature," I nevertheless believe that to this also there is a limit; and that the absolute sway of Matter is quite as mischievous an error as the unrelated nature of Mind; even that in its direct action upon personal conduct, it has the more ill effect of the two. For if the doctrine of free-will has raised up fanatics and persecutors, who, assuming that men may be good under all conditions if they merely wish to be so, have sought to persuade other men's wills with threats, fines, imprisonments, torture, the spike, the wheel, the axe, the fagot, in order to make them good and save them against their obdurate wills; if the doctrine of Spiritualism, the soul supreme, has done this, the doctrine of Materialistic Determinism has produced shifting, self-excusing, worthless, parasitical characters, who are *this* now and *that* at some other time, and anything and nothing upon principle. "My conditions have made me so," they cry, and there is no more to be said; poor mirror-ghosts! how could they help it! To be sure, the influence of such a character rarely reaches so far as that of the principled persecutor; but for every one of the latter, there are a hundred of these easy, doughy characters, who will fit any baking tin, to whom determinist self-excusing appeals; so the balance of evil between the two doctrines is *about* maintained.

What we need is a true appraisement of the power and rôle of the Idea. I do not think I am able to give such a true appraisement, I do not think that any one—even *much* greater intellects than mine—will be able to do it for a long time to come. But I am at least able to suggest it, to show its necessity, to give a rude approximation of it.

And first, against the accepted formula of modern Materialism, "Men are what circumstances make them," I set the opposing declaration, "Circumstances are what men make them"; and I contend that both these things are true up to the point where the combating powers are equalized, or one is overthrown. In other words, my conception of mind, or character, is not that it is a powerless reflection of a momentary condition of stuff and form, but an active modifying agent, reacting on its environment and transforming circumstances, sometimes slightly, sometimes greatly, sometimes, though not often, entirely.

All over the kingdom of life, I have said, one may see dominant ideas working, if one but trains his eyes to look for them and recognize them. In the human world there have been many dominant ideas. I cannot conceive that ever, at any time, the struggle of the body before dissolution can have been aught but agony. If the reasoning that insecurity of conditions, the expectation of suffering, are circumstances which make the soul of man uneasy, shrinking, timid, what answer will you give to the challenge of old Ragnar Lodbrog, to that triumphant death-song hurled out, not by one cast to his death in the heat of battle, but under slow prison torture, bitten by serpents, and yet singing: "The goddesses of death invite me away—now end I my song. The hours of my life are run out. I shall smile when I die"? Nor can it be said that this is an exceptional instance, not to be accounted for by the usual operation of general law, for old King Lodbrog the Skalder did only what his fathers did, and his sons and his friends and his enemies, through long generations; they set the force of a dominant idea, the idea of the super ascendant ego, against the force of torture and of death, ending life as they wished to end it, with a smile on their lips. But a few years ago, did we not read how the helpless Kaffirs, victimized by the English for the contumacy of the Boers, having been forced to dig the trenches wherein for pleasant sport they were to be shot, were lined up on the edge, and seeing death facing them, began to chant barbaric strains of triumph, smiling as they fell? Let us admit that such exultant defiance was owing to ignorance, to primitive beliefs in gods and hereafters; but let us admit also that it shows the power of an idea dominant.

Everywhere in the shells of dead societies, as in the shells of the sea-slime, we shall see the force of purposive action, of intent *within* holding its purpose against obstacles *without*.

I think there is no one in the world who can look upon the steadfast, far-staring face of an Egyptian carving, or read a description of Egypt's monuments, or gaze upon the mummied clay of its old dead men, without feeling that the dominant idea of that people in that age was to be enduring and to work enduring things, with the immobility of their great still sky upon them and the stare of the desert in them. One must feel that whatever other ideas animated them, and expressed themselves in their lives, this was the dominant idea. *That which was* must remain, no matter at what cost, even if it were to break the ever-lasting hills: an idea which made the live humanity beneath it, born and nurtured in the corns of caste, groan and writhe and gnaw its bandages, till in the fullness of time it passed away: and still the granite mould of it stares with empty eyes out across the world, the stern old memory of the *Thing-that-was*.

I think no one can look upon the marbles wherein Greek genius wrought the figuring of its soul without feeling an apprehension that the things are going to leap and fly; that in a moment one is like to be set upon by heroes with spears in their hands, by serpents that will coil around him; to be trodden by horses that may trample and flee; to be smitten by these gods that have as little of the idea of stone in them as a dragon-fly, one instant poised upon a wind-swayed petal edge. I think no one can look upon them without realizing at once that those figures came out of the boil of life; they seem like rising bubbles about to float into the air, but beneath them other bubbles rising, and others, and others,—there will be no end of it. When one's eyes are upon one group, one feels that behind one, perhaps, a figure is tiptoeing to seize the darts of the air and hurl them on one's head; one must keep whirling to face the miracle that appears about to be wrought—stone leaping! And this though nearly every one is minus some of the glory the old Greek wrought into it so long ago; even the broken stumps of arms and legs live. And the dominant idea is Activity, and the beauty and strength of it. Change, swift, ever-circling Change! The making of things and the casting of them away, as children cast away their toys, not interested that these shall endure, so that they themselves realize incessant activity. Full of creative power what matter if the creature perished. So there was an endless procession of changing shapes in their schools, their philosophies, their dramas, their poems, till at last it wore itself to death. And the marvel passed away from the world. But still their marbles live to show what manner of thoughts dominated them.

And if we wish to, know what master-thought ruled the lives of men when the mediæval period had had time to ripen it, one has only at this day to stray into some quaint, out-of-the-way English village, where a strong old towered Church yet stands in the midst of little straw-thatched cottages, like a brooding mother-hen surrounded by her chickens. Everywhere the greatening of God and the lessening of Man: the Church so looming, the home so little. The search for the spirit, for the *enduring* thing (not the poor endurance of granite which in the ages crumbles, but the eternal), the eternal,—and contempt for the body which perishes, manifest in studied uncleanliness, in mortifications of the flesh, as if the spirit should have spat its scorn upon it.

Such was the dominant idea of that middle age which has been too much cursed by modernists. For the men who built the castles and the cathedrals, were men of mighty works, though they made no books, and though their souls spread crippled wings, because of their very endeavors to soar too high. The spirit of voluntary subordination for the accomplishment of a great work, which proclaimed the aspiration of the common soul,—that was the spirit wrought into the cathedral stones; and it is not wholly to be condemned.

In waking dream, when the shadow-shapes of world-ideas swim before the vision, one sees the Middle-Age Soul an ill-contorted, half-formless thing, with dragon wings and a great, dark, tense face, strained sunward with blind eyes.

If now we look around us to see what idea dominates our own civilization, I do not know that it is even as attractive as this piteous monster of the old darkness. The relativity of things has altered: Man has risen and God has descended. The modern village has better homes and less pretentious churches. Also, the conception of dirt and disease as much-sought afflictions, the patient suffering of which is a meet offering to win God's pardon, has given place to the emphatic promulgation of cleanliness. We have Public School nurses notifying parents that "pediculosis capitis" is a very contagious and unpleasant disease; we have cancer associations gathering up such cancers as have attached themselves to impecunious persons, and carefully experimenting with a view to cleaning them out of the human race; we have tuberculosis societies attempting the Herculean labor of clearing the Augean stables of our modern factories of the deadly bacillus, and they have got as far as spittoons with water in them in some factories; and others, and others, and others, which, while not yet overwhelmingly successful in their avowed purposes, are evidence sufficient that humanity no longer seeks dirt as a means of grace. We laugh at those old superstitions and talk much about exact experimental knowledge. We endeavor to galvanize the Greek corpse, and pretend that we enjoy physical culture. We dabble in many things; but the one great real idea of our age, not copied from any other, not pretended, not raised to life by any conjuration, is the Much Making of Things,—not the making of beautiful things, not the joy of spending living energy in creative work; rather the shameless, merciless driving and over-driving, wasting and draining of the last bit of energy, only to produce heaps and heaps of things,—things ugly, things harmful, things useless, and at the best largely unnecessary. To what end are they produced? Mostly the producer does not know; still less does he care. But he is possessed with the idea that he must do it, every one is doing it, and every year the making of things goes on more and faster; there are mountain ranges of things made and making, and still men go about desperately seeking to increase the list of created things, to start fresh heaps and to add to the existing heaps. And with what agony of body, under what stress and strain of danger and fear of danger, with what mutilations and maimings and lamings they struggle on, dashing themselves out against these rocks of wealth! Verily, if the vision of the Mediæval Soul is painful in its blind staring and pathetic striving, grotesque in its senseless tortures, the Soul of the Modern is most amazing with its restless, nervous eyes, ever searching the corners of the universe, its restless, nervous hands ever reaching and grasping for some useless toil.

And certainly the presence of things in abundance, things empty and things vulgar and things absurd, as well as things convenient and useful, has produced the desire for the possession of things, the exaltation of the possession of things. Go through the business street of any city, where the tilted edges of the strata of things are exposed to gaze, and look at the faces of the people as they pass,—not at the hungry and smitten ones who fringe the sidewalks and plain dolefully for alms, but at the crowd,—and see what idea is written on their faces. On those of the women, from the ladies of the horse-shows to the shop girls out of the factory, there is a sickening vanity, a consciousness of their clothes, as of some jackdaw in borrowed feathers. Look for the pride and glory of the free, strong, beautiful body, lithe-moving and powerful. You will not see it. You will see mincing steps, bodies tilted to show the cut of a skirt, simpering, smirking faces, with eyes cast about seeking admiration for the gigantic bow of ribbon in the over-dressed hair. In the caustic words of an acquaintance, to whom I once said, as we walked, "Look at the amount of vanity on all these women's faces," "No: look at the little bit of womanhood showing out of all that vanity!"

And on the faces of the men, coarseness! Coarse desires for coarse things, and lots of them: the stamp is set so unmistakably that "the way-farer though a fool need not err therein." Even the frightful anxiety and restlessness begotten of the creation of all this, is less distasteful than the abominable expression of lust for the things created.

Such is the dominant idea of the western world, at least in these our days. You may see it wherever you look, impressed plainly on things and on men; very like if you look in the glass, you will see it there. And if some archaeologist of a long future shall some day unbury the bones of our civ-ilization, where ashes or flood shall have entombed it, he will see this frightful idea stamped on the factory walls he shall uncover, with their rows and rows of square light-holes, their tons upon tons of toothed steel, grinning out of the skull of this our life; its acres of silk and velvet, its square miles of tinsel and shoddy. No glorious marbles of nymphs and fawns, whose dead images are yet so sweet that one might wish to kiss them still; no majestic figures of winged horses, with men's faces and lions' paws casting their colossal symbolism in a mighty spell forward upon Time, as those old stone chimeras of Babylon yet do; but meaningless iron giants, of wheels and teeth, whose secret is forgotten, but whose business was to grind men up, and spit them out as housefuls of woven stuffs, bazaars of trash, wherethrough other men might wade. The statues he shall find will bear no trace of mythic dream or mystic symbol; they will be statues of merchants and ironmasters and militia-men, in tailored coats and pan-taloons and proper hats and shoes.

But the dominant idea of the age and land does not necessarily mean the dominant idea of any single life. I doubt not that in those long gone days, far away by the banks of the still Nile, in the abiding shadow of the pyramids, under the heavy burden of other men's stolidity, there went to and fro restless, active, rebel souls who hated all that the ancient society stood for, and with burning hearts sought to overthrow it.

I am sure that in the midst of all the agile Greek intellect created, there were those who went about with downbent eyes, caring nothing for it all, seeking some higher revelation, willing to abandon the joys of life, so that they drew near to some distant, unknown perfection their fellows knew not of. I am certain that in the dark ages, when most men prayed and cow-ered, and beat and bruised themselves, and sought afflictions, like that St. Teresa who said, "Let me suffer, or die," there were some, many, who looked on the world as a chance jest, who despised or pitied their ignorant comrades, and tried to compel the answers of the universe to their questionings, by the patient, quiet searching which came to be Modern Science. I am sure there were hundreds thousands of them, of whom we have never heard.

And now, to-day, though the Society about us is dominated by Thing-Worship, and will stand so marked for all time, that is no reason any single soul should be. Because the one thing seemingly worth doing to my neighbor, to all my neighbors, is to pursue dollars, that is no reason I should pursue dollars. Because my neighbors conceive they need an inordinate heap of carpets, furniture, clocks, china, glass, tapestries, mirrors, clothes, jewels and servants to care for them, and detectives to keep an eye on the servants, judges to try the thieves, and politicians to appoint the judges, jails to punish the culprits, and wardens to watch in the jails, and tax collectors to gather support for the wardens, and fees for the tax collectors, and strong houses to hold the fees, so that none but the guardians thereof can make off with them,—and therefore, to keep this host of parasites, need other men to work for them, and make the fees; because my neighbors want all this, is that any reason I should devote myself to such a barren folly? and bow my neck to serve to keep up the gaudy show?

Must we, because the Middle Age was dark and blind and brutal, throw away the one good thing it wrought into the fibre of Man, that the inside of a human being was worth more than the outside? that to conceive a higher thing than oneself and live toward that is the only way of living worthily? The goal strived for should, and must, be a very different one from that which led the mediæval fanatics to despise the body and belabor it with hourly crucifixions. But one can recognize the claims and the importance of the body without therefore sacrificing truth, honor, simplicity, and faith, to the vulgar gauds of body-service, whose very decorations debase the thing they might be supposed to exalt.

I have said before that the doctrine that men are nothing and circumstances all, has been, and is, the bane of our modern social reform movements.

Our youth, themselves animated by the spirit of the old teachers who believed in the supremacy of ideas, even in the very hour of throwing away that teaching, look with burning eyes to the social East, and believe that wonders of revolution are soon to be accomplished. In their enthusiasm they foreread the gospel of Circumstances to mean that very soon the pressure of material development must break down the social system—they give the rotten thing but a few years to last; and then, they themselves shall witness the transformation, partake in its joys. The few years pass away and nothing happens; enthusiasm cools. Behold these same idealists then, successful business men, professionals, property owners, money lenders, creeping into the social ranks they once despised, pitifully, contemptibly, at the skirts of some impecunious personage to whom they have lent money, or done some professional service gratis; behold them lying, cheating, tricking, flattering, buying and selling themselves for any frippery, any cheap little pretense. The Dominant Social Idea has seized them, their lives are swallowed up in it; and when you ask the reason why, they tell you that Circumstances compelled them so to do. If you quote their lies to them, they smile with calm complacency, assure you that when Circumstances demand lies, lies are a great deal better than truth; that tricks are sometimes more effective than honest dealing; that flattering and duping do not matter, if the end to be attained is desirable; and that under existing "Circumstances" life isn't possible without all this; that it is going to be possible whenever Circumstances have made truth-telling easier than lying, but till then a man must look out for himself, by all means. And so the cancer goes on rotting away the moral fibre, and the man becomes a lump, a squash, a piece of slippery slime taking all shapes and losing all shapes, according to what particular hole or corner he wishes to glide into,—a disgusting embodiment of the moral bankruptcy begotten by Thing-Worship.

Had he been dominated by a less material conception of life, had his will not been rotted by the intellectual reasoning of it out of its existence, by its acceptance of its own nothingness, the unselfish aspirations of his earlier years would have grown and strengthened by exercise and habit; and his protest against the time might have been enduringly written, and to some purpose.

Will it be said that the Pilgrim fathers did not hew, out of the New England ice and granite, the idea which gathered them together out of their scattered and obscure English villages, and drove them in their frail ships over the Atlantic in midwinter, to cut their way against all opposing forces? Were they not common men, subject to the operation of common law? Will it be said that Circumstances aided them? When death, disease, hunger, and cold had done their worst, not one of those remaining was willing by an *easy lie* to return to material comfort and the possibility of long days.

Had our modern social revolutionists the vigorous and undaunted conception of their own powers that these had, our social movements would not be such pitiful abortions,—core-rotten even before the outward flecks appear.

"Give a labor leader a political job, and the system becomes all right," laugh our enemies; and they point mockingly to Terence Powderly and his like; and they quote John Burns, who as soon as *he* went into Parliament declared: "The time of the agitator is past; the time of the legislator has come." "Let an Anarchist marry an heiress, and the country is safe," they sneer:—and they have the right to sneer. But would they have that right, could they have it, if our lives were not in the first instance dominated by more insistent desires than those we would fain have others think we hold most dear?

It is the old story: "Aim at the stars, and you may hit the top of the gatepost; but aim at the ground and you will hit the ground."

It is not to be supposed that any one will attain to the full realization of what he purposes, even when those purposes do not involve united action with others; he *will* fall short; he will in some measure be overcome by contending or inert opposition. But something he will attain, if he continues to aim high.

What, then, would I have? you ask. I would have men invest themselves with the dignity of an aim higher than the chase for wealth; choose a thing to do in life outside of the making of things, and keep it in mind,—not for a day, nor a year, but for a life-time. And then keep faith with themselves! Not be a light-o'-love, to-day professing this and to-morrow that, and easily reading oneself out of both whenever it becomes convenient; not advocating a thing to-day and to-morrow kissing its enemies' sleeve, with that weak, coward cry in the mouth, "Circumstances make me." Take a good look into yourself, and if you love Things and the power and the plenitude of Things better than you love your own dignity, human dignity, Oh, say so, say so! Say it to yourself, and abide by it. But do not blow hot and cold in one breath. Do not try to be a social reformer and a respected possessor of Things at the same time. Do not preach the straight and narrow way while going joyously upon the wide one. *Preach the wide one*, or do not preach at all; but do not fool yourself by saying you would like to help usher in a free society, but you cannot sacrifice an arm-chair for it. Say honestly, "I love arm-chairs better than free men, and pursue them because I choose; not because circumstances make me. I love hats, large, large hats, with many feathers and great bows; and I would rather have those hats than trouble myself about social dreams that will never be accomplished in my day. The world worships hats, and I wish to worship with them."

But if you choose the liberty and pride and strength of the single soul, and the free fraternization of men, as the purpose which your life is to make manifest then do not sell it for tinsel. Think that your soul is strong and will hold its way; and slowly, through bitter struggle perhaps the strength will grow. And the foregoing of possessions for which others barter the last possibility of freedom will become easy.

At the end of life you may close your eyes saying: "I have not been dominated by the Dominant Idea of my Age; I have chosen mine own allegiance, and served it. I have proved by a lifetime that there is that in man which saves him from the absolute tyranny of Circumstance, which in the end conquers and remoulds Circumstance, the immortal fire of Individual Will, which is the salvation of the Future."

Let us have Men, Men who will say a word to their souls and keep it— keep it not when it is easy, but keep it when it is hard—keep it when the storm roars and there is a white-streaked sky and blue thunder before, and one's eyes are blinded and one's ears deafened with the war of opposing things; and keep it under the long leaden sky and the gray dreariness that never lifts. Hold unto the last: that is what it means to have a Dominant Idea, which Circumstance cannot break. And such men make and unmake Circumstance.

Crime and Punishment

"Crime and Punishment," delivered as a lecture to the Social Science Club in Philadelphia on 15 March 1903, is probably Voltairine's most systematic essay, but it is also one of her most impassioned, which is saying something. In it, she addresses one of the most difficult questions in anarchist theory, and in political theory and practice in general: the treatment of "criminals." No doubt this essay is the best anarchist treatment of the subject, and its answer is the most radical possible: that we have no right to judge or punish others. Indeed, she suggests that if we want to understand crime, we look within ourselves. Empathy of the most intense variety thus becomes the basis of political theory. This is virtually a religious conviction for Voltairine, and though it seems on its face remarkably implausible, it receives here about as dazzling and sincere a defense as it is possible to give. In fact, Voltairine appeals to religious figures such as Jesus, Buddha, and the German Anabaptists.

"Peter Chilciky," to whom Voltairine refers, is usually called Peter of Chelcic, a radical church reformer, pacifist, anarchist, and primitive Christian of the fifteenth century associated with the Moravian Brotherhood.

The final quotation is from Arthur Hugh Clough's (1819–1861) poem "Say Not the Struggle Nought Availeth."

Crime and Punishment

Men are of three sorts: the turn backs, the rush-aheads, and the indifferents. The first and second are comparatively few in number. The really conscientious conservative, eternally looking backward for his models and trying hard to preserve that which is, is almost as scarce an article as the genuine radical, who is eternally attacking that which is and looking forward to some indistinct but glowing vision of a purified social life. Between them lies the vast nitrogenous body of the indifferents, who go through life with no large thoughts or intense feelings of any kind, the best that can be said of them being that they serve to dilute the too fierce activities of the other two. Into the callous ears of these indifferents, nevertheless, the opposing voices of conservative and radical are continually shouting; and for years, for centuries, the conservative wins the day, not because he really touches the consciences of the indifferent so much (though in a measure he does that) as because his way causes his hearer the least mental trouble. It is easier to this lazy, inert mentality to nod its head and approve the continuance of things as they are, than to listen to proposals for change, to consider, to question, to make an innovating decision. These require activity, application,—and nothing is so foreign to the hibernating social conscience of your ordinary individual. I say "social" conscience, because I by no means wish to say that these are conscienceless people; they have, for active use, sufficient conscience to go through their daily parts in life, and they think that is all that is required. Of the lives of others, of the effects of their attitude in cursing the existences of thousands whom they do not know, they have no conception; they sleep; and they hear the voices of those who cry aloud about these things, dimly, as in dreams; and they do not wish to awaken. Nevertheless, at the end of the centuries they always awaken. It is the radical who always wins at last. At the end of the centuries institutions are reviewed by this aroused social conscience, are revised, sometimes are utterly rooted out.

Thus it is with the institutions of Crime and Punishment. The conservative holds that these things have been decided from all time; that crime is a thing-in-itself, with no other cause than the viciousness of man; that punishment was decreed from Mt. Sinai, or whatever holy mountain happens to be believed in in his country; that society is best served by strictness and severity of judgment and punishment. And he wishes only to make his indifferent brothers keepers of other men's consciences along these lines. He would have all men be hunters of men, that crime may be tracked down and struck down.

The radical says: All false, all false and wrong. Crime has not been decided from all time: crime, like everything else, has had its evolution according to place, time, and circumstance. "The demons of our sires become the saints that we adore,"—and the saints, the saints and the heroes of our fathers, are criminals according to our codes. Abraham, David, Solomon,—could any respectable member of society admit that he had done the things they did? Crime is not a thing-in-itself, not a plant without roots, not a something proceeding from nothing; and the only true way to deal with it is to seek its causes as earnestly, as painstakingly, as the astronomer seeks the causes of the perturbations in the orbit of the planet he is observing, sure that there must be one, or many, somewhere. And Punishment, too, must be studied. The holy mountain theory is a failure. Punishment is a failure. And it is a failure not because men do not hunt down and strike enough, but because they hunt down and strike at all; because in the chase of those who do ill, they do ill themselves; they brutalize their own characters, and so much the more so because they are convinced that this time the brutal act is done in accord with conscience. The murderous deed of the criminal was *against* conscience, the torture or the murder of the criminal by the official is *with* conscience. Thus the conscience is diseased and perverted, and a new class of imbruted men created. We have punished and punished for untold thousands of years, and we have not gotten rid of crime, we have not diminished it. Let us consider then.

The indifferentist shrugs his shoulders and remarks to the conservative: "What have I to do with it? I will hunt nobody and I will save nobody. Let every one take care of himself. I pay my taxes; let the judges and the lawyers take care of the criminals. And as for you, Mr. Radical, you weary me. Your talk is too heroic. You want to play Atlas and carry the heavens on your shoulders. Well, do it if you like. But don't imagine I am going to act the stupid Hercules and transfer your burden to my shoulders. Rave away until you are tired, but let me alone."

"I will not let you alone. I am no Atlas. I am no more than a fly; but I will annoy you, I will buzz in your ears; I will not let you sleep. You must think about this."

That is about the height and power of my voice, or of any individual voice, in the present state of the question. I do not deceive myself. I do not imagine that the question of crime and punishment will be settled till long, long after the memory of me shall be as completely swallowed up by time as last year's snow is swallowed by the sea. Two thousand years ago a man whose soul revolted at punishment, cried out: "Judge not, that ye be not judged," and yet men and women who have taken his name upon their lips as holy, have for all those two thousand years gone on judging as if their belief in what he said was only lip-belief; and they do it to-day. And judges sit upon benches and send men to their death,—even judges who do not themselves believe in capital punishment; and prosecutors exhaust their eloquence and their tricks to get men convicted; and women and men bear witness against sinners; and then they all meet in church and pray, "Forgive us our trespasses *as* we forgive those who trespass against us!"

Do they mean anything at all by it?

And I know that just as the voice of Jesus was not heard, and is not heard; save here and there; just as the voice of Tolstoy is not heard, save here and there; and others great and small are lost in the great echoless desert of indifferentism, having produced little perceptible effect, so my voice also will be lost, and barely a slight ripple of thought be propagated over that dry and fruitless expanse; even that the next wind of trial will straighten and leave as unimprinted sand.

Nevertheless, by the continued and unintermitting action of forces infinitesimal compared with the human voice, the greatest effects are at length accomplished. A wave-length of light is but the fifty-thousandth part of an inch, yet by the continuous action of waves like these have been produced all the creations of light, the entire world of sight, out of masses irresponsive, dark, colorless. And doubt not that in time this cold and irresponsive mass of indifference will feel and stir and realize the force of the great sympathies which will change the attitude of the human mind as a whole towards Crime and Punishment, and erase both from the world.

Not by lawyers and not by judges shall the final cause of the criminal be tried; but lawyer and judge and criminal together shall be told by the Social Conscience, "Depart in peace."

A great ethical teacher once wrote words like unto these: "I have within me the capacity for every crime."

Few, reading them, believe that he meant what he said. Most take it as the sententious utterance of one who, in an abandonment of generosity, wished to say something large and leveling. But I think he meant exactly what he said. I think that with all his purity Emerson had within him the turbid stream of passion and desire; for all his hard-cut granite features he knew the instincts of the weakling and the slave; and for all the sweetness, the tenderness, and the nobility of his nature, he had the tiger and the jackal in his soul. I think that within every bit of human flesh and spirit that has ever crossed the enigma bridge of life, from the prehistoric racial morning until now, all crime and all virtue were germinal. Out of one great soul-stuff are we sprung, you and I and all of us; and if in you the virtue has grown and not the vice, do not therefore conclude that you are essentially different from him whom you have helped to put in stripes and behind bars. Your balance may be more even, you may be mixed in smaller proportions altogether, or the outside temptation has not come upon you.

I am no disciple of that school whose doctrine is summed up in the teaching that Man's Will is nothing, his Material Surroundings all. I do not accept that popular socialism which would make saints out of sinners only by filling their stomachs. I am no apologist for characterlessness, and no petitioner for universal moral weakness. I believe in the individual. I believe that the purpose of life (in so far as we can give it a purpose, and it has none save what we give it) is the assertion and the development of strong, self-centered personality. It is therefore that no religion which offers vicarious atonement for the misdoer, and no philosophy which rests on the cornerstone of irresponsibility, makes any appeal to me. I believe that immeasurable mischief has been wrought by the ceaseless repetition for the last two thousand years of the formula: "Not through any merit of mine shall I enter heaven, but through the sacrifice of Christ."—Not through the sacrifice of Christ, nor any other sacrifice, shall any one attain strength, save in so far as he takes the spirit and the purpose of the sacrifice into his own life and lives it. Nor do I see anything as the result of the teaching that all men are the helpless victims of external circumstance and under the same conditions will act precisely alike, than a lot of spineless, nerveless, bloodless crawlers in the tracks of stronger men,—too desirous of ease to be honest, too weak to be successful rascals.

Let this be put as strongly as it can now, that nothing I shall say hereafter may be interpreted as a gospel of shifting and shirking.

But the difference between us, the Anarchists, who preach self-government and none else, and Moralists who in times past and present have asked for individual responsibility, is this, that while they have always framed creeds and codes for the purpose of *holding others to account*, we draw the line upon ourselves. Set the standard as high as you will; live to it as near as you can; and if you fail, try yourself, judge yourself, condemn yourself, if you choose. Teach and persuade your neighbor if you can; consider and compare his conduct if you please; speak your mind if you desire; but if he fails to reach your standard or his own, try him not, judge him not, condemn him not. He lies beyond your sphere; you cannot know the temptation nor the inward battle nor the weight of the circumstances upon him. You do not know how long he fought before he failed. Therefore you cannot be just. Let him alone.

This is the ethical concept at which we have arrived, not by revelation from any superior power, not through the reading of any inspired book, not by special illumination of our inner consciousness; but by the study of the results of social experiment in the past as presented in the works of historians, psychologists, criminologists, sociologists and legalists.

Very likely so many "ists" sound a little oppressive, and there may be those to whom they may even have a savor of pedantry. It sounds much simpler and less ostentatious to say "Thus saith the Lord," or "The Good Book says." But in the meat and marrow these last are the real presumptions, these easy-going claims of familiarity with the will and intent of Omnipotence. It may sound more pedantic to you to say, "I have studied the accumulated wisdom of man, and drawn certain deductions therefrom," than to say "I had a talk with God this morning and he said thus and so"; but to me the first statement is infinitely more modest. Moreover there is some chance of its being true, while the other is highly imaginative fiction.

This is not to impugn the honesty of those who inherit this survival of an earlier mental state of the race, and who accept it as they accept their appetites or anything else they find themselves born with. Nor is it to belittle those past efforts of active and ardent souls who claimed direct divine inspiration as the source of their doctrines. All religions have been, in their great general outlines, the intuitive graspings of the race at truths which it had not yet sufficient knowledge to demonstrate,—rude and imperfect statements of ideas which were yet but germinal, but which, even then, mankind had urgent need to conceive, and upon which it afterwards spent the efforts of generations of lives to correct and perfect. Thus the very ethical concept of which I have been speaking as peculiarly Anarchistic, was preached as a religious doctrine by the fifteenth century Tolstoy, Peter Chilciky; and in the sixteenth century, the fanatical sect of the Anabaptists shook Germany from center to circumference by a doctrine which included the declaration that "pleadings in courts of law, oaths, capital punishment, and all absolute power were incompatible with the Christian faith." It was an imperfect illumination of the intellect, such only as was possible in those less enlightened days, but an illumination that defined certain noble conceptions of justice. They appealed to all they had, the Bible, the inner light, the best that they knew, to justify their faith. We to whom a wider day is given, who can appeal not to one book but to thousands, who have the light of science which is free to all that can command the leisure and the will to know, shining white and open on these great questions, dim and obscure in the days of Peter Chilciky, we should be the last to cast a sneer at them for their heroic struggle with tyranny and cruelty; though to-day the man who would claim their claims on their grounds would justly be rated atavist or charlatan.

Nothing or next to nothing did the Anabaptists know of history. For genuine history, history which records the growth of a whole people, which traces the evolution of its mind as seen in its works of peace,—its literature, its art, its constructions—is the creation of our own age. Only within the last seventy-five years has the purpose of history come to have so much depth as this. Before that it was a mere register of dramatic situations, with no particular connection, a chronicle of the deeds of prominent persons, a list of intrigues, scandals, murders big and little; and the great people, the actual builders and preservers of the race, the immense patient, silent mass who painfully filled up all the waste places these destroyers made, almost ignored. And no man sought to discover the relations of even the recorded acts to any general causes; no man conceived the notion of discovering what is political and moral growth or political and moral suicide. That they did not do so is because writers of history, who are themselves incarnations of their own time spirit, could not get beyond the unscientific attitude of mind, born of ignorance and fostered by the Christian religion, that man is something entirely different from the rest of organized life; that he is a free moral agent, good if he pleases and bad if he pleases, that is, according as he accepts or rejects the will of God; that every act is isolated, having no antecedent, morally, but the will of its doer. Nor until modern science had fought its way past prisons, exilements, stakes, scaffolds, and tortures, to the demonstration that man is no free-will freak thrust by an omnipotent joker upon a world of cause and sequence to play havoc therein, but just a poor differentiated bit of protoplasm as much subject to the general processes of matter and mind as his ancient progenitor in the depths of the Silurian sea, not until then was it possible for any real conception of the scope of history to begin. Not until then was it said: "The actions of men are the effects of large and general causes. Humanity as a whole has a regularity of movement as fixed as the movement of the tides; and given certain physical and social environments, certain developments may be predicted with the certainty of a mathematical calculation." Thus crime, which for so many ages men have gone on punishing more or less light-heartedly, so far from having its final cause in individual depravity, bears a steady and invariable relation to the production and distribution of staple food supplies, a thing over which society itself at times can have no control (as on the occasion of great natural disturbances), and in general does not yet know how to manage wisely: how much less, then, the individual! This regularity of the recurrence of crime was pointed out long before by the greatest statisticians of Europe, who, indeed, did not go so far as to question why it was so, nor to compare these regularities with other regularities, but upon whom the constant repetition of certain figures in the statistics of murder, suicide, assault, etc., made a profound impression. It was left to the new historians, the great pioneer among whom was H. T. Buckle in England, to make the comparisons in the statistics, and show that individual crimes as well as virtues are always calculable from general material conditions.

This is the basis from which we argue, and it is a basis established by the comparative history of civilizations. In no other way could it have been really established. It might have been guessed at, and indeed was. But only when the figures are before us, figures obtained "by millions of observations extending over different grades of civilization, with different laws, different opinions, different habits, different morals" (I am quoting Buckle), only then are we able to say surely that the human mind proceeds with a regularity of operation overweighing all the creeds and codes ever invented, and that if we would begin to understand the problem of the treatment of crime, we must go to something far larger than the moral reformation of the criminal. No prayers, no legal enactments, will ever rid society of crime. If they would, there have been prayers enough and preachments enough and laws enough and prisons enough to have done it long ago. But pray that the attraction of gravitation shall cease. Will it cease? Enact that water shall freeze at 100° heat. Will it freeze? And no more will men be sane and honest and just when they are compelled to live in an insane, dishonest, and unjust society, when the natural operation of the very elements of their being is warred upon by statutes and institutions which must produce outbursts destructive both to themselves and to others.

Away back in 1835 Quetelet, the French statistician, wrote: "Experience demonstrates, in fact, by every possible evidence, this opinion, which may seem paradoxical at first, that it is society which prepares the crime, and that the guilty one is but the instrument which executes it." Every crime, therefore, is a charge against society which can only be rightly replied to when society consents to look into its own errors and rectify the wrong it has done. This is one of the results which must, in the end, flow from the labors of the real historians; one of the reasons why history was worth writing at all.

Now the next point in the problem is the criminal himself. Admitting what cannot be impeached, that there is cause and sequence in the action of man; admitting the pressure of general causes upon all alike, what is the reason that one man is a criminal and another not?

From the days of the Roman jurisconsults until now the legalists themselves have made a distinction between crimes against the law of nature and crimes merely against the law of society. From the modern scientific standpoint no such distinction can be maintained. Nature knows nothing about crime, and nothing ever was a crime until the social Conscience made it so. Neither is it easy when one reads their law books, even accepting their view-point, to understand why certain crimes were catalogued as against the law of nature, and certain others as of the more artificial character. But I presume what were in general classed as crimes against nature were Acts of Violence committed against persons. Aside from these we have a vast, an almost interminable number of offenses big and little, which are in the main attacks upon the institution of property, concerning which some very different things have to be said than concerning the first. As to these first there is no doubt that these are real crimes, by which I mean simply anti-social acts. Any action which violates the life or liberty of any individual is an anti-social act, whether done by one person, by two, or by a whole nation. And the greatest crime that ever was perpetrated, a crime beside which all individual atrocities diminish to nothing, is War; and the greatest, the least excusable of murderers are those who order it and those who execute it. Nevertheless, this chiefest of murderers, the Government, its own hands red with the blood of hundreds of thousands, assumes to correct the individual offender, enacting miles of laws to define the varying degrees of his offense and punishment, and putting beautiful building stone to very hideous purposes for the sake of caging and tormenting him therein.

We do get a fig from a thistle—sometimes! Out of this noisome thing, the prison, has sprung the study of criminology. It is very new, and there is considerable painstaking nonsense about it. But the main results are interesting and should be known by all who wish to form an intelligent conception of what a criminal is and how he should be treated. These men who are cool and quiet and who move among criminals and study them as Darwin did his plants and animals, tell us that these prisoners are reducible to three types: The Born Criminal, the Criminaloid, and the Accidental Criminal. I am inclined to doubt a great deal that is said about the born criminal. Prof. Lombroso gives us very exhaustive reports of the measurements of their skulls and their ears and their noses and their thumbs and their toes, etc. But I suspect that if a good many respectable, decent, never-did-a-wrong-thing-in-their-lives people were to go up for measurement, malformed ears and disproportionately long thumbs would be equally found among them if they took the precaution to represent themselves as criminals first. Still, however few in number (and they are really very few), there are some born criminals,—people who through some malformation or deficiency or excess of certain portions of the brain are constantly impelled to violent deeds. Well, there are some born idiots and some born cripples. Do you punish them for their idiocy or for their unfortunate physical condition? On the contrary, you pity them, you realize that life is a long infliction to them, and your best and tenderest sympathies go out to them. Why not to the other, equally a helpless victim of an evil inheritance? Granting for the moment that you have the right to punish the mentally responsible, surely you will not claim the right to punish the mentally irresponsible! Even the law does not hold the insane man guilty. And the born criminal is irresponsible; he is a sick man, sick with the most pitiable chronic disease; his treatment is for the medical world to decide, and the best of them,—not for the prosecutor, the judge, and the warden.

It is true that many criminologists, including Prof. Lombroso himself, are of opinion that the best thing to do with the born criminal is to kill him at once, since he can be only a curse to himself and others. Very heroic treatment. We may inquire, Is he to be exterminated at birth because of certain physical indications of his criminality? Such neo-Spartanism would scarcely commend itself to any modern society. Moreover the diagnosis might be wrong, even though we had a perpetual and incorruptible commission of the learned to sit in inquiry upon every pink-skinned little suspect three days old! What then? Is he to be let go, as he is now, until he does some violent deed and then be judged more hardly because of his natural defect? Either proposition seems not only heartless and wicked but,—what the respectable world is often more afraid of being than either,—ludicrous. If one is really a born criminal he will manifest criminal tendencies in early life, and being so recognized should be cared for according to the most humane methods of treating the mentally afflicted.

The second, or criminaloid, class is the most numerous of the three. These are criminals, first, because being endowed with strong desires and unequal reasoning powers they cannot maintain the uneven battle against a society wherein the majority of individuals must all the time deny their natural appetites, if they are to remain unstained with crime. They are, in short, the ordinary man (who, it must be admitted, has a great deal of paste in him) plus an excess of wants of one sort and another, but generally physical. Society outside of prisons is full of these criminaloids, who sometimes have in place of the power of genuine moral resistance a sneaking cunning by which they manage to steer a shady course between the crime and the punishment.

It is true these people are not pleasant subjects to contemplate; but then, through that very stage of development the whole human race has had to pass in its progress from the beast to the man,—the stage, I mean, of overplus of appetite opposed by weak moral resistance; and if now some, it is not certain that their number is very great, have reversed the proportion, it is only because they are the fortunate inheritors of the results of thousands of years of struggle and failure, struggle and failure, but *struggle* again. It is precisely these criminaloids who are most sinned against by society, for they are the people who need to have the right of doing things made easy, and who, when they act criminally, need the most encouragement to help the feeble and humiliated moral sense to rise again, to try again.

The third class, the Accidental or Occasional Criminals, are perfectly normal, well balanced people, who, through tremendous stress of outward circumstance, and possibly some untoward mental disturbance arising from those very notions of the conduct of life which form part of their moral being, suddenly commit an act of violence which is at utter variance with their whole former existence; such as, for instance, the murder of a seducer by the father of the injured girl, or of a wife's paramour by her husband. If I believed in severity at all I should say that these were the criminals upon whom society should look with most severity, because they are the ones who have most mental responsibility. But that also is nonsense; for such an individual has within him a severer judge, a more pitiless jailer than any court or prison,—his conscience and his memory. Leave him to these; or no, in mercy take him away from these whenever you can; he will suffer enough, and there is no fear of his action being repeated.

Now all these people are with us, and it is desirable that something be done to help the case. What does Society do? Or rather what does Government do with them? Remember we are speaking now only of crimes of violence. It hangs, it electrocutes, it exiles, it imprisons. Why? For punishment. And why punishment? "Not," says Blackstone, "by way of atonement or expiation for the crime committed, for that must be left to the just determination of the Supreme Being, but as a precaution against future offenses of the same kind." This is supposed to be effected in three ways: either by reforming him, or getting rid of him altogether, or by deterring others by making an example of him.

Let us see how these precautions work. Exile, which is still practised by some governments, and imprisonment are, according to the theory of law, for the purpose of reforming the criminal that he may no longer be a menace to society. Logic would say that anyone who wished to obliterate cruelty from the character of another must himself show no cruelty; one who would teach regard for the rights of others must himself be regardful. Yet the story of exile and prison is the story of the lash, the iron, the chain and every torture that the fiendish ingenuity of *the non-criminal class can devise by way of teaching criminals to be good!* To teach men to be good, they are kept in airless cells, made to sleep on narrow planks, to look at the sky through iron grates, to eat food that revolts their palates, and destroys their stomachs,—battered and broken down in body and soul; and this is what they call reforming men!

Not very many years ago the Philadelphia dailies told us (and while we cannot believe all of what they say, and are bound to believe that such cases are exceptional, yet the bare facts were true) that Judge Gordon ordered an investigation into the workings of the Eastern Penitentiary officials; and it was found that an insane man had been put into a cell with two sane ones, and when he cried in his insane way and the two asked that he be put elsewhere, the warden gave them a strap to whip him with; and they tied him in some way to the heater, with the strap, so that his legs were burned when he moved; all scarred with the burns he was brought into the court, and the other men frankly told what they had done and why they had done it. This is the way they reform men.

Do you think people come out of a place like that better? with more respect for society? with more regard for the rights of their fellow men? I don't. I think they come out of there with their hearts full of bitterness, much harder than when they went in. That this is often the case is admitted by those who themselves believe in punishment, and practice it. For the fact is that out of the Criminaloid class there develops the Habitual Criminal, the man who is perpetually getting in prison; no sooner is he out than he does something else and gets in again. The brand that at first scorched him has succeeded in searing. He no longer feels the ignominy. He is a "jail-bird," and he gets to have a cynical pride in his own degradation. Every man's hand is against him, and his hand is against every man's. Such are the reforming effects of punishment. Yet there was a time when he, too, might have been touched, had the right word been spoken. It is for society to find and speak that word.

This for prison and exile. Hanging? electrocution? These of course are not for the purpose of reforming the criminal. These are to deter others from doing as he did; and the supposition is that the severer the punishment the greater the deterrent effect. In commenting upon this principle Blackstone says: "We may observe that punishments of unreasonable severity.... have less effect in preventing crimes and amending the manners of a people than such as are more merciful in general...." He further quotes Montesquieu: "For the excessive severity of laws hinders their execution; when the punishment surpasses all measure, the public will frequently, out of humanity, prefer impunity to it." Again Blackstone: "It is a melancholy truth that among the variety of actions which men are daily liable to commit, no less than one hundred and sixty have been declared by act of Parliament to be felonies ... worthy of instant death. So dreadful a list instead of diminishing *increases* the number of offenders."

Robert Ingersoll, speaking on "Crimes Against Criminals" before the New York Bar Association, a lawyer addressing lawyers, treating of this same period of which Blackstone writes, says: "There is something in injustice, in cruelty, which tends to defeat itself. There never were so many traitors in England as when the traitor was drawn and quartered, when he was tortured in every possible way,—when his limbs, torn and bleeding, were given to the fury of mobs, or exhibited pierced by pikes or hung in chains. The frightful punishments, produced intense hatred of the government, and traitors increased until they became powerful enough to decide what treason was and who the traitors were and to inflict the same torments on others."

The fact that Blackstone was right and Ingersoll was right in saying that severity of punishment increases crime, is silently admitted in the abrogation of those severities by acts of Parliament and acts of Congress. It is also shown by the fact that there are no more murders, proportionately, in States where the death penalty does not exist than in those where it does. Severity is therefore admitted by the State itself to have no deterrent influence on the intending criminal. And to take the matter out of the province of the State, we have only to instance the horrible atrocities perpetrated by white mobs upon negroes charged with outrage. Nothing more fiendishly cruel can be imagined; yet these outrages multiply. It would seem, then, that the notion of making a horrible example of the misdoer is a complete failure. As a specific example of this, Ingersoll (in this same lecture) instanced that "a few years before a man was hanged in Alexandria, Va. One who witnessed the execution on that very day murdered a peddler in the Smithsonian grounds at Washington. He was tried and executed; and one who witnessed his hanging went home and on the same day murdered his wife." Evidently the brute is rather aroused than terrified by scenes of execution.

What then? If extreme punishments do not deter, and if what are considered mild punishments do not reform, is any measure of punishment conceivable or attainable which will better our case?

Before answering this question let us consider the class of crimes which so far has not been dwelt upon, but which nevertheless comprises probably nine-tenths of all offenses committed. These are all the various forms of stealing,—robbery, burglary, theft, embezzlement, forgery, counterfeiting, and the thousand and one ramifications and offshoots of the act of taking what the law defines as another's. It is impossible to consider crimes of violence apart from these, because the vast percentage of murders and assaults committed by the criminaloid class are simply incidental to the commission of the so-called lesser crime. A man often murders in order to escape with his booty, though murder was no part of his original intention. Why, now, have we such a continually increasing percentage of stealing?

Will you persistently hide your heads in the sand and say it is because men grow worse as they grow wiser? that individual wickedness is the result of all our marvelous labors to compass sea and land, and make the earth yield up her wealth to us? Dare you say that?

It is not so. THE REASON MEN STEAL IS BECAUSE THEIR RIGHTS ARE STOLEN FROM THEM BEFORE THEY ARE BORN.

A human being comes into the world; he wants to eat, he wants to breathe, he wants to sleep; he wants to use his muscles, his brain; he wants to love, to dream, to create. These wants constitute him, the whole man; he can no more help expressing these activities than water can help running down hill. If the freedom to do any of these things is denied him, then by so much he is a crippled creature, and his energy will force itself into some abnormal channel or be killed altogether. Now I do not mean that he has a "natural right" to do these things inscribed on any lawbook of Nature. Nature knows nothing of rights, she knows power only, and a louse has as much natural right as a man to the extent of its power. What I do mean to say is that man, in common with many other animals, has found that by associative life he conquers the rest of nature, and that this society is slowly being perfected; and that this perfectionment consists in realizing that the solidarity and safety of the whole arises from the freedom of the parts; that such freedom constitutes Man's Social Right; and that any institution which interferes with this right will be destructive of the association, will breed criminals, will work its own ruin. This is the word of the sociologist, of the greatest of them, Herbert Spencer.

Now do we see that all men eat,—eat well? You know we do not. Some have so much that they are sickened with the extravagance of dishes, and know not where next to turn for a new palatal sensation. They cannot even waste their wealth. Some, and they are mostly the hardest workers, eat poorly and fast, for their work allows them no time to enjoy even what they have. Some,—I have seen them myself in the streets of New York this winter, and the look of their wolfish eyes was not pleasant to see—stand in long lines waiting for midnight and the plate of soup dealt out by some great newspaper office, stretching out, whole blocks of them, as other men wait on the first night of some famous star at the theater! Some die because they cannot eat at all. Pray tell me what these last have to lose by becoming thieves. And why shall they not become thieves? And is the action of the man who takes the necessities which have been denied to him really criminal? Is he morally worse than the man who crawls in a cellar and dies of starvation? I think not. He is only a little more assertive. Cardinal Manning said: "A starving man has a natural right to his neighbor's bread." The Anarchist says: "A hungry man has a social right to bread." And there have been whole societies and races among whom that right was never questioned. And whatever were the mistakes of those societies, whereby they perished, this was not a mistake, and we shall do well to take so much wisdom from the dead and gone, the simple ethics of the stomach which with all our achievement we cannot despise, or despising, shall perish as our reward.

"But," you will say, and say truly, "to begin by taking loaves means to end by taking everything and murdering, too, very often." And in that you draw the indictment against your own system. If there is no alternative between starving and stealing (and for thousands there is none), then there is no alternative between society's murdering its members, or the members disintegrating society. Let Society consider its own mistakes, then: let it answer itself for all these people it has robbed and killed: let it cease its own crimes first!

To return to the faculties of Man. All would breathe; and some do breathe. They breathe the air of the mountains, of the seas, of the lakes,— even the atmosphere in the gambling dens of Monte Carlo, for a change!

Some, packed thickly together in closed rooms where men must sweat and faint to save tobacco, breathe the noisome reek that rises from the spittle of their consumptive neighbors. Some, mostly babies, lie on the cellar doors along Bainbridge street, on summer nights, and bathe their lungs in that putrid air where a thousand lungs have breathed before, and grow up pale and decayed looking as the rotting vegetables whose exhalations they draw in. Some, far down underground, meet the choke-damp, and—do not breathe at all! Do you expect healthy morals out of all these poisoned bodies?

Some sleep. They have so much time that they take all manner of expensive drugs to try what sleeping it off a different way is like! Some sleep upon none too easy beds a few short hours, too few not to waken more tired than ever, and resume the endless grind of waking life. Some sleep bent over the books they are too tired to study, though the mind clamors for food after the long day's physical toil. Some sleep with hand upon the throttle of the engine, after twenty-six hours of duty, and—crash!—they have sleep enough!

Some use their muscles: they use them to punch bags, and other gentlemen's stomachs when their heads are full of wine. Some use them to club other men and women, at $2.50 a day. Some exhaust them welding them into iron, or weaving them into wool, for ten or eleven hours a day. And some become atrophied sitting at desks till they are mere specters of men and women.

Some love; and there is no end to the sensualities of their love, because all normal expressions have lost their savor through excess. Some love, and see their love tried and worn and threadbare, a skeleton of love, because the practicality of life is always there to repress the purely emotional. Some are stricken in health, so robbed of power to feel, that they never love at all.

And some dream, think, create; and the world is filled with the glory of their dreams. But who knows the glory of the dream that never was born, lost and dead and buried away somewhere there under the roofs where the exquisite brain was ruined by the heavy labor of life? And what of the dream that turned to madness and destroyed the thing it loved the best?

These are the things that make criminals, the perverted forces of man, turned aside by the institution of property, which is the giant social mistake to-day. It is your law which keeps men from using the sources and the means of wealth production unless they pay tribute to other men; it is this, and nothing else, which is responsible for all the second class of crimes and all those crimes of violence incidentally committed while carrying out a robbery. Let me quote here a most sensible and appropriate editorial which recently appeared in the Philadelphia *North American*, in comment upon the proposition of some foolish preacher to limit the right of reproduction to rich families:

"The earth was constructed, made habitable, and populated without the advice of a commission of superior persons, and until they appeared and began meddling with affairs, making laws and setting themselves up as rulers, poverty and its evil consequences were unknown to humanity. When social science finds a way to remove obstructions to the operation of natural law and to the equitable distribution of the products of labor, poverty will cease to be the condition of the masses of people, and misery, CRIME and problems of population will disappear."

And they will never disappear until it does. All hunting down of men, all punishments, are but so many ineffective efforts to sweep back the tide with a broom. The tide will fling you, broom and all, against the idle walls that you have built to fence it in. Tear down those walls or the sea will tear them down for you.

Have you ever watched it coming in,—the sea? When the wind comes roaring out of the mist and a great bellowing thunders up from the water? Have you watched the white lions chasing each other towards the walls, and leaping up with foaming anger as they strike, and turn and chase each other along the black bars of their cage in rage to devour each other? And tear back? And leap in again? Have you ever wondered in the midst of it all *which particular drops of water* would strike the wall? If one could know all the factors one might calculate even that. But who can know them all? Of one thing only we are sure: *some must strike it.*

They are the criminals, those drops of water pitching against that silly wall and broken. Just why it was these particular ones we cannot know; but some had to go. Do not curse them; you have cursed them enough. Let the people free.

There is a class of crimes of violence which arises from another set of causes than economic slavery—acts which are the result of an antiquated moral notion of the true relations of men and women. These are the Nemesis of the institution of property in love. If every one would learn that the limit of his right to demand a certain course of conduct in sex relations is himself; that the relation of his beloved ones to others is not a matter for him to regulate, any more than the relations of those whom he does not love; if the freedom of each is unquestioned, and whatever moral rigors are exacted are exacted of oneself only; if this principle is accepted and followed, crimes of jealousy will cease. But religions and governments uphold this institution and constantly tend to create the spirit of ownership, with all its horrible consequences.

Ah, you will say, perhaps it is true; perhaps when this better social condition is evolved, and this freer social spirit, we shall be rid of crime,—at least nine-tenths of it. But meanwhile must we not punish to protect ourselves?

The protection does not protect. The violent man does not communicate his intention; when he executes it, or attempts its execution, more often than otherwise it is some unofficial person who catches or stops him. If he is a born criminal, or in other words an insane man, he should, I reiterate, be treated as a sick person—not punished, not made to suffer. If he is one of the accidental criminals, his act will not be repeated; his punishment will always be with him. If he is of the middle class, your punishment will not reform him, it will only harden him; and it will not deter others.

As for thieves, the great thief is within the law, or he buys it; and as for the small one, see what you do! To protect yourself against him, you create a class of persons who are sworn to the service of the club and the revolver; a set of spies; a set whose business it is to deal constantly with these unhappy beings, who in rare instances are softened thereby, but in the majority of cases become hardened to their work as butchers to the use of the knife; a set whose business it is to serve cell and lock and key; and lastly, the lowest infamy of all, the hangman. Does any one want to shake his hand, the hand that kills for pay?

Now against all these persons individually there is nothing to be said: they may probably be very humane, well-intentioned persons when they start in; but the end of all this is imbrutement. One of our dailies recently observed that "the men in charge of prisons have but too often been men who ought themselves to have been prisoners." The Anarchist does not agree with that. He would have no prisons at all. But I am quite sure that if that editor himself were put in the prison-keeper's place, he too would turn hard. And the opportunities of the official criminal are much greater than those of the unofficial one. Lawyer and governmentalist as he was, Ingersoll said: "It is safe to say that governments have committed far more crimes than they have prevented." Then why create a second class of parasites worse than the first? Why not put up with the original one?

Moreover, you have another thing to consider than the simple problem of a wrong inflicted upon a guilty man. How many times has it happened that the innocent man has been convicted! I remember an instance of a man so convicted of murder in Michigan. He had served twenty-seven years in Jackson penitentiary (for Michigan is not a hang-State) when the real murderer, dying, confessed. And the State *pardoned* that innocent man! Because it was the quickest legal way to let him out! I hope he has been able to pardon the State.

Not very long ago a man was hanged here in this city. He had killed his superintendent. Some doctors said he was insane; the government experts said he was not. They said he was faking insanity when he proclaimed himself Jesus Christ. And he was hanged. Afterwards the doctors found two cysts in his brain. The State of Pennsylvania had killed a sick man! And as long as punishments exist, these mistakes will occur. If you accept the principle at all, you must accept with it the blood-guilt of innocent men.

Not only this, but you must accept also the responsibility for all the misery which results to others whose lives are bound up with that of the convict, for even he is loved by some one, much loved perhaps. It is a foolish thing to turn adrift a house full of children, to become criminals in turn, perhaps, in order to frighten some indefinite future offender by making an example of their father or mother. Yet how many times has it not happened!

And this is speaking only from the practical, selfish side of the matter. There is another, one from which I would rather appeal to you, and from which I think you would after all prefer to be appealed to. Ask yourselves, each of you, whether you are quite sure that you have feeling enough, understanding enough, and *have you suffered* enough, to be able to weigh and measure out another man's life or liberty, no matter what he has done? And if you have not yourself, are you able to delegate to any judge the power which you have not? The great Russian novelist, Dostoyevsky, in his psychological study of this same subject, traces the sufferings of a man who had committed a shocking murder; his whole body and brain are a continual prey to torture. He gives himself up, seeking relief in confession. He goes to prison, for in barbarous Russia they have not the barbarity of capital punishment for murderers, unless political ones. But he finds no relief. He remains for a year, bitter, resentful, a prey to all miserable feelings. But at last he is touched by love, the silent, unobtrusive, all-conquering love of one who knew it all and forgave it all. And the regeneration of his soul began.

"The criminal slew," says Tolstoy: "are you better, then, when you slay? He took another's liberty; and is it the right way, therefore, for you to take his? Violence is no answer to violence."

> "Have good will
> To all that lives, letting unkindness die,
> And greed and wrath; so that your lives be made
> As soft airs passing by."

So said Lord Buddha, the Light of Asia.

And another said: "Ye have heard that it hath been said 'an eye for an eye, and a tooth for a tooth'; but I say unto you, resist not him that is evil."

Yet the vengeance that the great psychologist saw was futile, the violence that the greatest living religious teacher and the greatest dead ones advised no man to wreak, that violence is done daily and hourly by every little-hearted prosecutor who prosecutes at so much a day, by every petty judge who buys his way into office with common politicians' tricks, and deals in men's lives and liberties as a trader deals in pins, by every neat-souled and cheap-souled member of the "unco guid" whose respectable bargain-counter maxims of morality have as much effect to stem the great floods and storms that shake the human will as the waving of a lady's kid glove against the tempest. Those who have not suffered cannot understand how to punish; those who have understanding *will* not.

I said at the beginning and I say again, I believe that in every one of us all things are germinal: in judge and prosecutor and prison-keeper too, and even in those small moral souls who cut out one undeviating pattern for all men to fit, even in them there are the germs of passion and crime and sym-pathy and forgiveness. And some day things will stir in them and accuse them and awaken them. And that awakening will come when suddenly one day there breaks upon them with realizing force the sense of the unison of life, the irrevocable relationship of the saint to the sinner, the judge to the criminal; that all personalities are intertwined and rushing upon doom together. Once in my life it was given to me to see the outward manifesta-tion of this unison. It was in 1897. We stood upon the base of the Nelson monument in Trafalgar Square. Below were ten thousand people packed together with upturned faces. They had gathered to hear and see men and women whose hands and limbs were scarred all over with the red-hot irons of the tortures in the fortress of Montjuich. For the crime of an unknown person these twenty-eight men and women, together with four hundred others, had been cast into that terrible den and tortured with the infamies of the inquisition to make them reveal that of which they knew nothing. After a year of such suffering as makes the decent human heart sick only to contemplate, with nothing proven against them, some even without trial, they were suddenly released with orders to leave the country within twenty-four hours. They were then in Trafalgar Square, and to the credit of old England be it said, harlot and mother of harlots though she is, for there was not another country among the great nations of the earth to which those twenty-eight innocent people could go. For they were paupers impover-ished by that cruel State of Spain in the terrible battle for their freedom; they would not have been admitted to free America. When Francesco Gana, speaking in a language which most of them did not understand, lifted his poor, scarred hands, the faces of those ten thousand people moved together like the leaves of a forest in the wind. They waved to and fro, they rose and fell; the visible moved in the breath of the invisible. It was the rev-elation of the action of the Unconscious, the fatalistic unity of man.

Sometimes, even now as I look upon you, it is as if the bodies that I see were as transparent bubbles wherethrough the red blood boils and flows, a turbulent stream churning and tossing and leaping, and behind us and our generation, far, far back, endlessly backwards, where all the bubbles are broken and not a ripple remains, the silent pouring of the Great Red River, the unfathomable River,—backwards through the unbroken forest and the untilled plain, backwards through the forgotten world of savagery and animal life, back somewhere to its dark sources in deep Sea and old Night, the rushing River of Blood—no fancy—real, tangible blood, the blood that hurries in your veins while I speak, bearing with it the curses and the blessings of the Past. Through what infinite shadows has that river rolled! Through what desolate wastes has it not spread its ooze! Through what desperate passages has it been forced! What strength, what invincible strength is in that hot stream! You are just the bubble on its crest; where will the current fling you ere you die? At what moment will the fierce impurities borne from its somber and tenebrous past be hurled up in you? Shall you then cry out for punishment if they are hurled up in another? if, flung against the merciless rocks of the channel, while you swim easily in the midstream, they fall back and hurt other bubbles?

Can you not feel that

"Men are the heart-beats of Man, the plumes that feather his wings,
Storm-worn since being began with the wind and the thunder of things.
Things are cruel and blind; their strength detains and deforms.
And the wearying wings of the mind still beat up the stream of their
    storms.
Still, as one swimming up-stream, they strike out blind in the blast,
In thunder of vision and dream, and lightning of future and past.
We are baffled and caught in the current and bruised upon edges of
    shoals:
As weeds or as reeds in the torrent of things are the wind-shaken souls.
Spirit by spirit goes under, a foam-bell's bubble of breath,
That blows and opens asunder and blurs not the mirror of Death."

Is it not enough that "things are cruel and blind"? Must we also be cruel and blind? When the whole thing amounts to so little at the most, shall we embitter it more, and crush and stifle what must so soon be crushed and stifled anyhow? Can we not, knowing what remnants of things dead and drowned are floating through us, haunting our brains with specters of old deeds and scenes of violence, can we not learn to pardon our brother to whom the specters are more real, upon whom greater stress was laid? Can we not, recalling all the evil things that we have done, or left undone only because some scarcely perceptible weight struck down the balance, or because some kindly word came to us in the midst of our bitterness and showed that not all was hateful in the world; can we not understand him for whom the balance was not struck down, the kind word unspoken? Believe me, forgiveness is better than wrath,—better for the wrong-doer, who will be touched and regenerated by it, and better for you. And you are wrong if you think it is hard: it is easy, far easier than to hate. It may sound like a paradox, but the greater the injury the easier the pardon.

Let us have done with this savage idea of punishment, which is without wisdom. Let us work for the freedom of man from the oppressions which make criminals, and for the enlightened treatment of all the sick. And though we may never see the fruit of it, we may rest assured that the great tide of thought is setting our way, and that

> "While the tired wave, vainly breaking,
>   Seems here no painful inch to gain,
> Far back, through creeks and inlets making,
>   Comes silent, flooding in, the main."

In Defense of
Emma Goldman

Voltairine's writing style seems at a glance to be florid and romantic. That is certainly true of her poetry, which has not aged well. But in her prose, the long sentences and poetic turns of phrase are always put into the service of a barely-controlled emotion. There is, as I have said, muscle driving the poetic gesture. Nowhere is that more true than in this masterful prose poem. Delivered in New York on 16 December 1893, and self-published as a pamphlet, this is a response to the arrest of Emma Goldman, who urged the starving to "take bread."

The "Cardinal Manning" referred to is Henry Edward Manning (1808–1892), a British Roman Catholic prelate.

The "Timmermann" referred to is Claus Timmermann, a friend of Emma's who was arrested for concealing her whereabouts.

In Defense of Emma Goldman and the Right of Expropriation

The light is pleasant, is it not, my friends? It is good to look into each other's faces, to see the hands that clasp our own, to read the eyes that search our thoughts, to know what manner of lips give utterance to our pleasant greetings. It is good to be able to wink defiance at the Night, the cold, unseeing Night. How weird, how gruesome, how chilly it would be if I stood here in blackness, a shadow addressing shadows, in a house of blindness! Yet each would know that he was not alone; yet might we stretch hands and touch each other, and feel the warmth of human presence near. Yet might a sympathetic voice ring thro' the darkness, quickening the dragging moments.—The lonely prisoners in the cells of Blackwell's Island have neither light nor sound! The short day hurries across the sky, the short day still more shortened in the gloomy walls. The long chill night creeps up so early, weaving its sombre curtain before the imprisoned eyes. And thro' the curtain comes no sympathizing voice, beyond the curtain lies the prison silence, beyond that the cheerless, uncommunicating land, and still beyond the icy, fretting river, black and menacing, ready to drown. A wall of night, a wall of stone, a wall of water! Thus has the great State of New York answered EMMA GOLDMAN; thus have the classes replied to the masses; thus do the rich respond to the poor; thus does the Institution of Property give its ultimatum to Hunger!

"Give us work," said EMMA GOLDMAN; "if you will not give us work, then give us bread; if you do not give us either work or bread, then we shall take bread." It wasn't a very wise remark to make to the State of New York, that is—Wealth and its watch-dogs, the Police. But I fear me much that the apostles of liberty, the fore-runners of revolt, have never been very wise. There is a record of a seditious person, who once upon a time went about with a few despised followers in Palestine, taking corn out of other people's corn-fields, (on the Sabbath day, too). That same person, when he wished to ride into Jerusalem told his disciples to go forward to where they would find a young colt tied, to unloose it and bring it to him, and if any one interfered or said anything to them, were to say: "My master hath need of it." That same person said: "Give to him that asketh of thee, and from him that taketh away thy goods ask them not back again." That same person once stood before the hungry multitudes of Galilee and taught them, saying: "The Scribes and the Pharisees sit in Moses' seat; therefore whatever they bid you observe, that observe and do. But do not ye after their works, for they say, and do not. For they bind heavy burdens, and grievous to be borne, and lay them on men's shoulders; but they themselves will not move them with one of their fingers. But all their works they do to be seen of men; they make broad their phylacteries, and enlarge the borders of their garments: and love the uppermost rooms at feasts, and the chief seats in the synagogues, and greeting in the markets, and to be called of men, 'Rabbi, Rabbi.'" And turning to the Scribes and the Pharisees, he continued: "Woe unto you, Scribes and Pharisees, hypocrites! for ye devour widows' houses, and for a pretense make long prayers: therefore shall ye receive the greater damnation. Woe unto you Scribes and Pharisees, hypocrites! for ye pay tithe of mint, and anise, and cummin, and have omitted the weightier matters of the law, judgement, and mercy, and faith: these ought ye to have done and not left the other undone. Ye blind guides, that strain at a gnat and swallow a camel! Woe unto you, Scribes and Pharisees, hypocrites! for ye make clean the outside of the cup and platter, but within they are full of extortion and excess. Woe unto you, Scribes and Pharisees, hypocrites! For ye are like unto whited sepulchres, which indeed appear beautiful outward, but within are full of dead men's bones and all uncleanness. Even so ye outwardly appear righteous unto men, but within ye are full of hypocrisy and iniquity. Woe unto you, Scribes and Pharisees, hypocrites! Because ye build the tombs of the prophets and garnish the sepulchres of the righteous; and say 'If we had been in the days of our fathers we would not have been partakers with them in the blood of the prophets'. Wherefore ye be witnesses unto yourselves that ye are the children of them which killed the prophets. Fill ye up then the measure of your fathers! Ye serpents! Ye generation of vipers! How can ye escape the damnation of hell!"

Yes; these are the words of the outlaw who is alleged to form the foundation stone of modern civilization, to the authorities of his day. Hypocrites, extortionists, doers of iniquity, robbers of the poor, blood-partakers, serpents, vipers, fit for hell!

It wasn't a very wise speech, from beginning to end. Perhaps he knew it when he stood before Pilate to receive his sentence, when he bore his heavy crucifix up Calvary, when nailed upon it, stretched in agony, he cried: "My God, my God, why hast thou forsaken me!"

No, it wasn't wise—but it was very grand.

This grand, foolish person, this beggar-tramp, this thief who justified the action of hunger, this man who set the Right of Property beneath his foot, this Individual who defied the State, do you know why he was so feared and hated, and punished? Because, as it is said in the record, "the common people heard him gladly"; and the accusation before Pontius Pilate was, "we found this fellow perverting the whole nation. He stirreth up the people, teaching throughout all Jewry."

Ah, the dreaded "common people"!

When Cardinal Manning wrote: "Necessity knows no law, and a starving man has a natural right to a share of his neighbor's bread," who thought of arresting Cardinal Manning? His was a carefully written article in the *Fortnightly Review*. Who read it? Not the people who needed bread. Without food in their stomachs, they had not fifty cents to spend for a magazine. It was not the voice of the people themselves asserting their rights. No one for one instant imagined that Cardinal Manning would put himself at the head of ten thousand hungry men to loot the bakeries of London. It was a piece of ethical hair-splitting to be discussed in after-dinner speeches by the wine-muddled gentlemen who think themselves most competent to consider such subjects when their dress-coats are spoiled by the vomit of gluttony and drunkenness. But when EMMA GOLDMAN stood in Union Square and said, "If they do not give you work or bread, take bread," the common people heard her gladly; and as of old the wandering carpenter of Nazareth addressed his own class, teaching throughout all Jewry, stirring up the people against the authorities, so the dressmaker of New York addressing the unemployed working-people of New York was the menace of the depths of society, crying in its own tongue. The authorities heard and were afraid: therefore the triple wall.

It is the old, old story. When Thomas Paine, one hundred years ago, published the first part of "The Rights of Man," the part in which he discusses principles only, the edition was a high-priced one, reaching comparatively few readers. It created only a literary furore. When the second part appeared, the part in which he treats of the application of principles, in which he declares that "men should not petition for rights but take them," it came out in a cheap form, so that one hundred thousand copies were sold in a few weeks. That brought down the prosecution of the government. It had reached the people that might act, and prosecution followed prosecution till Botany Bay was full of the best men of England. Thus were the limitations of speech and press declared, and thus will they ever be declared so long as there are antagonistic interests in human society.

Understand me clearly. I believe that the term "constitutional right of free speech" is a meaningless phrase, for this reason: the Constitution of the United States, and the Declaration of Independence, and particularly the latter, were, in their day, progressive expressions of progressive ideals. But they are, throughout, characterized by the metaphysical philosophy which dominated the thought of the last century. They speak of "inherent rights," "inalienable rights," "natural rights," etc. They declare that men are equal because of a supposed metaphysical something-or-other, called equality, existing in some mysterious way apart from material conditions, just as the philosophers of the eighteenth century accounted for water being wet by alleging a metaphysical wetness, existing somehow apart from matter. I do not say this to disparage those grand men who dared to put themselves against the authorities of the monarchy, and to conceive a better ideal of society, one which they certainly thought would secure equal rights to men; because I realize fully that no one can live very far in advance of the time-spirit, and I am positive in my own mind that, unless some cataclysm destroys the human race before the end of the twentieth century, the experience of the next hundred years will explode many of our own theories. But the experience of this age has proven that metaphysical quantities do not exist apart from materials, and hence humanity can not be made equal by declarations on paper. Unless the material conditions for equality exist, it is worse than mockery to pronounce men equal. And unless there is equality (and by equality I mean equal chances for every one to make the most of himself), unless, I say, these equal chances exist, freedom, either of thought, speech, or action, is equally a mockery.

I once read that one million angels could dance at the same time on the point of a needle; possibly one million angels might be able to get a decent night's lodging by virtue of their constitutional rights; one single tramp couldn't. And whenever the tongues of the non-possessing class threaten the possessors, whenever the disinherited menace the privileged, that moment you will find that the Constitution isn't made for you. Therefore I think Anarchists make a mistake when they contend for their constitutional rights. As a prominent lawyer, Mr. Thomas Earle White, of Philadelphia, himself an Anarchist, said to me not long since: "What are you going to do about it? Go into the courts, and fight for your legal rights? Anarchists haven't got any." "Well," says the governmentalist, "you can't consistently claim any. You don't believe in constitutions and laws." Exactly so; and if any one will right my constitutional wrongs, I will willingly make him a present of my constitutional rights. At the same time I am perfectly sure no one will ever make this exchange; nor will any help ever come to the wronged class from the outside. Salvation on the vicarious plan isn't worth despising. Redress of wrongs will not come by petitioning "the powers that be." "He has rights who dare maintain them." "The Lord helps them who help themselves." (And when one is able to help himself, I don't think he is apt to trouble the Lord much for his assistance.) As long as the working people fold hands and pray the gods in Washington to give them work, so long they will not get it. So long as they tramp the streets, whose stones they lay, whose filth they clean, whose sewers they dig, yet upon which they must not stand too long lest the policeman bid them "move on"; so long as they go from factory to factory, begging for the opportunity to be a slave, receiving the insults of bosses and foremen, getting the old "No," the old shake of the head, in these factories which they build, whose machines they wrought; so long as they consent to herd like cattle, in the cities, driven year after year, more and more, off the mortgaged land, the land they cleared, fertilized, cultivated, rendered of value; so long as they stand shivering, gazing through plate glass windows at overcoats, which they made but cannot buy, starving in the midst of food they produced but cannot have; so long as they continue to do these things vaguely relying upon some power outside themselves, be it god, or priest, or politician, or employer, or charitable society, to remedy matters, so long deliverance will be delayed. When they conceive the possibility of a complete international federation of labor, whose constituent groups shall take possession of land, mines, factories, all the instruments of production, issue their own certificates of exchange, and, in short, conduct their own industry without regulative interference from law-makers or employers, then we may hope for the only help which counts for aught—self-help; the only condition which can guarantee free speech (and no paper guarantee needed).

But meanwhile, while we are waiting, for there is yet much grist of the middle class to be ground between the upper and nether millstones of economic evolution; while we await the formation of the international labor trust; while we watch for the day when there are enough of people with nothing in their stomachs and desperation in their heads, to go about the work of expropriation; what shall those do who are starving now?

That is the question which EMMA GOLDMAN had to face; and she answered it by saying: "Ask, and if you do not receive, take—take bread."

I do not give you that advice. Not because I do not think the bread belongs to you; not because I do not think you would be morally right in taking it; not that I am not more shocked and horrified and embittered by the report of one human being starving in the heart of plenty, than by all the Pittsburgs, and Chicagos, and Homesteads, and Tennessees, and Cœur d'Alenes, and Buffalos, and Barcelonas, and Parises; not that I do not think one little bit of sensitive human flesh is worth all the property rights in New York city; not that I do not think the world will ever be saved by the sheep's virtue of going patiently to the shambles; not that I do not believe the expropriation of the possessing classes is inevitable, and that that expropriation will begin by just such acts as EMMA GOLDMAN advised, viz.: the taking possession of wealth already produced; not that I think you owe any consideration to the conspirators of Wall Street, or those who profit by their operations, as such, nor ever will till they are reduced to the level of human beings having equal chances with you to earn their share of social wealth, and no more.

I have said that I do not give you the advice given by EMMA GOLDMAN, not that I would have you forget the consideration the expropriators have shown to you; that they have advised lead for strikers, strychnine for tramps, bread and water as good enough for working people; not that I cannot hear yet in my ears the words of one who said to me of the Studebaker Wagon Works' strikers, "If I had my way I'd mow them down with Gatling guns", not that I would have you forget the electric wire of Fort Frick, nor the Pinkertons, nor the militia, nor the prosecutions for murder and treason; not that I would have you forget the 4th of May, when your constitutional right of free speech was vindicated, nor the 11th of November when it was assassinated; not that I would have you forget the single dinner at Delmonico's which Ward McAllister tells us cost ten thousand dollars! Would I have you forget that the wine in the glasses was your children's blood? It must be a rare drink—children's blood! I have read of the wonderful sparkle on costly champagne—I have never seen it. If I did I think it would look to me like mothers' tears over the little, white, wasted forms of dead babies—dead because there was no milk in their breasts! Yes, I want you to remember that these rich are blood-drinkers, tearers of human flesh, gnawers of human bones! Yes, if I had the power I would burn your wrongs upon your hearts in characters that should glow like coals in the night!

I have not a tongue of fire as EMMA GOLDMAN has; I cannot "stir the people"; I must speak in my own cold, calculated way. (Perhaps that is the reason I am allowed to speak at all.) But if I had the power, my will is good enough. You know how Shakespeare's Marc Antony addressed the populace at Rome:

> "I am no orator, as Brutus is,
> But as you know me well, a plain blunt man
> That love my friend. And that they know full well
> That gave me public leave to speak of him.
> For I have neither wit, nor words, nor worth,
> Action, nor utterance, nor the power of speech
> To stir men's blood. I only speak right on.
> I tell you that which you yourselves do know,
> Show you sweet Cæsar's wounds, poor, poor dumb mouths,
> And bid them speak for me. But were I Brutus
> And Brutus Antony, there were an Antony
> Would ruffle up your spirits, and put a tongue
> In every wound of Cæsar's, that should move
> The stones of Rome to rise and mutiny."

If, therefore, I do not give you the advice which EMMA GOLDMAN gave, let not the authorities suppose it is because I have any more respect for their constitution and their law than she has, or that I regard them as having any rights in the matter.

No! My reasons for not giving that advice are two. First, if I were giving advice at all, I would say: "My friends, that bread belongs to you. It is you who toiled and sweat in the sun to sow and reap the wheat; it is you who stood by the thresher, and breathed the chaff-filled atmosphere in the mills, while it was ground to flour; it is you who went into the eternal night of the mine and risked drowning, fire damp, explosion, and cave-in, to get the fuel for the fire that baked it; it is you who stood in the hell-like heat, and struck the blows that forged the iron for the ovens wherein it is baked; it is you who stand all night in the terrible cellar shops, and tend the machines that knead the flour into dough; it is you, you, you, farmer, miner, mechanic, who make the bread; but you haven't the power to take it. At every transformation wrought by toil, some one who didn't toil has taken part from you; and now he has it all, and you haven't the power to take it back! You are told you have the power because you have the numbers. Never make so silly a blunder as to suppose that power resides in numbers. One good, level-headed policeman with a club, is worth ten excited, unarmed men; one detachment of well-drilled militia has a power equal to that of the greatest mob that could be raised in New York City. Do you know I admire compact, concentrated power. Let me give you an illustration. Out in a little town in Illinois there is a certain capitalist, and if ever a human creature sweat and ground the grist of gold from the muscle of man, it is he. Well, once upon a time, his workmen, (not his slaves, his workmen,) were on strike; and fifteen hundred muscular Polacks armed with stones, brickbats, red-hot pokers, and other such crude weapons as a mob generally collects, went up to his house for the purpose of smashing the windows, and so forth; possibly to do as those people in Italy did the other day with the sheriff who attempted to collect the milk tax. He alone, one man, met them on the steps of his porch, and for two mortal hours, by threats, promises, cajoleries held those fifteen hundred Poles at bay. And finally they went away, without smashing a pane of glass or harming a hair of his head. Now that was power; and you can't help but admire it, no matter if it was your enemy who displayed it; and you must admit that so long as numbers can be overcome by such relative quantity, power does not reside in numbers. Therefore, if I were giving advice, I would not say, "take bread," but take counsel with yourselves how to get the power to take bread.

There is no doubt but that power is latently in you; there is no doubt it can be developed; there is no doubt the authorities know this, and fear it, and are ready to exert as much force as is necessary to repress any signs of its development. And this is the explanation of EMMA GOLDMAN's imprisonment. The authorities do not fear you as you are; they only fear what you may become. The dangerous thing was "the voice crying in the wilderness", foretelling the power which was to come after it. You should have seen how they feared it in Philadelphia. They got out a whole platoon of police and detectives, and executed a military manœuvre to catch the woman who had been running around under their noses for three days. And when she walked up to them, then they surrounded and captured her, and guarded the city hall where they kept her over night, and put a detective in the next cell to make notes. Why so much fear? Did they shrink from the stab of the dressmaker's needle? Or did they dread some stronger weapon?

Ah! the accusation before the New York Pontius Pilate was: "She stirreth up the people." And Pilate sentenced her to the full limit of the law, because, he said, "You are more than ordinarily intelligent." Why is intelligence dealt thus harshly with? Because it is the beginning of power. Strive, then, for power.

My second reason for not repeating EMMA GOLDMAN's words is, that I, as an Anarchist, have no right to advise another to do anything involving a risk to himself; nor would I give a fillip for an action done by the advice of some one else, unless it is accompanied by a well-argued, well settled conviction on the part of the person acting, that it really is the best thing to do. Anarchism, to me, means not only the denial of authority, not only a new economy, but a revision of the principles of morality. It means the development of the individual, as well as the assertion of the individual. It means self-responsibility, and not leader-worship. I say it is your business to decide whether you will starve and freeze in sight of food and clothing, outside of jail, or commit some overt act against the institution of property and take your place beside TIMMERMANN and GOLDMAN. And in saying this I mean to cast no reflection whatever upon MISS GOLDMAN for doing otherwise. She and I hold many different views on both Economy and Morals; and that she is honest in her's she has proved better than I have proved mine. MISS GOLDMAN is a Communist; I am an Individualist. She wishes to destroy the right of property; I wish to assert it. I make my war upon privilege and authority, whereby the right of property, the true right in that which is proper to the individual, is annihilated. She believes that co-operation would entirely supplant competition; I hold that competition in one form or another will always exist, and that it is highly desirable it should. But whether she or I be right, or both of us be wrong, of one thing I am sure: *the spirit which animates Emma Goldman is the only one which will emancipate the slave from his slavery, the tyrant from his tyranny—the spirit which is willing to dare and suffer.*

That which dwells in the frail body in the prison-room to-night is not the New York dressmaker alone. Transport yourselves there in thought a moment; look steadily into those fair, blue eyes, upon the sun-brown hair, the sea-shell face, the restless hands, the woman's figure; look steadily till in place of the person, the individual of time and place, you see that which transcends time and place, and flits from house to house of life, mocking at death. Swinburne in his magnificent "Before a Crucifix," says:

"With iron for thy linen bands,
And unclean cloths for winding-sheet,
They bind the people's nail-pierced hands,
They hide the people's nail-pierced feet:
And what man, or what angel known
Shall roll back the sepulchral stone?"

Perhaps in the presence of this untrammeled spirit we shall feel that something has rolled back the sepulchral stone; and up from the cold wind of the grave is borne the breath that animated ANAXAGORAS, SOCRATES, CHRIST, HYPATIA, JOHN HUSS, BRUNO, ROBERT EMMET, JOHN BROWN, SOPHIA PEROVSKAYA, PARSONS, FISCHER, ENGEL, SPIES, LINGG, BERKMAN, PALLAS; and all those, known and unknown, who have died by tree, and axe, and fagot, or dragged out forgotten lives in dungeons, derided, hated, tortured by men. Perhaps we shall know ourselves face to face with that which leaps from the throat of the strangled when the rope chokes, which smokes up from the blood of the murdered when the axe falls; that which has been forever hunted, fettered, imprisoned, exiled, executed, and never conquered. Lo, from its many incarnations it comes forth again, the immortal Race-Christ of the Ages! The gloomy walls are glorified thereby, the prisoner is transfigured, and we say, reverently we say:

"O sacred Head, O desecrate,
O labor-wounded feet and hands,
O blood poured forth in pledge to fate
Of nameless lives in divers lands!
O slain, and spent, and sacrificed
People! The grey-grown, speechless Christ."

Part IV

Neither Gods nor Superstitions

Freethought and Religion

Introduction

"The world's our church, to do good is our creed."
—from the poem, "The Freethinkers Plea"

Voltairine de Cleyre hated the Church and religion with a white-hot intensity. The three years she spent as a teenager in a stifling, rigidly authoritarian Catholic convent made her into a freethinker without even the influence of a book or word from the outside. Her rebellious and independent nature and her constantly questioning intelligence brought her continued punishment from the nuns and, because of her already frail health, nearly made her a nervous wreck. In her essay "The Making of an Anarchist," she writes, "It had been like the Valley of the Shadow of Death, and there are white scars on my soul yet, where Ignorance and Superstition burnt me with their hell-fire in those stifling days." Through sheer force of will, Voltairine refused to let this atmosphere crush her, rejecting not only the superstition of religion but blossoming into one of the freethought movement's most articulate speakers and writers, as well as an unflinching atheist and advocate of the separation of church and state.

The affinity between anarchism and freethought was a natural one. Both have a strongly anti-authoritarian base—the one rejecting the authority of the state and the other rejecting the authority of the church. The word "freethought" means the use of reason in forming opinions about religion, rather than basing belief on faith, authority or tradition. Although many nineteenth century freethinkers were atheists, their ranks also included agnostics, rationalists, and deists. Never a popular tradition but certainly a honorable one in American history, its forebears included Thomas Paine, Thomas Jefferson, George Washington, John Adams, Benjamin Franklin, and James Madison, all of whom were deists.

In twenty-first century America, some readers may fail to appreciate not only how radical freethought was in the nineteenth century, but how dangerous it could be to hold such views. Atheists in America today may not be very popular—they may be despised in certain quarters—but they are usually able to be heard and are rarely in physical danger. Not so in the nineteenth century. In a time when even what are now moderate Christian denominations, such as Methodism and Presbyterianism, were rigid and puritanical, freethought was reviled and vehemently opposed.

Though largely unacknowledged today, even by most male freethought historians, women played a large role in freethought movement of the nineteenth century. Before Voltairine and even Robert Ingersoll, the most influential freethinker, there was the unabashedly atheist activist Ernestine Rose, a champion of women's rights. There was Ella Gibson, who wrote the first book with a feminist analysis of the Bible in 1870, and, of course, the infamous Victoria Woodhull, the first woman to run for President of the US. Active in abolitionism and the free love (sexual freedom) movement, the women of freethought were also the first to speak out for women's rights, a debt still unacknowledged by today's mainstream women's movement. From deist Mary Wollstonecraft, author of the first feminist manifesto, *A Vindication of the Rights of Women*, and anti-cleric socialist Frances Wright to Quaker heretic Lucretia Mott; from Elizabeth Cady Stanton, author of the *Women's Bible*, condemning the role of religion in women's lives, to the largely forgotten but crucially important Matilda Joslyn Gage, the women freethinkers made a significant impact on American political culture.

It was into the vibrant and exciting intellectual milieu of freethought that Voltairine stepped when she left the convent. For Voltairine, writes her biographer Paul Avrich, "plunging into the freethought movement was part of her struggle to liberate herself from the shackles of religious tyranny ... her poems of this period, especially 'The Christian's Faith' and 'The Freethinker's Plea,' both written in 1887, show her wrestling free of the lingering effects of the convent, completing the burial of her 'past self.'" As her reputation grew, her lectures, including frequent tours for the American Secular Union, a nationwide freethought organization, took her to many Midwestern and Eastern states. In the days before radio and television, such public lectures were enormously popular and well-attended.

Voltairine's thoughts about religious education were later published in *The Truth Seeker* in 1887 as the essay, "Secular Education," which appears in this volume. This essay discusses the dangers of intruding religion into public education and the importance of keeping religion and education, Church and State, separate. Commenting on the early influence of parents in inculcating religious notions, she asserts: "Oh, it is a power, this early influence! And therein lies the hidden strength of the church ..." As an alternative to this pernicious influence, Voltairine calls for teaching critical and independent thinking to children: "Secularism owes this duty to itself—that it instruct its children in their earliest infancy to think—think for themselves." No admonition could be more relevant to current public education, now under attack by fundamentalist forces, and with a curriculum that rarely encourages critical or independent thinking.

"The Economic Tendency of Freethought," a lecture originally given before the Boston Secular Society, was later published in Benjamin Tucker's individualist anarchist periodical, *Liberty*, in 1890. Voltairine believed that the "God-Idea" is destructive to human freedom and to women's emancipation. In this essay, she details her logical argument against the idea of God, discussing why she thinks it is dangerous to society and calling for the embracing of reason and science as opposed to faith and superstition. She also vindicates several charges often leveled against freethought—that it would lead to atheism, to anarchism, and to the destruction of marriage. All three institutions—church, government, and marriage—rest on the slavery of authority, she believed. Truth, Voltairine writes, is a result of liberty, not force; "true economy lies in Liberty." Rejecting the notion that these institutions have brought great good to society, she echoes Thoreau when she asserts that "It is not slavery that produced the means of transportation, communication, production, and exchange, and all the thousand and one economic... contrivances of civilization. No—nor is it government. It is *Self-Interest.*"

Voltairine, impeccably consistent, believed that rejection of authority and acceptance of independent thought meant rejecting all of the manifestations of authority—most especially government, church and patriarchy—and embracing anarchism, freethought, and feminism. In her view, these ideas were inextricably intertwined. "I see no reason, absolutely none," she concluded in her essay, "The Case of Woman vs. Orthodoxy," "why women have clung to the doom of the gods. I cannot understand why they have not rebelled."

—Sharon Presley

REFERENCES

Gage, Matilda Joslyn. *Women, Church and State,* Watertown, NY: Persephone Press, 1980; reprint of 1893 edition.

Gaylor, Annie Laurie (ed.). *Women Without Superstition: The Collected Writings of Women Freethinkers of the Nineteenth and Twentieth Centuries.* Madison, Wisconsin: Freedom From Religion Foundation, 1997.

Sears, Hal. *The Sex Radicals,* Lawrence, KS: The Regents Press of Kansas, 1977.

Stanton, Elizabeth Cady. *The Original Feminist Attack on the Bible (The Woman's Bible),* New York: Arno Press, 1974.

The Economic Tendency
of Freethought

"The Economic Tendency of Freethought" was published in *Liberty*, Boston, Mass., Vol. XI, No. 25, Feb. 15, 1890. It gives a capsule history of the freethought movement, the main tenet of which she defines as follows: "the right to believe as the evidence, coming in contact with the mind, forces it to believe." She argues that such a principle, first applied to religious matters, extends to political and economic convictions as well.

Thomas Paine (1737–1809), a great hero of Voltairine's and activist in both the American and French revolutions, was the author of the classic anti-authoritarian tracts *Common Sense* and *The Rights of Man*.

Giordano Bruno (1548–1600) was an Italian philosopher and supporter of Copernicus. He was burned at the stake for his pantheism.

Martin Luther (1483–1546) was the spearhead of the Protestant reformation and champion of individual conscience in religious matters.

Cardinal (Henry Edward) Manning (1808–1892) was an English Catholic prelate.

Benjamin Harrison (1833–1901) was the Republican president of the United States at the time the essay was published.

The Mussel Slough affair was a misrepresentation of land prices by the Southern Pacific Railroad, originally granted by Congress. Settlers found themselves without clear title to land they thought they owned.

"Gould" is Jay Gould (1836–1892), an American financier most famous for trying to corner the gold market, causing a panic in 1869.

"Vanderbilt," of course, is Cornelius Vanderbilt (1794–1877), American railroad magnate.

The Economic Tendency
of Freethought

FRIENDS,-On page 286, Belford-Clarke edition, of the "Rights of Man," the words which I propose as a text for this discourse may be found. Alluding to the change in the condition of France brought about by the Revolution of '93, Thomas Paine says:

> The mind of the nation had changed beforehand, and a new order of things had naturally followed a new order of thoughts.

Two hundred and eighty-nine years ago, a man, a student, a scholar, a thinker, a philosopher, was roasted alive for the love of God and the preservation of the authority of the Church; and as the hungry flames curled round the crisping flesh of martyred Bruno, licking his blood with their wolfish tongues, they shadowed forth the immense vista of "a new order of things": they lit the battle-ground where Freedom fought her first successful revolt against authority.

That battle-ground was eminently one of thought. Religious freedom was the rankling question of the day. "Liberty of conscience! Liberty of conscience! Non-interference between worshipper and worshipped!" That was the voice that cried out of dungeons and dark places, from under the very foot of prince and ecclesiastic. And why? Because the authoritative despotisms of that day were universally ecclesiastic despotisms; because Church aggression was grinding every human right beneath its heel, and every other minor oppressor was but a tool in the hands of the priesthood; because Tyranny was growing towards its ideal and crushing out of existence the very citadel of Liberty,—individuality of thought; Ecclesiasticism had a corner on ideas.

But individuality is a thing that cannot be killed. Quietly it may be, but just as certainly, silently, perhaps, as the growth of a blade of grass, it offers its perpetual and unconquerable protest against the dictates of Authority. And this silent, unconquerable, menacing thing, that balked God, provoked him to the use of rack, thumb-screw, stock, hanging, drowning, burning, and other instruments of "infinite mercy," in the seventeenth century fought a successful battle against that authority which sought to control this fortress of freedom. It established its right to be. It overthrew that portion of government which attempted to guide the brains of men. It "broke the corner." It declared and maintained the *anarchy*, or non-rulership, of thought.

Now you who so fear the word *an-arche*, remember! the whole combat of the seventeenth century, of which you are justly proud, and to which you never tire of referring, was waged for the sole purpose of realizing anarchism in the realm of thought.

It was not an easy struggle,—this battle of the quiet thinkers against those who held all the power, and all the force of numbers, and all of the strength of tortures! It was not easy for them to speak out of the midst of faggot flames, "We believe differently, and we have the right". But on their side stood Truth! And there lies more inequality between her and Error, more strength for Truth, more weakness for Falsehood, than all the fearful disparity of power that lies between the despot and the victim. So theirs was the success. So they paved the way for the grand political combat of the eighteenth century.

Mark you! The seventeenth century made the eighteenth possible, for it was the "new order of thoughts," which gave birth to a "new order of things". Only by deposing priests, only by rooting out their authority, did it become logical to attack the tyranny of kings: for, under the old regime, kingcraft had ever been the tool of priestcraft, and in the order of things but a secondary consideration. But with the downfall of the latter, kingcraft rose into prominence as the pre-eminent despot, and against the pre-eminent despot revolt always arises.

The leaders of that revolt were naturally those who carried the logic of their freethought into the camp of the dominant oppressor; who thought, spoke, wrote freely of the political fetish, as their predecessors had of the religious mockery; who did not waste their time hugging themselves in the camps of dead enemies, but accepted the live issue of the day, pursued the victories of Religion's martyrs, and carried on the war of Liberty in those lines most necessary to the people at the time and place. The result was the overthrow of the principle of kingcraft. (Not that all kingdoms have been overthrown, but find me one in a hundred of the inhabitants of a kingdom who will not laugh at the farce of the "divine appointment" of monarchs.) So wrought the new order of thoughts.

I do not suppose for a moment that Giordano Bruno or Martin Luther foresaw the immense scope taken in by their doctrine of individual judgment. From the experience of men up to that date it was simply impossible that they could foresee its tremendous influence upon the action of the eighteenth century, much less upon the nineteenth. Neither was it possible that those bold writers who attacked the folly of "hereditary government" should calculate the effects which certainly followed as their thoughts took form and shape in the social body. Neither do I believe it possible that any brain that lives can detail the working of a thought into the future, or push its logic to an ultimate. But that many who think, or think they think, do not carry their syllogisms even to the first general conclusion, I am also forced to believe. If they did, the freethinkers of today would not be digging, mole-like, through the substratum of dead issues; they would not waste their energies gathering the ashes of fires burnt out two centuries ago; they would not lance their shafts at that which is already bleeding at the arteries; they would not range battalions of brains against a crippled ghost that is "laying" itself as fast as it decently can, while a monster neither ghostly nor yet like the rugged Russian bear, the armed rhinoceros, or the Hyrcan tiger, but rather like a terrible anaconda, steel-muscled and iron-jawed, is winding its horrible folds around the human bodies of the world, and breathing its devouring breath into the faces of children. If they did, they would understand that the paramount question of the day is not political, is not religious, but is economic. That the crying-out demand of today is for a circle of principles that shall forever make it impossible for one man to control another by controlling the means of his existence. They would realize that, unless the freethought movement has a practical utility in rendering the life of man more bearable, unless it contains a principle which, worked out, will free him from the all-oppressive tyrant, it is just as complete and empty a mockery as the Christian miracle or Pagan myth. Eminently is this the age of utility; and the freethinker who goes to the Hovel of Poverty with metaphysical speculations as to the continuity of life, the transformation of matter, etc.; who should say, "My dear friend, your Christian brother is mistaken; you are not doomed to an eternal hell; your condition here is your misfortune and can't be helped, but when you are dead, there's an end of it," is of as little use in the world as the most irrational religionist. To him would the hovel justly reply: "Unless you can show me something in freethought which commends itself to the needs of the race, something which will adjust my wrongs, 'put down the mighty from his seat,' then go sit with priest and king, and wrangle out your metaphysical opinions with those who mocked our misery before."

The question is, does freethought contain such a principle? And right here permit me to introduce a sort of supplementary text, taken, I think, from a recent letter of Cardinal Manning, but if not Cardinal Manning, then some other of the various dunce-capped gentlemen who recently "biled" over the Bruno monument.

Says the Cardinal: "Freethought leads to Atheism, to the destruction of social and civil order, and to the overthrow of government." I accept the gentleman's statement; I credit him with much intellectual acumen for perceiving that which many freethinkers have failed to perceive: accepting it, I shall do my best to prove it, and then endeavor to show that this very iconoclastic principle is the salvation of the economic slave and the destruction of the economic tyrant.

FIRST: DOES FREETHOUGHT LEAD TO ATHEISM?

Freethought, broadly defined, is the right to believe as the evidence, coming in contact with the mind, forces it to believe. This implies the admission of any and all evidence bearing upon any subject which may come up for discussion. Among the subjects that come up for discussion, the moment so much is admitted, is the existence of a God.

Now, the idea of God is, in the first place, an exceeding contradiction. The sign God, so Deists tell us, was invented to express the inexpressible, the incomprehensible and infinite! Then they immediately set about defining it. These definitions prove to be about as self-contradictory and generally conflicting as the original absurdity. But there is a particular set of attributes which form a sort of common ground for all these definitions. They tell us that God is possessed of supreme wisdom, supreme justice, and supreme power. In all the catalogue of creeds, I never yet heard of one that had not for its nucleus unlimited potency.

Now, let us take the deist upon his own ground and prove to him either that his God is limited as to wisdom, or limited as to justice, or limited as to power, or else there is no such thing as justice.

First, then, God, being all-just, wishes to do justice; being all-Wise, knows what justice is; being all-powerful, can do justice. Why then injustice? Either your God can do justice and won't or doesn't know what justice is, or he can not do it. The immediate reply is: "What appears to be injustice in our eyes, in the sight of omniscience may be justice.—God's ways are not our ways."

Oh, but if he is the all-wise pattern, they should be; what is good enough for God ought to be good enough for man; but what is too mean for man won't do in a God. Else there is no such thing as justice or injustice, and every murder, every robbery, every lie, every crime in the calendar is right and upon that one premise of supreme authority you upset every fact in existence.

What right have you to condemn a murderer if you assume him necessary to "God's plan"? What logic can command the return of stolen property, or the branding of a thief, if the Almighty decreed it? Yet here, again, the Deist finds himself in a dilemma, for to suppose crime necessary to God's purpose is to impeach his wisdom or deny his omnipotence by limiting him as to means. The whole matter, then, hinges upon the one attribute of authority of the central idea of God.

But, you say, what has all this to do with the economic tendency of freethought? Everything. For upon that one idea of supreme authority is based every tyranny that was ever formulated. Why? Because, if God is, no human being no thing that lives, ever had a right! He simply had a privilege, bestowed, granted, conferred, gifted to him, for such a length of time as God sees fit.

This is the logic of my textator, the logic of Catholicism, the only logic of Authoritarianism. The Catholic Church says: "You who are blind, be grateful that you can hear: God could have made you deaf as well. You who are starving, be thankful that you can breathe; God could deprive you of air as well as food. You who are sick, be grateful that you are not dead: God is very merciful to let you live at all. Under all times and circumstances take what you can get, and be thankful." These are the beneficences, the privileges, given by Authority.

Note the difference between a right and a privilege. A right, in the abstract, is a fact; it is not a thing to be given, established, or conferred; it is. Of the exercise of a right power may deprive me; of the right itself, never. Privilege, in the abstract, does not exist; there is no such thing. Rights recognized, privilege is destroyed.

But, in the practical, the moment you admit a supreme authority, you have denied rights. Practically the supremacy has all the rights, and no matter what the human race possesses, it does so merely at the caprice of that authority. The exercise of the respiratory function is not a right, but a privilege granted by God; the use of the soil is not a right, but a gracious allowance of Deity; the possession of product as the result of labor is not a right, but a boon bestowed. And the thievery of pure air, the withholding of land from use, the robbery of toil, are not wrongs (for if you have no rights, you cannot be wronged), but benign blessings bestowed by "the Giver of all Good" upon the air-thief, the landlord, and the labor-robber.

Hence the freethinker who recognizes the science of astronomy, the science of mathematics, and the equally positive and exact science of justice, is logically forced to the denial of supreme authority. For no human being who observes and reflects can admit a supreme tyrant and preserve his self-respect. No human mind can accept the dogma of divine despotism and the doctrine of eternal justice at the same time; they contradict each other, and it takes two brains to hold them. The cardinal is right: freethought does logically lead to atheism, if by atheism he means the denial of supreme authority.

I will now take his third statement, leaving the second for the present; freethought, he says, leads to the overthrow of government.

I am sensible that the majority of you will be ready to indignantly deny the cardinal's asseveration; I know that the most of my professedly atheistic friends shrink sensitively from the slightest allusion that sounds like an attack on government; I am aware that there are many of you who could eagerly take this platform to speak upon "the glorious rights and privileges of American citizenship"; to expatiate upon that "noble bulwark of our liberties—the constitution"; to defend "that peaceful weapon of redress, the ballot"; to soar off rhapsodically about that "starry banner that floats 'over the land of the free and the home of the brave.'" We are so free! and so brave! We don't hang Brunos at the stake any more for holding heretical opinions on religious subjects. No! But we imprison men for discussing the social question, and we hang men for discussing the economic question! We are so very free and so very brave in this country! "Ah"! we say in our nineteenth century freedom (?) and bravery (?), "it was a weak God, a poor God, a miserable, quaking God, whose authority had to be preserved by the tortuous death of a creature!" Aye! the religious question is dead, and the stake is no longer fashionable. But is it a strong State, a brave State, a conscience-proud State, whose authority demands the death of five creatures? Is the scaffold better than the faggot? Is it a very free mind which will read that infamous editorial in the Chicago "Herald": "It is not necessary to hold that Parsons was legally, rightfully, or wisely hanged: he was mightily hanged. The State, the sovereign, need give no reasons; the State need abide by no law; the State is the law!"—to read that and applaud, and set the Cain-like curse upon your forehead and the red "damned spot" upon your hand? Do you know what you do?—Craven, you worship the fiend, Authority, again! True, you have not the ghosts, the incantations, the paraphernalia and mummery of the Church. No: but you have the "precedents," the "be it enacted," the red-tape, the official uniforms of the State; and you are just as bad a slave to statecraft as your Irish Catholic neighbor is to popecraft. Your Government becomes your God, from whom you accept privileges, and in whose hands all rights are vested. Once more the individual has no rights; once more intangible, irresponsible authority assumes the power of deciding what is right and what is wrong. Once more the race must labor under just such restricted conditions as the law—the voice of the Authority, the governmentalist's bible—shall dictate. Once more it says: "You who have not meat, be grateful that you have bread; many are not allowed even so much. You who work sixteen hours a day, be glad it is not twenty; many have not the privilege to work. You who have not fuel, be thankful that you have shelter; many walk the street! And you, street-walkers, be grateful that there are well-lighted dens of the city; in the country you might die upon the roadside. Goaded human race! Be thankful for your goad. Be submissive to the Lord, and kiss the hand that lashes you!" Once more misery is the diet of the many, while the few receive, in addition to their rights, those rights of their fellows which government has wrested from them. Once more the hypothesis is that the Government, or Authority, or God in his other form, owns all the rights, and grants privileges according to its sweet will.

The freethinker who should determine to question it would naturally suppose that one difficulty in the old investigation was removed. He would say, "at least this thing Government possesses the advantage of being of the earth,—earthy. This is something I can get hold of, argue, reason, discuss with. God was an indefinable, arbitrary, irresponsible something in the clouds, to whom I could not approach nearer than to his agent, the priest. But this dictator surely I shall be able to meet it on something like possible ground." Vain delusion! Government is as unreal, as intangible, as unapproachable as God. Try it, if you don't believe it. Seek through the legislative halls of America and find, if you can, the Government. In the end you will be doomed to confer with the agent, as before. Why, you have the statutes! Yes, but the statutes are not the government; where is the power that made the statutes? Oh, the legislators! Yes, but the legislator, per se, has no more power to make a law for me than I for him. I want the power that gave him the power. I shall talk with him; I go to the White House; I say: "Mr. Harrison, are you the government?" "No, madam, I am its representative." "Well, where is the principal?—Who is the government?" "The people of the United States." "The whole people?" "The whole people." "You, then, are the representative of the people of the United States. May I see your certificate of authorization?" "Well, no; I have none. I was elected." "Elected by whom? the whole people?" "Oh, no. By some of the people,—some of the voters." (Mr. Harrison being a pious Presbyterian, he would probably add: "The majority vote of the whole was for another man, but I had the largest electoral vote.") "Then you are the representative of the electoral college, not of the whole people, nor the majority of the people, nor even a majority of the voters. But suppose the largest number of ballots cast had been for you: you would represent the majority of the voters, I suppose. But the majority, sir, is not a tangible thing; it is an unknown quantity. An agent is usually held accountable to his principals. If you do not know the individuals who voted for you, then you do not know for whom you are acting, nor to whom you are accountable. If any body of persons has delegated to you any authority, the disposal of any right or part of a right (supposing a right to be transferable), you must have received it from the individuals composing that body; and you must have some means of learning who those individuals are, or you cannot know for whom you act, and you are utterly irresponsible as an agent.

"Furthermore, such a body of voters can not give into your charge any rights but their own; by no possible jugglery of logic can they delegate the exercise of any function which they themselves do not control. If any individual on earth has a right to delegate his powers to whomsoever he chooses, then every other individual has an equal right; and if each has an equal right, then none can choose an agent for another, without that other's consent. Therefore, if the power of government resides in the whole people, and out of that whole all but one elected you as their agent, you would still have no authority whatever to act for the one. The individuals composing the minority who did not appoint you have just the same rights and powers as those composing the majority who did; and if they prefer not to delegate them at all, then neither you, nor any one, has any authority whatever to coerce them into accepting you, or any one, as their agent—for upon your own basis the coercive authority resides, not in the majority, not in any proportion of the people, but in the whole people."

Hence "the overthrow of government" as a coercive power, thereby denying God in another form.

Upon this overthrow follows, the Cardinal says, the disruption of social and civil order!

Oh! it is amusing to hear those fellows rave about social order! I could laugh to watch them as they repeat the cry, "Great is Diana of the Ephesians!" "Down on your knees and adore this beautiful statue of Order," but that I see this hideous, brainless, disproportion idol come rolled on the wheels of Juggernaut over the weak and the helpless, the sorrowful and the despairing. Hate burns, then, where laughter dies.

Social Order! Not long ago I saw a letter from a young girl to a friend; a young girl whose health had been broken behind a counter, where she stood eleven and twelve hours a day, six days in the week, for the magnificent sum of $5. The letter said: "Can't you help me to a position? My friends want me to marry a man I do not like, because he has money. Can't you help me? I can sew, or keep books. I will even try clerking again rather than that!" Social Order! When the choice for a young girl lies between living by inches and dying by yards at manual labor, or becoming the legal property of a man she does not like because he has money!

Walk up Fifth Avenue in New York some hot summer day, among the magnificent houses of the rich; hear your footsteps echo for blocks with the emptiness of it! Look at places going to waste, space, furniture, draperies, elegance,—all useless. Then take a car down town; go among the homes of the producers of that idle splendor; find six families living in a five-room house,—the sixth dwelling in the cellar. Space is not wasted here,—these human vermin rub each other's elbows in the stifling narrows; furniture is not wasted,—these sit upon the floor; no echoing emptiness, no idle glories! No—but wasting, strangling, choking, vicious human life! Dearth of vitality there—dearth of space for it here! This is social order!

Next winter, when the "annual output" of coal has been mined, when the workmen are clenching their hard fists with impotent anger, when the coal in the ground lies useless, hark to the cry that will rise from the freezing western prairies, while the shortened commodity goes up, up, up, eight, nine, ten, eleven dollars a ton; and while the syndicate's pockets are filling, the grave-yards fill, and fill. Moralize on the preservation of social order!

Go back to President Grant's administration,—that very "pure republican" administration;—see the settlers of the Mussel Slough compelled to pay thirty-five, forty dollars an acre for the land reclaimed from almost worthlessness by hard labor,—and to whom? To a corporation of men who never saw it! whose "grant" lay a hundred miles away, but who, for reasons of their own, saw fit to hire the "servants of the people" to change it so. See those who refused to pay it shot down by order of "the State"; watch their blood smoke upward to the heavens, sealing the red seal of Justice against their murderers; and then—watch a policeman arrest a shoeless tramp for stealing a pair of boots. Say to your self, this is civil order and must be preserved. Go talk with political leaders, big or little, on methods of "making the slate," and "railroading" it through the ward caucus or the national convention. Muse on that "peaceful weapon of redress," the ballot.

Consider the condition of the average "American sovereign" and of his "official servant," and prate then of civil order.

Subvert the social and civil order! Aye, I would destroy, to the last vestige, this mockery of order, this travesty upon justice!

Break up the home? Yes, every home that rests on slavery! Every marriage that represents the sale and transfer of the individuality of one of its parties to the other! Every institution, social or civil, that stands between man and his right; every tie that renders one a master, another a serf; every law, every statute, every be-it-enacted that represents tyranny; everything you call American privilege that can only exist at the expense of international right. Now cry out, "Nihilist— disintegrationist!" Say that I would isolate humanity, reduce society to its elemental state, make men savage! It is not true. But rather than see this devastating, cankering, enslaving system you call social order go on, rather than help to keep alive the accursed institutions of Authority, I would help to reduce every fabric in the social structure to its native element.

But is it true that freedom means disintegration? Only to that which is bad. Only to that which ought to disintegrate.

What is the history of free thought?

Is it not so, that since we have Anarchy there, since all the children of the brain are legitimate, that there has been less waste of intellectual

energy, more cooperation in the scientific world, truer economy in utiliz-
ing the mentalities of men, than there ever was, or ever could be, under
authoritative dominion of the church? Is it not true that with the liberty of
thought, Truth has been able to prove herself without the aid of force?
Does not error die from want of vitality when there is no *force* to keep it
alive? Is it not true that natural attractions have led men into associative
groups, who can best follow their chosen paths of thought, and give the
benefit of their studies to mankind with better economy than if some coercive power had said, "You think in this line—you in that"; or what the
majority had by ballot decided it was best to think about?

I think it is true.

Follow your logic out; can you not see that *true economy lies in
Liberty,*—whether it be in thought or action? It is not slavery that has
made men unite for cooperative effort. It is not slavery that produced the
means of transportation, communication, production, and exchange, and
all the thousand and one economic, or what ought to be economic, contrivances of civilization. No—nor is it government. It is *Self-interest.* And
would not self-interest exist if that institution which stands between man
and his right to the free use of the soil were annihilated? Could you not see
the use of a bank if the power which renders it possible for the national
banks to control land, production and everything else, were broken down?

Do you suppose the producers of the east and west couldn't see the
advantage of a railroad, if the authority which makes a systematizer like
Gould or Vanderbilt a curse were swept away? Do you imagine that government has a corner on ideas, now that the Church is overthrown; and that the
people could not learn the principles of economy, if this intangible giant
which has robbed and slaughtered them, wasted their resources and distributed opportunities so unjustly, were destroyed? I don't think so. I believe that
legislators as a rule have been monuments of asinine stupidity, whose principal business has been to hinder those who were not stupid, and get paid for
doing it. I believe that the so-called brainy financial men would rather buy the
legislators than be the legislators; and the real thinkers, the genuine improvers
of society, have as little to do with law and politics as they conveniently can.

I believe that "Liberty is the mother, not the daughter, of Order."

"But," some one will say, "what of the criminals? Suppose a man
steals." In the first place, a man won't steal, ordinarily, unless that which he
steals is something he can not as easily get without stealing; in liberty the
cost of stealing would involve greater difficulties than producing, and
consequently he would not be apt to steal. But suppose a man steals. Today
you go to a representative of that power which has robbed you of the earth,
of the right of free contract of the means of exchange, taxes you for everything you eat or wear (the meanest form of robbery),—you go to him for

redress from a thief! It is about as logical as the Christian lady whose husband had been "removed" by Divine Providence, and who thereupon prayed to said Providence to "comfort the widow and the fatherless." In freedom we would not institute a wholesale robber to protect us from petty larceny. Each associative group would probably adopt its own methods of resisting aggression, that being the only crime. For myself, I think criminals should be treated as sick people.

"But suppose you have murderers, brutes, all sorts of criminals. Are you not afraid to lose the restraining influence of the law?" First, I think it can be shown that the law makes ten criminals where it restrains one. On that basis it would not, as a matter of policy merely, be an economical institution. Second, this is not a question of expediency, but of right. In antebellum days the proposition was not, Are the blacks good enough to be free? but, Have they the right? So today the question is not, Will outrages result from freeing humanity? but, Has it the right to life, the means of life, the opportunities of happiness?

In the transition epoch, surely crimes will come. Did the seed of tyranny ever bear good fruit? And can you expect Liberty to undo in a moment what Oppression has been doing for ages? Criminals are the crop of despots, as much a necessary expression of the evil in society as an ulcer is of disease in the blood; and so long as the taint of the poison remains, so long there will be crimes.

"For it must needs that offences come, but woe to him through whom the offence cometh." The crimes of the future are the harvests sown of the ruling classes of the present. Woe to the tyrant who shall cause the offense!

Sometimes I dream of this social change. I get a streak of faith in Evolution, and the good in man. I paint a gradual slipping out of the *now*, to that beautiful *then*, where there are neither kings, presidents, landlords, national bankers, stockbrokers, railroad magnates, patent-right monopolists, or tax and title collectors; where there are no over-stocked markets or hungry children, idle counters and naked creatures, splendor and misery, waste and need. I am told this is farfetched idealism, to paint this happy, povertyless, crimeless, diseaseless world; I *have* been told I "ought to be behind the bars" for it.

Remarks of that kind rather destroy the white streak of faith. I lose confidence in the slipping process, and am forced to believe that the rulers of the earth are sowing a fearful wind, to reap a most terrible whirlwind. When I look at this poor, bleeding, wounded World, this world that has suffered so long, struggled so much, been scourged so fiercely, thorn-pierced so deeply, crucified so cruelly, I can only shake my head and remember:

The giant is blind, but he's thinking: and his locks are growing, fast.

Secular Education

"Secular Education" was originally published in *The Truth Seeker*, Vol.14, No. 49, December 3, 1887. It expresses the importance that Voltairine attributed to education. But more, it expresses the importance that she attributed to independent thought—thought independent of any authority and specifically of religion. The essay also gives a sense of the resentment with which she regarded her own education by the church.

Stephen Girard: French sea captain and captain of American industry, d. 1831.

Secular Education

There are four instruments which, wielded by dominant minds, bend and mold the sentiments of the masses to meet the form and spirit of the times: The force of early influence, the school, the platform, and the press.

These are the four grand educators, and education is the strong right arm of progress, that arm which bares its mighty muscles and strikes upon the hewn rock of time the chisel-blows which carve the tablets of an advancing era, there to remain until the surges of the incoming ages shall have swept them away, leaving a smooth face whereon shall be inscribed the newer thought, the better hope, the fuller life of the millennium.

To underestimate the power of anyone of these four is to commit oneself to an error in judgment which betrays a lack of generalship, since a good general will never underrate the strength of either his own or his enemy's forces; and whether influence, school, press, and platform are ranged on the side of your battalions or against them, they exert a power which it will not do to overlook if you desire to win the conflict.

To the public school system the nation looks, and in a measure has a right to look, for the formation of the character of its youth. I say it has a right to look in a measure. But there is an education which begins before that, an education which is rooted deeper, which reaches farther, which endures longer than that, and might be called the education of early circumstances; the education of parental influence; the education which makes the child of Catholic parents get down upon its knees while yet scarcely able to lisp its mother's name, and make the sign of the cross while that mother repeats: *In nomine patris, et filius, et spirituus sanctus;* the education which makes the child of Calvinistic parents afraid to be happy on Sunday for fear of offending an all-loving father; the education which should make the child of Secular parents understand that it is better to study how to live rather than how to die; that it is better to have a religion of deeds rather than a religion of creeds; that it is better to work for humanity than for God.

Secularism owes this duty to itself—that it instruct its children in their earliest infancy to think—think for themselves. One of our Secular papers has for its motto, "The agitation of thought is the beginning of wisdom."

Once the people begin to understand that; once they begin to appreciate the fact that aroused thought creates questions, that questions provoke answers, and that unsatisfactory answers call forth a denial from reason; once they get waked up to the propriety of asking the clergy questions, you will see the frock-coated gentlemen coming down mightily from their clerical stilts. They'll get down at about the rate the old Scottish minister did with the foxes' tails. I suppose you've all heard of that. A certain Scotch clergyman who, after the manner of ministers in general and particular, was very fond of hearing himself praised, said one day to the sexton, whom he met in the vestibule after service, "Well, Sandy, an' how did ye like the sermon the day?"

"A weel, meenister, it were vera guid."

This tickled the old gentleman immensely, and he wanted to hear it again, so pretty soon he recommenced,

"An' so, Sandy, ye likit the sermon, did ye?"

"Weel, meenister, I didna say that, but it were better nor usual. I didna see sae mony folk asleep."

"What, Sandy! asleep in the kirk?"

"Aye, meenister. Ye ken that sometimes ye are a wee bit gien to exaggeration an'———"

"Exagger—what?"

"Weel, meenister, I didna mean tae pit it ower strang, but ye ken that—weel, ye sometimes stretch the truth a bit."

"What, Sandy? Me stretch the truth, an' me a meenister! Sandy, I'll tell ye. Ye ken that ye sit in the kirk afornent the pulpit. Weel, the next time that ye hear me exaggeratin' wull ye look up and whustle?"

"I wull."

So the next Sunday our minister had a very carefully-prepared sermon, taking his text from that part of the scripture which tells about Samson catching the three hundred foxes and tying their tails together; and had he but stuck to his notes he would hav been all right. But no; he could not forbear to extemporize; and closing the big Bible he leaned forward upon it, remarking as he did so, "Noo, brethren, this is wi' mony a vera sair pint; how Samson could ha' caught the three hun'erd foxes, and having caught them, tied their tails thegither. For ye ken that, in this country, it taks a grat mony men an' a grat mony houn's to catch one fox, let alone three hun'erd foxes. But, brethren, if ye'll gie me yer attention for a few munits I'll make that a' perfectly plain to ye. We're tauld in the scriptures that Samson was the strongest mon that ever lived; noo, while we're *not* tauld that he was the gratest runner that ever lived, we're *not* tauld that he *wasn't*; and so I infer from that that Samson was the gratest runner that ever lived. But noo we come to a mair sair pint still. Having caught the three hun'erd foxes, how was it that he tied their tails thegither, for ye maun ken that it wad be a vera difficult matter for a mon to tie twa foxes' tails thegither, let alone three hun'erd foxes. But ha' patience wi' me, brethren, and I'll make that plain to ye. Noo, there ha' been mun who ha' na staid on thar farms and dairies like yersel's, who ha'na been to the univarsities like mysel', but ha' been away au' traveled i' foreign countries, i' Palestine and the Holy Land. An' these travelers tell us that thar foxes there are nae like the foxes here, that they are a vera different creetyer; that their tails are vera much longer than they are here; that, in fact, thae foxes there hae tails f-o-r-t-y feet long!"

(A prolonged whistle.)

"Wait a meenit, brethren. Some writers tell us that thae foxes ha' tails forty feet long, but ither writers inform us that this is a grat exaggeration. That thae foxes' tails are nae mair than t-w-e-n-t-y feet long!"

(Another whistle.)

"Wait, brethren! While some writers hae tauld us that thae foxes' tails are forty feet long, and ither writers hae tauld us that thae foxes' tails are twenty feet long, I mysel' hae studied the matter, and I hae come to the conclusion that this is a vera grat exaggeration. That, in fact, the foxes' tails are nae mair than t-e-n feet long!"

(Another prolonged whistle.)

"Sandy McDonald, I'll nae tak' anither inch off thae foxes' tails if ye whustle till ye whustle off the top o' the kirk! Wad ye hae the foxes wi' nae tails at a'?"

Well, if the people will only keep on whistling, they will get the preachers down to within five or ten feet of the truth.

Secularism owes this duty to itself, that it educate its children in the bottom facts of truth, and not leave them exposed to the deceitful allurements of well-masked falsehood.

Oh, it is a power, this early influence! And therein lies the secret strength of the church; therein lies the hidden source of might to that magnificent organization—the finest which this world has ever seen—that teacher of the dark and damnable doctrins of ignorance, the Roman Catholic church. Therein lies the power which enables it to stretch out a long arm under the Atlantic ocean, to reach a hand beneath the people of the United States, to press its fingers down upon our political parties and its thumb upon our political liberties, and when the opportune moment comes, will enable it to drag them all back, back under the iron heel of the Italian despot.

Do you think them unable to do it, simply because a few Freethinkers oppose a feeble remonstrance? You might as well hope to keep out the storm tides of the ocean with a few poor, rotten dykes. It is going to take the barrier of well-educated minds to stem that torrent; and education, to be most effective, must begin in childhood. Earliest impressions are most enduring, and earliest superstitions are hardest to be rid of.

Do not deceive yourselvs. If you do not educate your children, the church will do it for you, and with an object.

Think you, when their numbers are grown vast enough, that they will hesitate to roll their car of Juggernaut over the writhing form of mental liberty? Think you that they will pause out of respect to your sentiments; do you suppose they are afraid of hurting your feelings? Oh, no, "they ain't built that way!" Think you that this vast array of falsely instructed minds, fortified with the barrier, "Thou shalt not think," grounded upon ignorance just as firmly as the adamantine rock is grounded upon its base— think you that it will hesitate to work out its nefarious schemes on account of any so poor a barrier as Secularists have thus far interposed? Ah! you fail to comprehend the power of your enemy's forces.

There are 225,000,000 Catholics in the world, and the United States has its full proportion of them. Do you realize the power of that army of dupes in the hands of pope and cardinal? Do you realize that they multiply like rats, and are daily and hourly making proselytes? Do you realize that they are constantly working in the ditches and sewers and underground cities of thought? Do you realize that the stratum of our liberties has a sub-stratum, and that that sub-stratum is being honeycombed, tunneled through and through by these never-ceasing, never-tiring forces of what Mr. Putnam so aptly styles "organized ignorance?" Do you realize that the sentiment of this overwhelming mass, only waiting to elect a majority in senate and house to establish this government upon a Christian basis, with that high-handed outlaw God upon the throne of the Constitution, with the Catholic church the power behind the throne—do you realize that this vast sentiment, held in check by the one article of the Constitution which guarantees that there shall be no union of church and state, in the sword of Damocles suspended by a hair?

Ah! we have need of secular education; we have need of a Secular Union; we have need to throw ourselvs in the breach; we are standing with our hand on the throttle of the avalanche. And what in true of the Catholic church is true of the Protestant in a less degree. It isn't because they lack the will; it's because they lack the power of organization. Nor does its activity end with the matter of influence. It has wedged itself into our public schools; it has been wrought into the scientific brains of their faculties (yes, and very poor faculties some of them have, too), until our schools have become, not institutions devoted to purely secular teaching, but actually Christian places of worship. Yes, indeed, Christian places of worship; where the Protestant God, and the Protestant Jesus, and the Protestant Bible are set up as little idols for Jew, Catholic, and Infidel alike to fall down and worship. The approved text books of the common schools are in general such as are fraught with reverential nonsense concerning the bounty and goodness of a supreme being in fitting up the beautiful home for man's abode; when everybody possessed with common sense knows that unless he has a lot of rich relations, God won't help him a bit about getting a home. And some of the more advanced works on zoology, chemistry, and geology have spent much valuable space and printers' ink in the silly endeavor to reconcile Darwin, rock literature, and common sense with that snake-apple yarn. It's high time all this foolishness was abandoned. If scientists will continue to make books pandering to the follies of Christian prejudice, it is the duty of Secularists to demand and to earnestly support that demand that religious sentiment be kept entirely out of educational works. It is enough that our schools should teach concerning the here and the now; it is enough that they should deal with known quantities and assured facts. There are quite enough of them to keep any ordinary mind well employed for some time, without speculating concerning the pin-feathers of an angel's wing. It has more to do with the specific gravity of a comet's tail. It is out of the province of a public school system to decide whether the pavements of the New Jerusalem are 18 k, fine or weighed by the table of 24 grs. make 1 pwt., 20 pwt., 1 oz,., 12 oz. 1 lb.

It is an inconsistency to declare ourselves a nation of freemen so long as the precepts of truth are incumbered by religious falsehood, and the whole incorporated into the mental food which is ladled out to our youth by teachers who *believe* because their salary depends upon the precarious foothold of popular favor. And we, as Secularists, are inconsistent when a religious system is taught in our public schools in any form, and yet we raise no voice of protest. If the faithful want their children instructed in the "mysteries of religion" let them go to those who make that their business; but it were better for them to beware how they endeavor to foist this *ism* or that upon an institution which *must* and *shall* be committed to purely secular teaching.

It is much to be regretted that so-called Liberals and Freethinkers do not seem to appreciate the necessity of colleges which shall be established upon an entirely secular basis, to the exclusion of all chimerical and—yes, parasitical theology. There are certain moneyed Freethinkers in these United States who have given more or less to the support of various churches which might much better have been used to found a college of this kind. But no; these gentlemen prefer to see their names in print as the "generous Mr. So-and-so," patron of the Methodist God, or the Presbyterian God, or the Congregationalist God, or some other poor little god who needs patronizing, rather than as founders of secular colleges. Too much laxity in this matter has led to serious backsliding. (I know that is a

Methodist term, but, however, it applies.) We have not only failed to advance, but have actually lost ground. Girard College, once the stronghold of secular training, has become a religious institution—a soft snap for priests; and though the design of its founder is thwarted, and the original bequest forfeited thereby, yet those who pretend to venerate that great and noble man stand idly by, witnessing the defeat of his life object, watching this rank and sickly growth of superstition springing green over the ashes of Truth's fallen empire. Where are your Secular principles? Where is your enthusiasm for the liberation of mankind from mental slavery, that you do not at least reclaim the gift of Stephen Girard? I know of one but one college in this supposed realm of thought liberty which is wholly free from superstitious fetters—that is at Liberal, Mo.

Ah! if only our Liberal friends were but half as anxious to propagate truth as our orthodox opponents are to promulgate falsehood. If only they were half as willing to work with mind and heart and pocketbook for the elevation of humanity as to listen to pretty speeches about it. When I see the money that is spent in dotting our cities, towns, villages, and farm lands with church spires, and church colleges, and church institutions of all kinds, even to church gambling houses, and then compare the spectacle with the few, the very, very few, Free-thought institutions, I am forced to believe that a little hell fire doctrine is a pretty good thing to burn holes through pockets. Why, you people who talk so much about elevating humanity are not half as anxious to do something practical in the line as your opponents are about sending us to hell. What is the reason we can't have secular colleges?

The churches have theirs, and they've a great big stumbling block to get over, too, which isn't in our way because there's nothing about Secularism to provoke theological disputes, simply because there is no theology to dispute about; while a Baptist must draw back from a Presbyterian institution with a shake of his head at the idea of foreordination, and a Presbyterian will look at a Baptist college with a contemptuous, "Take no stock in you, it's too well watered." But pray, what is there to keep anyone out of an exclusivly Secular institution? I fear again that the power of such education is not fully appreciated, and remember it is in the hands of the church to use for the advancement of their objects. And they use it. Here again comes in the power of Rome. They have sprinkled our country with monastic and conventual institutions which exert a secret, deadly influence which makes itself felt to an extent you are little aware of. I know of what I speak. I spent four years in a convent, and I have seen the watch-works of their machinations. I have seen bright intellects, intellects which might have been brilliant stars in the galaxies of genius, loaded down with chains, made abject, prostrate nonentities. I have seen frank, generous dispositions made morose, sullen, and deceitful; and I have seen rose-leaf cheeks turn to a sickly pallor, and glad eyes lose their brightness, and elastic youth lose its vitality and go down to an early grave, murdered—murdered by the church. Can you hesitate to work for secular schools when you recognize the power of this instrument in the hands of the enemy?

Once the minds of the people have been educated in the principles of truth by a thorough system of early training, they will be enabled to judge better of those matters of interest which are brought before the people by the two other great instruments—platform and press. These work together, and surely the power of eloquence, that subtle, transcendent power, which appeals to both mind and heart, which locks sentiment and reason in each other's arms, should use its every fiber, its every nerve, its every sinew, to draw the rapt and listening soul toward the gate of liberty. And the free press! Ah! that is the grandest of them all! That is the power which penetrates the darkest hovels, the deepest dungeons, the lowest cesspool of humanity. That is the sublime educator of the masses; that is the hand which is stretched out to each and every one. That is the guerdon of our liberties.

And inasmuch as it is the noblest and highest instrument when rightly used, so when perverted and turned from its course does it become the most baneful. A few months since an influential, wide-awake Michigan newspaper made the statement that religion was even more essential than education to the welfare of the state, and if not otherwise provided it would be a necessity for the state to furnish it. That paper had a very poor opinion of itself as an educator; it had a *very* poor opinion of the press of this country. Unfortunately there seemed to be a little policy in the matter, as the said paper has a large Christian support; but I'm thinking if the worthy editor who wrote the article were asked which the world could do without best, religion or the Detroit *Evening News,* he would have reconsidered his decision.

He would have said as I say, "That is false!" The press and the platform are the *vox populi,* the call of humanity; the cry for liberty; the cry which goes up from the weary, struggling, surging sea of life; the cry which catches the ear when we wake and listen and hear the mourning of the desolate homes, laid waste by that rich, grinding, hated, accursed monopoly, the church.

Part V

No Authority but Oneself

The Anarchist Feminist Philosophy
of Autonomy and Freedom

Introduction

Voltairine de Cleyre's passionate yearning for individual freedom was nowhere more evident than in her writings on feminism (then called the Woman Question) and nowhere more at home than the anarchist movement. The anarchist feminist movement of the late nineteenth century was a haven in the storm for women who longed to be free of the strictures of the stifling gender roles of that time. Unlike most women in socialist and mainstream feminist organizations of the time, the anarchist feminists were not afraid to question traditional gender roles. Anticipating the twentieth century feminist idea that the "personal is the political," they carried the anarchist questioning of authority into the personal realm as well.

Today it is hard to imagine how difficult the lives of women were a century ago. Lack of legal rights and economic opportunities, combined with stifling puritanical sexual mores, kept most women confined to the narrow and dependent role of wife and mother. It was in this context that the anarchist feminists rebelled against conventional American culture as well as government, demanding not the vote as did the more mainstream feminists, but something far more sweeping and radical—an end to gender roles, the right to control their own lives and destinies completely, the right to be free and autonomous individuals.

Though Emma Goldman is the anarchist feminist best remembered today, Voltairine's role as an advocate of liberation for women was second only to Emma's in the turn-of-the-century American anarchist movement. From the 1890s till her death in 1912, Voltairine spoke and wrote eloquently on the Woman Question in individualist anarchist journals such as Moses Harman's *Lucifer* and Benjamin Tucker's *Liberty*, as well as communist anarchist journals such as *The Rebel* and Emma Goldman's *Mother Earth*. These writings on feminism were among Voltairine's most important theoretical contributions.

Voltairine's importance as a feminist rests primarily on her willingness to confront issues such as female sexuality and the emotional and psychological, as well as economic, dependence on men within the family structure.

Though a few other writers, most notably socialist feminist Charlotte Perkins Gilman, dealt with issues of the family and women's economic dependence, much of the organized women's movement of that time was far more wrapped up in the issue of women's suffrage. Most of them either ignored or had no disagreement with the traditional gender roles of the time.

Voltairine and the anarchist feminists did not just question the unfair nature of marriage laws of that time, they repudiated institutional marriage and the conventional family structure, seeing in these institutions the same authoritarian oppression as they saw in the institution of the State. Voltairine, while valuing love, was among those most vehemently opposed to marriage of any kind, a theme best explicated in "Those Who Marry Do Ill." In an age when the husband had almost total control over the family as well as the wife, when most women were economically dependent on men, and when a woman's chief duty was to her husband and family, even to the point of self-sacrifice, Voltairine understandably viewed marriage as slavery, a theme she developed further in "The Woman Question." In the latter essay, inspired by her hero, Mary Wollstonecraft, she even advocated living separately from one's lover or husband, an idea still radical today.

The theme of economic independence was a repeated theme in Voltairine's essays, including "The Case of Women vs. Orthodoxy" and "The Political Equality of Woman." In "Political Equality of Woman," she rejects the concept of "natural rights" as a basis for social change, arguing instead on a practical basis that, in "standing alone" and becoming strong, women will be better able to press their "claim of equality." In "The Case of Women vs. Orthodoxy," Voltairine asserts that material conditions determine the social relations of men and women, suggesting that if economic conditions change, women's inequality would disappear. Though she, like her compatriots in both the communist and individualist camps, deplored the wretched living conditions of the working classes in the big cities and had a negative view of the monopoly capitalism of that time, Voltairine blessed capitalists for making women's economic independence possible. As unpleasant as the jobs might be, at least they were jobs actually available to women, a rarity in that time.

Radical as her other feminist essays were, "Sex Slavery" is, in important ways, the most radical of all. It is an essay that is both striking in its modernity—expounding on the "constructed crime" of pornography, marital rape, gender role socialization, and the double standard—and breathtaking in its still radical rejection of both Church and State. In this essay, Voltairine also attacks the idea that gender roles are inherent in human nature, seeing them as the result of socialization. In a comment that reminds us that we haven't come as far as we sometimes think, she notes that little girls are taught not to be tomboys and boys aren't allowed to have dolls.

"Women can't rough it like men" it is said. "Train any animal, or any plant as you train your girls, and it won't be able to rough it either."

In "Sex Slavery," we find Voltairine's most radical position of all, a position that not only differentiated her from most of the mainstream feminists of her day but today as well—Voltairine's denunciation of the twin roles of the Church and the State in oppressing women. Declaring that "We are tired of promises, God is deaf, and his church is our worst enemy," she pointed out how it colludes with the State to keep women in bondage. The Church teaches the inferiority of women while the State-constructed crime of "obscenity" keeps people from hearing the truth about marital rape (a forbidden topic at the time) and the slavery of marriage. The State, she also believed, keeps women and men from having economic independence through its protection of monopoly capitalism and the subsequent detrimental effect on the ability to earn a living.

Most radical of all in a feminist context is Voltairine's anarchism itself. Few feminists today, even the most radical, are willing to explore the role of the State in oppressing women. Then as now, anarchists differ as to exactly what that oppression consists of, but modern anarchist feminists of all philosophical persuasions agree that the State is women's enemy. The communist and social anarchist feminists believe that the State protects capitalism, which in turn exploits women. The individualist anarchist feminists believe that the State has fostered economic oppression and institutionalized gender role stereotypes through laws that restrict women's choices, for example, protective labor legislation, which perpetuate the idea that women are weak, and which protect men's interests at the expense of women.

—Sharon Presley

REFERENCES

Brown, Susan L. *The Politics of Individualism: Liberalism, Liberal Feminism and Anarchism*, Montreal: Black Rose Books, 1973.

Ehrlich, Howard J. "Toward A General Theory of Anarchafeminism," *Social Anarchism*, v19, 1994.

Gaylor, Annie Laurie (ed.). *Women Without Superstition*, Madison, WI: Freedom From Religion Foundation, 1997.

Gilman, Charlotte Perkins, in Carl Degler (ed.). *Women and Economics*, New York: Harper & Row, 1966.

Kornegger, Peggy, "Anarchism: the Feminist Connection" and Marion Leighton, "Anarcho-feminism" in *Reinventing Anarchy* edited by Howard Ehrlich, Carol Ehrlich, David DeLeon, & Glenda Morris, London: Routledge & Kegan Paul, 1979.

Marsh, Margaret, *Anarchist Women 1870–1920*, Philadelphia: Temple University Press, 1981.

Presley, Sharon, "Feminism in *Liberty*" in Michael Coughlin, Charles Hamilton & Mark Sullivan (eds.). *Benjamin R. Tucker and the Champions of* Liberty, St. Paul and New York: Michael Coughlin & Mark Sullivan Publishers, 1987.

Presley, Sharon and Kinsky, Lynn, "Government is Women's Enemy," and Joan Kennedy Taylor, "Protective Labor Legislation" in Wendy McElroy (ed.). *Freedom, Feminism and the State*, Washington, DC: Cato Institute, 1982.

Reichert, William O. *Partisans of Freedom: A Study in American Anarchism*, Bowling Green, OH: Bowling Green University Popular Press, 1976.

Sears, Hal. *The Sex Radicals: Free Love in High Victorian America*, Lawrence, KS: The Regents Press of Kansas, 1977.

Taylor, Joan Kennedy. *Reclaiming the Mainstream: Individualist Feminism Rediscovered*, Buffalo, NY: Prometheus Books, 1992.

Those Who Marry Do Ill

Voltairine delivered this lecture as part of a debate at the Radical Liberal League on 28 April 1907. Her opponent was Dr. Henrietta Westbrook, whose talk was titled, of course, "Those Who Marry Do Well." The lecture was published in *Mother Earth* in January 1908. In it, Voltairine states her view that morality is socially constructed, and, roughly, that moral notions are deployed for utilitarian purposes: right conduct is that which best serves the needs of society. This she identifies as being at the current time the development of the free individual, a purpose to which she believes marriage runs counter, for both men and women, though for women in particular.

"Huxley" is Thomas Huxley (1825–1895), British freethinker and evolutionist.

"Von Hartman" is presumably Karl Eduard Robert Von Hartmann (1842–1906), German philosopher who denied the afterlife.

"Lum" is Dyer B. Lum (see intro to "Events Are the True Schoolmasters").

Alice Roosevelt (1884–1981) was the sparkling daughter of Teddy Roosevelt. She married Ohio Congressman Nicholas Longworth, later Speaker of the House.

Ernest Howard Crosby (1856–1907) was an anti-imperialist writer.

Leonard D. Abbott was an editor of radical periodicals and friend of Emma Goldman. It was he who coined the phrase "priestess of pity and vengeance" to refer to Voltairine de Cleyre.

Hugh O. Pentecost was an American religious leader with anarchist leanings and publisher of *Twentieth Century*.

Those Who Marry Do Ill

Let me make myself understood on two points, now, so that when discussion arises later, words may not be wasted in considering things not in question:

First—How shall we measure doing well or doing ill;

Second—What I mean by marriage.

So much as I have been able to put together the pieces of the universe in my small head, there is no absolute right or wrong; there is only a relativity, depending upon the continuously though very slowly altering condition of a social race in respect to the rest of the world. Right and wrong are social conceptions: mind, I do not say *human* conceptions. The names "right" and "wrong," truly, are of human invention only; but the conception "right" and "wrong," dimly or clearly, has been wrought out with more or less effectiveness by all intelligent social beings. And the definition of Right, as sealed and approved by the successful conduct of social beings, is: That mode of behavior which best serves the growing need of that society.

As to what that need is, certainly it has been in the past, and for the most part is now indicated by the unconscious response of the structure (social or individual) to the pressure of its environment. Up till a few years since I believed with Huxley, Von Hartman, and my teacher, Lum, that it was wholly so determined; that consciousness might discern, and obey or oppose, but had no voice in deciding the course of social development: if it decided to oppose, it did so to its own ruin, not to the modification of the unconsciously determined ideal.

Of late years I have been approaching the conclusion that consciousness has a continuously increasing part in the decision of social problems; that while it is still a minor voice, and must be for a long time to come, it is, nevertheless, the dawning power which threatens to over-hurl old processes and old laws, and supplant them by other powers and other ideals. I know no more fascinating speculation than this, of the rôle of consciousness in present and future evolution. However, it is not our present speculation. I speak of it only because in determining what constitutes well-being at present, I shall maintain that the old ideal has been considerably modified by conscious reaction against the superfluities produced by unconscious striving towards a certain end.

The question now becomes: What is the growing ideal of human society, unconsciously indicated and consciously discerned and illuminated?

By all the readings of progress, this indication appears to be the *free individual*; a society whose economic, political, social, and sexual organization shall secure and constantly increase the scope of being to its several units; whose solidarity and continuity depend upon the free attraction of its component parts, and in no wise upon compulsory forms.

Unless we are agreed that this is the discernible goal of our present social striving, there is no hope that we shall agree in the rest of the argument. For it would be vastly easy to prove that if the maintenance of the old divisions of society into classes, each with specialized services to perform—the priesthood, the military, the wage earner, the capitalist, the domestic servant, the breeder, etc.—is in accord with the growing force of society, then marriage is the thing, and they who marry do well.

But this is the point at which I stand, and from which I shall measure well and ill-doing; viz.: that the aim of social striving now is the free individual, implying all the conditions necessary to that freedom.

Now the second thing: What shall we understand as marriage?

Some fifteen or eighteen years ago, when I had not been out of a convent long enough to forget its teachings, nor lived and experienced enough to work out my own definitions, I considered that marriage was "a sacrament of the Church," or it was "a civil ceremony performed by the State," by which a man and a woman were united for life, or until the divorce court separated them. With all the energy of a neophyte freethinker, I attacked religious marriage as a piece of unwarranted interference on the part of the priest with the affairs of individuals, condemned the "until-death-do-us-part" promise as one of the immoralities which made a person a slave through all his future to his present feelings, and urged the miserable vulgarity of both the religious and civil ceremony, by which the intimate personal relations of two individuals are made topic of comment and jest by the public.

By all this I still hold. Nothing is more disgustingly vulgar to me than the so-called sacrament of marriage; outraging all delicacy with the trumpeting of private matters in the general ear. Need I recall, as an example, the unprinted and unprintable floating literature concerning the marriage of Alice Roosevelt, when the so-called "American princess" was targeted by every lewd jester in the country, because, forsooth, the whole world had to be informed of her forthcoming union with Mr. Longworth! But it is neither a religious nor a civil ceremony that I refer to now, when I say that "those who marry do ill." The ceremony is only a form, a ghost, a meatless shell. By marriage I mean the real thing, the permanent relation of a man and a woman, sexual and economical, whereby the present home and family life is maintained. It is of no importance to me whether this is a polygamous, polyandric, or monogamous marriage, nor whether it was blessed by a priest, permitted by a magistrate, contracted publicly or privately, or not contracted at all. It is the permanent dependent relationship which, I affirm, is detrimental to the growth of individual character, and to which I am unequivocally opposed. Now my opponents know where to find me.

In the old days to which I have alluded, I contended, warmly and sincerely, for the exclusive union of one man and one woman as long as they were held together by love, and for the dissolution of the arrangement upon desire of either. We talked in those days most enthusiastically about the bond of love, and it only. Nowadays I would say that I prefer to see a marriage based purely on business considerations, than a marriage based on love. That is not because I am in the least concerned for the success of the marriage, but because I am concerned with the success of love. And I believe that the easiest, surest and most applicable method of killing love is marriage—marriage as I have defined it. I believe that the only way to preserve love in anything like the ecstatic condition which renders it worthy of a distinctive name—otherwise it is either lust or simply friendship—is to maintain the distances. Never allow love to be vulgarized by the common indecencies of continuous close communion. Better be in familiar contempt of your enemy than of the one you love.

I presume that some who are unacquainted with my opposition to legal and social forms, are ready to exclaim: "Do you want to do away with the relation of the sexes altogether, and cover the earth with monks and nuns?" By no means. While I am not over and above anxious about the repopulation of the earth, and should not shed any tears if I knew that the last man had already been born, I am not advocating sexual total abstinence. If the advocates of marriage had merely to prove a case against complete sexual continence, their task would be easy. The statistics of insanity, and in general of all manner of aberrations, would alone constitute a big item in the charge. No: I do not believe that the highest human being is the unsexed one, or the one who extirpates his passions by violence, whether religious or scientific violence. I would have people regard all their normal instincts in a normal way, neither gluttonizing nor starving them, neither exalting them beyond their true service nor denouncing them as servitors of evil, both of which mankind are wont to do in considering the sexual passion. In short, I would have men and women so arrange their lives that they shall always, at all times, be free beings in this regard as in all others. The limit of abstinence or indulgence can be fixed by the individual alone, what is normal for one being excess for another, and what is excess at one period of life being normal at another. And as to the effects of such normal gratification of normal appetite upon population, I would have them consciously controlled, as they can be, are to some extent now, and will be more and more through the progress of knowledge. The birth-rate of France and of native Americans gives evidence of such conscious control.

"But," say the advocates of marriage, "what is there in marriage to interfere with the free development of the individual? What does the free development of the individual mean, if not the expression of manhood and womanhood? And what is more essential to either than parentage and the rearing of young? And is not the fact that the latter requires a period of from fifteen to twenty years, the essential need which determines the per-manent home?" It is the scientific advocate of marriage that talks this way. The religious man bases his talk on the will of God, or some other such metaphysical matter. I do not concern myself with him; I concern myself only with those who contend that as Man is the latest link in evolution, the same racial necessities which determine the social and sexual relations of allied races will be found shaping and determining these relations in Man; and that, as we find among the higher animals that the period of rearing the young to the point of caring for themselves usually determines the period of conjugality, it must be concluded that the greater attainments of Man, which have so greatly lengthened the educational period of youth, must likewise have fixed the permanent family relation as the ideal condition for humanity. This is but the conscious extension of what unconscious, or per-haps semi-conscious adaptation, had already determined in the higher ani-mals, and in savage races to an extent. If people are reasonable, sensible, self-controlled (as to other people they will keep themselves in trouble any-way, no matter how things are arranged), does not the marriage state secure this great fundamental purpose of the primal social function, which is at the same time an imperative demand of individual development, better than any other arrangement? With all its failures, is it not the best that has been tried, or with our present light has been conceived?

In endeavoring to prove the opposite of this contention, I shall not go to the failures to prove my point. It is not my purpose to show that a vast number of marriages do not succeed; the divorce court records do that. But as one swallow doesn't make a summer, nor a flock of swallows either, so divorces do not prove that marriage in itself is a bad thing, only that a goodly number of individuals make mistakes. This is, indeed, an unan-swerable argument against the indissolubility of marriage, but none against marriage itself. I will go to the successful marriages—the marriages in which whatever the friction, man and wife have spent a great deal of agreeable time together; in which the family has been provided for by honest work decently paid (as the wage-system goes), of the father, and preserved within the home by the saving labor and attention of the mother; the children given a reasonable education and started in life on their own account, and the old folks left to finish up life together, each resting secure in the knowledge that he has a tried friend until death severs the bond. This, I conceive, is the best form that marriage can present, and I opine it is oftener dreamed of than realized. But sometimes it is realized. Yet from the viewpoint that the object of life should be the development of individuality, such have lived less successfully than many who may not have lived so happily.

And to the first great point—the point that physical parentage is one of the fundamental necessities of self-expression: here, I think, is where the factor of consciousness is in process of overturning the methods of life. Life, working unconsciously, blindly sought to preserve itself by generation, by manifold generation. The mind is simply staggered at the productivity of a single stalk of wheat, or of a fish, or of a queen bee, or of a man. One is smitten by the appalling waste of generative effort; numbed with helpless pity for the little things, the infinitude of little lives, that must come forth and suffer and die of starvation, of exposure, as a prey to other creatures, and all to no end but that out of the multitude a few may survive and continue the type! Man, at war with Nature and not yet master of the situation, obeyed the same instinct, and by prolific parentage maintained his war. To the Hebrew patriarch as to the American pioneer, a large family meant strength, the wealth of brawn and sinew to continue the conquest of forest and field. It was the only resource against annihilation. Therefore, the instinct towards physical creation was one of the most imperative determinants of action.

Now the law of all instinct is, that it survives long after the necessity which created it has ceased to exist, and acts mischievously. The usual method of reckoning with such a survival is that since such and such a thing exists, it is an essential part of the structure, not obliged to account for itself and bound to be gratified. I am perfectly certain, however, that the more conscious consciousness becomes, or in other words, the more we become aware of the conditions of life and our relations therein, their new demands and the best way of fulfilling them, the more speedily will instincts no longer demanded be dissolved from the structure.

How stands the war upon Nature now? Why, so,—that short of a planetary catastrophe, we are certain of the conquest. And what is perfecting the conquest? Consciousness! The alert brain! The dominant will! Invention, discovery, mastery of hidden forces. We are no longer compelled to use the blind method of limitless propagation to equip the race with hunters and trappers and fishers and sheep-keepers and soil-tillers and breeders. Therefore, the original necessity which gave rise to the instinct of prolific parentage is gone; the instinct itself is bound to die, and is dying, but will die the faster as men grasp more and more the whole situation. In proportion as the parenthood of the brain becomes more and more prolific, as ideas spread, multiply, and conquer, the necessity for great physical production declines. This is my first contention. Hence the development of individuality does no longer *necessarily* imply numerous children, nor indeed, *necessarily* any children at all. That is not to say that no one will want children, nor to prophesy race suicide. It is simply to say that there will be fewer born, with better chances of surviving, developing, and achieving. Indeed, with all its clash of tendencies, the consciousness of our present society is having this driven home to it.

Supposing that the majority will still desire, or let me go further and say *do* still desire, this limited parentage, the question now becomes: Is this the overshadowing need in the development of the individual, or are there other needs equally imperative? If there are other needs equally imperative, must not these be taken equally into account in deciding the best manner of conducting one's life? If there are not other needs equally imperative, is it not still an open question whether the married state is the best means of securing it? In answering these questions, I think it will again be safe to separate into a majority and a minority. There will be a minority to whom the rearing of children will be the great dominant necessity of their being, and a majority to whom this will be one of their necessities. Now what are the other necessities? The other physical and mental appetites! The desire for food and raiment and housing after the individual's own taste; the desire for sexual association, not for reproduction; the artistic desires; the desire to know, with its thousand ramifications, which may carry the soul from the depths of the concrete to the heights of the abstract; the desire to do, that is, to imprint one's will upon the social structure, whether as a mechanical contriver, a force harnesser, a social rebuilder, a combiner, a dream translator—whatever may be the particular mode of the personal organization.

The necessity for food, shelter, and raiment, it should at all times lie within the individual's power to furnish for himself. But the method of home-keeping is such that after the relation has been maintained for a few years, the interdependence of one on the other has become so great that each is somewhat helpless when circumstance destroys the combination, the man less so, and the woman wretchedly so. She has done one thing in a secluded sphere, and while she may have learned to do that thing well (which is not certain, the method of training is not at all satisfactory), it is not a thing which has equipped her with the confidence necessary to go about making an independent living. She is timid above all, incompetent to deal with the conditions of struggle. The world of production has swept past her; she knows nothing of it. On the other hand, what sort of an occupation is it for her to take domestic service under some other woman's rule? The conditions and pay of domestic service are such that every independent spirit would prefer to slave in a factory, where at least the slavery ends with the working hours. As for men, only a few days since a staunch free unionist told me, apparently without shame, that were it not for his wife he would be a tramp and a drunkard, simply because he is unable to keep a home; and in his eyes the chief merit of the arrangement is that his stomach is properly cared for. This is a degree of a helplessness which I should have thought he would have shrunk from admitting, but is nevertheless probably true. Now this is one of the greatest objections to the married condition, as it is to any other condition which produces like results. In choosing one's economic position in society, one should always bear in mind that it should be such as should leave the individual uncrippled—an all-around person, with both productive and preservative capacities, a being pivoted within.

Concerning the sexual appetite, irrespective of reproduction, the advocates of marriage claim, and with some reason, that it tends to preserve normal appetite and satisfaction, and is both a physical and moral safeguard against excesses, with their attendant results, disease. That it does not do so entirely, we have ample and painful proof continuously before our eyes. As to what it may accomplish, it is almost impossible to find out the truth; for religious asceticism has so built the feeling of shame into the human mind, on the subject of sex, that the first instinct, when it is brought under discussion, seems to be to lie about it. This is especially the case with women. The majority of women usually wish to create the impression that they are devoid of sexual desires, and think they have paid the highest compliment to themselves when they say, "Personally, I am very cold; I have never experienced such attraction." Sometimes this is true; but oftener it is a lie—a lie born of centuries of the pernicious teaching of the Church. A roundly developed person will understand that she pays no honor to herself by denying herself fulness of being, whether to herself or of herself; though, without doubt, where such a deficiency really exists, it may give room for an extra growth of some other qualities, perhaps of higher value. In general, however, notwithstanding women's lies, there is no such deficiency. In general, young, healthy beings of both sexes desire such relations. What then? Is marriage the best answer to the need? Suppose they marry, say at twenty years, or thereabout, which will be admitted as the time when sexual appetite is usually most active: the consequence is (I am just now leaving children out of account) that the two are thrown too much and too constantly in contact, and speedily exhaust the delight of each other's presence. Then irritations begin. The familiarities of life in common breed contempt. What was once a rare joy becomes a matter of course, and loses all its delicacy. Very often it becomes a physical torture to one (usually the woman), while it still retains some pleasure to the other, for the reason that bodies, like souls, do most seldom, almost never, parallel each other's development. And this lack of parallelism is the greatest argument to be produced against marriage. No matter how perfectly adapted to each other two people may be at any given time, it is not the slightest evidence that they will continue to be so. And no period of life is more deceptive as to what future development may be than the age I have just been speaking of, the age when physical desires and attractions being strongest, they obscure or hold in abeyance the other elements of being.

The terrible tragedies of sexual antipathy, mostly for shame's sake, will never be revealed. But they have filled the earth with murder. And even in those homes where harmony has been maintained, and all is apparently peaceful, it is mainly so through the resignation and self-suppression of either the man or the woman. One has consented to be largely effaced, for the preservation of the family and social respect.

But awful as these things are, these physical degradations, they are not so terrible as the ruined souls. When the period of physical predominence is past, and soul-tendencies begin more and more strongly to assert themselves, how dreadful is the recognition that one is bound by the duties of common parentage and the necessities of home-keeping to remain in the constant company of one from whom one finds oneself going farther away in thought every day.—"Not a day," exclaim the advocates of "free unions." I find such exclamation worse folly than the talk of "holy matrimony" believers. The bonds are there, the bonds of life in common, the love of the home built by joint labor, the habit of association and dependence; they are very real chains, binding both, and not to be thrown off lightly. Not in a day nor a month, but only after long hesitation, struggle, and grievous, grievous pain, can the wrench of separation come. Oftener it does not come at all.

A chapter from the lives of two men recently deceased will illustrate my meaning. Ernest Crosby, wedded, and I presume happily, to a lady of conservative thought and feeling, himself then conservative, came into his soul's own at the age of thirty-eight, while occupying the position of Judge of the International Court at Cairo. From then on, the whole radical world knows Ernest Crosby's work. Yet what a position was his, compelled by honor to continue the functions of a social life which he disliked! To quote the words of his friend, Leonard Abbott, "a prisoner in his palatial home, waited on by servants and lackeys. Yet to the end he remained enslaved by his possessions." Had Crosby not been bound, had not union and family relations with one who holds very different views of life in faith and honor held him, should we not have had a different life-sum? Like his great teacher, Tolstoi, likewise made absurd, his life contradicted by his works, because of his union with a woman who has not developed along parallel lines.

The second case, Hugh O. Pentecost. From the year 1887 on, whatever were his special tendencies, Pentecost was in the main a sympathizer with the struggle of labor, an opposer of oppression, persecution and prosecution in all forms. Yet through the influence of his family relations, because he felt in honor bound to provide greater material comfort and a better standing in society than the position of a radical speaker could give, he consented at one time to be the puppet of those he had most strenuously condemned, to become a district attorney, a prosecutor. And worse than that, to paint himself as a misled baby for having done the best act of his life, to protest against the execution of the Chicago Anarchists. That this influence was brought to bear upon him, I know from his own lips; a repetition, in a small way, of the treason of Benedict Arnold, who for his Tory wife's sake laid everlasting infamy upon himself. I do not say there was no self-excusing in this, no Eve-did-tempt-me taint, but surely it had its influence. I speak of these two men because these instances are well known; but everyone knows of such instances among more obscure persons, and often where the woman is the one whose higher nature is degraded by the bond between herself and her husband.

And this is one side of the story. What of the other side? What of the conservative one who finds himself bound to one who outrages every principle of his or hers? People will not, and cannot, think and feel the same at the same moments, throughout any considerable period of life; and therefore, their moments of union should be rare and of no binding nature.

I return to the subject of children. Since this also is a normal desire, can it not be gratified without the sacrifice of individual freedom required by marriage? I see no reason why it cannot. I believe that children may be as well brought up in an individual home, or in a communal home, as in a dual home; and that impressions of life will be far pleasanter if received in an atmosphere of freedom and independent strength than in an atmosphere of secret repression and discontent. I have no very satisfactory solutions to offer to the various questions presented by the child-problem; but neither have the advocates of marriage. Certain to me it is, that no one of the demands of life should ever be answered in a manner to preclude future free development. I have seen no great success from the old method of raising children under the indissoluble marriage yoke of the parents. (Our conservative parents no doubt consider their radical children great failures, though it probably does not occur to them that their system is in any way at fault.) Neither have I observed a gain in the child of the free union. Neither have I observed that the individually raised child is any more likely to be a success or a failure. Up to the present, no one has given a scientific answer to the child-problem. Those papers which make a specialty of it, such as *Lucifer*, are full of guesses and theories and suggested experiments; but no infallible principles for the guidance of intentional or actual parents have as yet been worked out. Therefore, I see no reason why the rest of life should be sacrificed to an uncertainty.

That love and respect may last, I would have unions rare and impermanent. That life may grow, I would have men and women remain separate personalities. Have no common possessions with your lover more than you might freely have with one not your lover. Because I believe that marriage stales love, brings respect into contempt, outrages all the privacies and limits the growth of both parties, I believe that "they who marry do ill."

The Case of Woman Versus
Orthodoxy

Previously given as a lecture, this article was published in the *Boston Investigator* in 1896.

George Jacob Holyoake, a freethought writer, bookseller and publisher, was the last man in Britain to be imprisoned for blasphemy.

The Open Court was an American freethought publishing house.

The long list of heroic women at the end of Voltairine's essay include Hypatia of Alexandria, a mathematician, astronomer, and philosopher, who was killed by Christian monks in 415 CE and Mary Wollstonecraft, the author of the first feminist book, "A Vindication of the Rights of Women," published in 1792 in England. The other women listed at the end of this article were all active in social movements of the nineteenth century.

Frances Wright (1795–1852), the first woman in the U.S. to publicly advocate women's rights, was a leader in the freethought movement, an abolitionist activist, and a social reformer.

Harriet Martineau (1802–1876), the author of 50 books and over 1600 articles, was a British freethought advocate and sometimes considered the world's first sociologist.

Ernestine L. Rose (1810–1892) was America's first lobbyist for women's rights, an outspoken atheist, and eloquent speaker for abolitionism, women's rights and freethought.

Lucretia Mott (1793–1880) was one of the major leaders of the American women's rights and suffrage movement.

Sojourner Truth (1797(?)–1883), a former slave, was one of the women's rights movement's most eloquent speakers.

Lucy N. Coleman (1817–1906) was an ardent abortionist and activist in the freethought and women's rights movements.

The Case of Woman Versus Orthodoxy

"I will greatly multiply thy sorrow and thy conception; in sorrow shalt thou bring forth children, and thy desire shall be unto thy husband, and he shall rule over thee." Thus descended the anathema from the voice which thundered upon Sinai; and thus has the curse gone echoing from away back there in the misty darkness before the morning of history rose upon men. Sorrow, sorrow, sorrow—and oh! how many million voices wail, wail endlessly. "Sorrow is my portion and pain is my burden; for so it was decreed of the Lord God, the Lord God who ruleth and whose creature am I. But oh, the burden is heavy, very heavy. I have been patient; I have borne it long; I have not complained; I have not rebelled; if I have wept, it has been at night and alone; if I have stumbled, I have gone on the faster. When I have lain down in the desert and closed my eyes and known no more, I have rebuked myself. I have remembered my mother, and been patient and waited, waited. But the waiting is very long."

This is the cry of the woman heard in the night of the long ages; ghost-forms flitting through the abyss, ghost-hands wrung in the ancient darkness come close and are laid upon the living, and the mournful cadence is reintoned from the dead by the quick, and the mournful, hopeless superstition which bound the hearts and the souls of our foremothers, lengthens out its weary chain and binds us, too. Why it should be so, why it has done so for so long, is one of the mysteries which a sage of the future may solve, but not I. I can see no reason, absolutely none, why women have clung to the doom of the gods. I cannot understand why they have not rebelled. I cannot imagine what they ever hoped to gain by it, that they should have watered their footsteps with tears, and borne their position with such abnegation. It is true that we are often offered explanations, and much force may be in them, but these explanations may serve only to account for the position. They do not account for woman's centurian acceptance of, and resignation to, it. Women are, we know, creatures of their environments, the same as are men; and they react on their environment in proportion to their capacities.

We know that women are not now, and, with some few tribal exceptions, probably never were, as strong as men are physically. But why in common sense sorrow should therefore be their lot, and their husbands should rule over them, and why they should uncomplainingly accept this regime, is one of the, to me, incomprehensible phenomena of human history. Men, enslaved, have, to speak expressively, "kicked"—kicked vigorously, even when the kicking brought to them heavier chains; but we have never, till very recently, had anything like a revolt of women. They have bowed, and knelt and kissed the hand which smote them. Why? Notwithstanding all of its pretensions to be the uplifter and the glorifier of women, there ever has been, there never will be, anything for them in orthodoxy but slavery. And whether that slavery is of the sordid, gloomy, leaden, work-a-day sort or of the gilded toy-shop variety, whether it be the hard toil and burden of workwomen or the canary-bird style of the upper classes, who neither toil nor spin, the undertone and the overtone are still the same: "Be in subjection; for such is the Lord's will." In order to maintain this ideal of the relation of master and of subject between men and women, a different method of education, a different code of morals and a different sphere exertion were mapped out for women, because of their sex, without reference to individual qualifications. If a horse is designed to draw wheels because it is a horse, so have women been allotted certain tasks, mostly menial, because they are women. The majority of men actually hold to that analogy, and without in the least believing themselves tyrannical or meddle-some, conceived themselves to be justified in making a tremendous row if the horse attempted to get over the traces.

That splendid old veteran of Freethought, George Jacob Holyoake, in a recent article, one of a series running in the Open Court, has pertinently observed that the declaration that thought is by its very essence free is an error, because as long as speech, which is the necessary tool of thought, is not free, the intellect is as much hampered in its effort to think as a shoe maker without tools is in attempting to make a pair of shoes. By this same method, viz., the denial of the means of altering it, was the position of woman sustained, by subordinating her physical development to what was called delicacy, which *ought* to have been called by its proper name, *weakness*, by inculcating a scheme of morals which made obedience the first virtue, suppression of the will in deference to her husband (or father, or brother, or, failing these, her nearest male relative) the first deduction therefrom, by a plan of education which omitted all of those branches of knowledge which require the application of reason and of judgment, by all of these deprivals of the tools of thinking the sphere was circumscribed and guarded well. And by the penalties inflicted for the breaking through of these prescriptions, whether said penalties were legal or purely social and voluntary, the little spirit which was left in woman by these limitations was almost hopelessly broken. It is apparent, therefore, that if in all these ages of submission women have hopelessly accepted that destiny, if they have never tried to break these forbidding barriers, they will not do so now, with all of their added centuries of inheritance, unless the relentless iron of circumstance drives them across. (Later, it will be my endeavor to show that this iron is already pressing down.)

It may not be flattering to have this conviction thrust upon us; but it may be less disagreeable if I explain what I mean. In former times, when people trod upon the toes of gods every time they turned about, moral ideals and social ideals were looked upon as things in themselves descended from on high, the gift of the gods, Divine patterns laid down without reference to climate, to race, to social development, or to other material things, matters of the soul without relation to bodily requirements. But now that gods speaking the tongues of men have vanished like vapors at sunrise, it is necessary, since it is evident that morality of some sort exists everywhere, of very different sorts under different conditions, to find some explanation of these psychic phenomena correlated with the explanation of physical phenomena. For souls are no longer perceived as monarchs of bodies laying down all manner of laws for the bringing into subjection of the physical members, but rather soul, or mind, or whatever name may be given to the psychological aspect of the bundle called an ego, is one with the body, subject to growth, to expansion and to decay, adapting itself seasonably to time and to circumstances, modified always by material conditions, intimately connected with the stomach, indissolubly related to the weather, to the crops, and to all other baldly commonplace things. In contemplating this revised version of the soul one will, according to the bent of one's nature, regard this view as a descent from spiritual heights, rendering things coarse and gross, or, on the other hand, he will see all things clothed in the glory of superb equality, he will not say: "I am sunken to the indignity of a cabbage," but "this common plant is my brother and the brother of things greater than I, serving equally well his part; there is no *more* or *less, smaller* or *greater*; Life is common to us all."

Now, therefore, upon this basis, the basis of the perpetual relation between physical foundations and ethical superstructures, it is seen that if this be an acting principle now, so it has ever been, and will be as long as mind and matter constitute reality. Hence the ethics said to have been delivered by Jehovah upon Sinai was truly the expression of social ideas compatible with the existing physical conditions. Not less so the ethics of bees, of ants, of birds, and of the Fiji Islanders; and not less so the ethics of to-day, which, despite the preservation of the outward shell of the decalogue, are indeed vastly changed.

The conclusion to be drawn from the foregoing in regard to the status of woman is this:—Material conditions determine the social relations of men and women; and if material conditions are such as to make these relations impossible of maintenance, they will be compelled to assume others. This is the explanation of the expression, "driven across the barriers." What no amount of unseasonable preaching can accomplish material necessity will force even in the face of sermons to the contrary. Not that I undervalue the service of the advance guard, the preaching of new thought. On the contrary, the first and best of praise is due to the "voice crying in the wilderness." And I say that such a voice is the first faint vibration of the world-soul in response to the unease of world-body created by the shifting of conditions,—whether it so proclaims or not, whether it cries wisely or not. I say that those who call for the breaking of the barriers will always precede the general action of the masses; but I add that were it not for the compulsion of material necessity the preaching would be barren. What I wish to express in order to illustrate my point clearly is, first, that the orthodox view of the ethics of woman's relations and her social usefulness was a view compatible with a tribal organization, narrow geographical limits, the reign of muscular force, the necessity of rapid reproduction; second, that those conditions have given place to others demanding an utterly different human translation.

Before the invention of the means of transportation, when, according to the story, it took forty years for the Israelites to explore a tract some 300 miles in length (though one may perhaps venture to credit them with better time than they credit themselves with), when, at any rate, a high mountain was a serious obstacle and a good-sized river a natural boundary for tribal wanderings, people were necessarily very ignorant of the outside world. Within the limits valuable pasture and farm lands were debatable grounds, debatable by different tribes, in terms of hue and cry, of slingshot and arrows, and other such arguments. War was a constant condition, the chief occupation of men. Now we who are evolutionists know that those tribes and species survived in the world which obeyed the fundamental necessity of adaptation; and it is easy to see that with a rapid rate of mortality and a non-correspondent rate of increase a tribe must have rapidly gone to the wall. Any nation which might have put its mothers up in battle would have been weeded out simply because the part played by the mother in reproduction requires so much longer a period than that played by the father. To produce warriors—that was the chief purpose of a woman's existence! Nothing in herself, she became everything when regarded as the race preserver. Therein lay her great usefulness; and in reading the sometimes nauseating accounts of the behavior of women in ancient times in Judah, the phase of human development in its entirety should be borne in mind. The mothers of Isaac and of Ishmael, Tamar, the daughter-in-law of Judah, the daughters of Lot, should never be viewed from the standpoint of nineteenth century morals, but from that of the tribal organization and the tribal necessities, which forced upon them the standard of "Multiply and replenish the earth" as the highest possible conception of conduct.

Yet, singular to observe, co-existent with this very ideal and with the very polygamous practices of the patriarchs, are found records of the most horrible punishments inflicted upon women for the breaking of the seventh commandment. As may be seen in the story of Tamar and Judah, the punishment to be inflicted upon her was burning alive, though nothing is said of Judah's. The Talmud has many accounts of tests by "the bitter water" for women, while men were subjected to nothing more than a fine. (Bitter water was simply poisoned water; the innocent were supposed not to be injured, the guilty to fall dead in the market-place, exposed to the public gaze.) Nevertheless, such was the stringent necessity for rapid reproductions that women defied danger and instinctively continued to fulfill that race-purpose, though the law of Moses, already codifying the conditions of peace (not as yet existent), recognized war and its accompaniments as transient, and giving place to a stricter moral behavior.

As I said before, I do not perceive for the life of me what the women saw in all of this for them; I don't see why they should have been interested in the tribal welfare at all, or in the dreary business of bearing sons for other women's sons to slay. But since the war-environment was the one under which they were born and reared, since no other purpose for them had ever been thought of, by either the dead or the living, it is not surprising that they did not see matters at all as I do. Nowadays, that the majority of English and of French speaking peoples at least see that the requisite ethics is the *limitation of population* within the means of subsistence, these direct descendants of the Judaic ideal are subject rather to a jest among the enlightened of their own race. Thus Zangwill, in the "Children of the Ghetto," puts this speech in the mouth of one of the Jewish grandmothers: "How is Fanny?" inquired the visitor. "Ah, poor Pesach! He has never done well in business! But blessed be He. I am soon to have my seventh grand-child." How fearfully potent is the force of heredity may thus be seen, since to this day these women walk through your streets, wan, faded, humped, distorted, hideous women—women all bone and jaw and flabby flesh, grotesque shadows from the past, creatures once trim and beautiful, but whose beauty went long ago to fulfill the order of the Lord of Sinai.

The primal division of labor is thus seen to have been one of sex. The business of men was to fight, of women to produce fighters. To men were the arts of war; to women were those of peace. Later in the time of Solomon, when material conditions among the Jews had already altered, we see the effect of the continuance of this division beyond the epoch which created it. Already monadism has been abandoned; and the settled mode of life has been begun. The conditions of war, though still often maintaining, bore no comparison to former prevalence; and the aforeward warrior was hence frequently idle. Was it thus with woman? Oh, no,

> Men may come and men may go,
> But she goes on forever

With her work.

Listen to this delectable account in Solomon, said to be the opinion of King Lemuel concerning a truly blessed woman; behold how her duties have gone on increasing. 'Tis the thirty-first chapter of Proverbs; and let no one with an appreciation of the humorous miss it. It begins rather inconsequently with something about wine-drinking, and runs into the question at issue in the tenth verse; just why, no one is able to understand. It bears no relation to what has preceded it. Here it is:

"Who can find a virtuous woman? for her price is far above rubies." (You'll be convinced of that before you've done;—diamonds either.)

"The heart of her husband doth safely trust in her, so that he shall have no need of spoil." (They don't generally need much of that if Lemuel means the sort of "spoil" which most modern husbands get.)

"She will do him good and not evil all the days of her life." (That's in general; what follows is specific.)

"She seeketh flax and wool, and worketh willingly with her hands." (So much for clothes; victuals now.)

"She is like the merchants' ships; she bringeth food from afar." (Goes where she can get it cheap, of course.)

"She riseth also while it is night, and giveth meat to her household, and a portion to her maidens." (Careful that they should not overeat and get sluggish. It is well to keep the girls tolerably hungry if you want them up before daylight.)

"She considereth a field and buyeth it; with the fruit of her hands she planteth a vineyard." (Trades, too, see?)

"She girdeth her loins with strength and strengtheneth her arms." (Nowadays she'd do that with a bicycle instead of a plow.)

"She perceiveth that her merchandise is good; her candle goeth not out by night." (That means that she works all night, too; for she wouldn't burn candles for nothing, being economical.)

"She layeth her hands to the spindle, and her hands hold the distaff." (The woman is all hands!)

"She stretcheth out her hands to the poor; yea, she reacheth forth her hands to the needy." (Hands again!)

"She is not afraid of the snow for her household, for all her household are clothed in scarlet." (How Mephistophelian the whole household must have seemed.)

"She maketh herself coverings of tapestry; her clothing is silk and purple." (The woman must have had forty days in a month and thirteen months in a year.)

"Her husband is known in the gates when he sitteth among the elders of the land." (I thought that he'd be up somewhere about the gates! I thought that he wouldn't be having much to do but to sit with the elders! I thought that he'd not be stopping about the house much!)

"She maketh fine linen and selleth it, and delivereth girdles unto the merchant." (I should think that she might send him around delivering.)

"Strength and honor are her clothing, and she shall rejoice in time to come." (There is certainly not much chance for her to rejoice in the time which has already come.)

"She openeth her mouth with wisdom, and in her tongue is the law of kindness." (Verily, I should have expected her to be shrewish.)

"She looketh well to the ways of her household, and eateth not the bread of idleness." (This paragraph was unnecessary; we had reached that conclusion before.)

"Her children arise up and call her blessed; her husband also, and he praiseth her." (Well, in all conscience, 'tis as little as he could do; and he ought to do it well, since there is a deal of fine rhetoric usually going about among the elders and around the gates; and he has plenty of leisure to "get onto it.")

"Many daughters have done virtuously; but thou excellest them all." ("Sure.")

"Favor is deceitful and beauty is vain; but a woman that feareth the Lord, she shall be praised." (That is to console her for getting ugly with all of that work.)

"Give her of the fruit of her hands; and let her own works praise her in the gates." Oh, thou who hast bought and planted and reaped and sold, spun and woven and girdled and clothed, risen and travelled and gathered and given, borne all, done all, ordered all, saved all, we will *"give* thee of the fruit of thy hands," and prate about it up at the gates! Verily, verily, the woman is far above rubies.

But alas for Lemuel and for Solomon, conditions then were also mutable. And perhaps a friend of mine who has expressed herself upon this passage, is right in her judgment that, as men never exalt a thing until it is beginning to wane and to vanish away, therefore it must have been that this sort of woman was on the decrease before Solomon began to repeat Lemuel. It does not lie within the scope of my lecture to trace the economic development which multiplied the diversion of labor, creating classes having separate and conflicting political interests, which will continue to clash until the process has either, by being pushed to its extremity, destroyed itself and reaccomplished independent production, or until some more correct political solution be found than any at present existing. What I wish to observe is merely that up to the dawn of the Revolutionary period this manifold splitting of humanity's occupations did not affect the primal division of the complementary labors of the sexes. Within the limits set by the original division, however, classes did arise. Among women these classes were principally two; the overworked drudges of the poor, and the pampered daughters of wealth. Is it not possible to say whose condition was the most lamentable. For to both was still maintained by preacher, by teacher, by lawyer and by doctor the old decree: "Thy husband shall rule over thee." Of the latter class there were but few previous to the Revolution. The rugged condition of pioneer life in the New World afforded small opportunity for the growth of a purely parasite class; that has arisen since. But in the Old World the women of the landed aristocracy, as likewise those of the developing mercantile class, constituted, though not a majority, yet a good percentage of the whole sex. So large a portion, in fact, that a whole stock of literature, which might have been labelled, "The Gospel of Jesus specially adapted to the use of society women," arose and flourished; preachers busied themselves with it; doctors wrote scores of verses on the preservation of the beauty and the delicacy of the lazy; rhetoricians frilled and furbelowed the human toy by way of exercising their art; lawyers rendered learned opinions upon "lovely woman"—they all took their turn and they all did her a bad turn. The entire science of life, as laid down in this literature for these women, was to make husband-traps of themselves. Their home training and their educational facilities were in line therewith. Nothing solid, nothing to develop or even to awaken the logical faculties, everything to develop the petty and the frivolous. The art of dressing, the tricks of assumed modesty, the degradation of intellect by continually curbing and straining it in to fit the patterns of God and of his servants—that the servant said that is was God's pattern—such was the feminine code.

About this time there arose the inevitable protest which conditions were bound to force. It was all very well for the dumb drudges and the well-fed toys; but society has ever between its extremes a middle product which fits in nowhere. This is recruited from both sides, but, at that time mostly from the upper classes being squeezed down into the ranks of the non-possessors. There were women, daughters of the formerly well-to-do, incapable of the very laborious life of the lowly, unable to reascend to their former superior position; upon these were forced the necessity of self-support. Most of them regarded it as a hard and bitter lot, and something to be ashamed of. Even literature, now considered a very fine source of support for women, was then a thing for a woman to keep still about if she engaged in it. The proper thing to do was to lay hold of an honorary sort of husband, support one's self and him, and pretend that he did it. So disgraceful was social usefulness in woman! Such was the premium on worthlessness!

Now, out of this class one who did not do the proper thing, one who protested against the whole scheme arose,—the woman whose name many now delight to honor as the author of the "Vindication of the Rights of Women,"—Mary Wollstonecraft. One of her biographers, Mrs. Pennel, states that she was the first woman in England who openly followed literature as a means of livelihood. (It is worthy of note that Mr. Jonson, her employer, was one of the Freethinkers of the time, Paine's printer, as well as Mary Wollstonecraft's.)

Nowadays the idea conveyed by the expression, "Women's Rights" is the idea of casting a ballot. Then it meant the right to be treated as serious beings having some faint claim to comprehension. The orthodox code never had, never has, admitted, and never will admit, anything of the kind until it is forced to do so. It is not surprising, therefore, to know that this woman was not orthodox. She found out that if ever a woman expected to have rights she must first pitch the teachings of the priests overboard. And not only priests, but their coadjutors, men of the scientific "cloth" indeed, who see that priestcraft is all wrong for them, but all right for women—men who hunt scientific justifications for keeping up the orthodox standard.

For a long time the seed sown by the author of the "Rights of Women" lay on seemingly barren ground; and the great prophet of the coming woman was, as usual, maligned, travestied, hissed and hooted, save by the select few. The reason for this is now apparent. Conditions had not so far developed as to create a *class* of women having none to depend upon except themselves; there were only sporadic specimens here and there, thence the old traditions fortified by the ancient possibilities remained firm. But now that the irresistible tide of economic development is driving women out of the corner wherein they lay drifted for so many thousand years, the case is different. And I, for one, bless the hour when a stinging lash drove women forth into the industrial arena. I know that it is the habit of our labor reformers to bewail the fact that men can no longer "support their wives and their daughters"; it is held up as the chief iniquity of the capitalist that he has broken up the poor man's family life; the "queen," poor tinsel queen, has been taken from her realm, the home, into the factory. But while I credit the capitalist with no better motive than that of buying in the cheapest market, I bless him from the crown of his head to the sole of his foot for this unintentional good. This iron-shod heel has crushed the shell of "woman's sphere"; and the wings will grow—never fear, they will grow. No one will accuse me of loving the horrors of modern society, no one will suppose that I want them to continue for one moment after the hour when it is possible to be rid of them. I know all of the evils resultant to woman from the factory system; I would not prolong them. But I am glad that by these very horrors, these gigantic machines which give to me the nightmare with their jaws and teeth, these monstrous buildings, bare and many-windowed, stretching skyward, brick, hard and loveless, which daily swallow and spew out again thousands upon thousands of frail lives, each day a little frailer, weaker, more exhausted, these unhealthy, man-eating traps which I cannot see blotting the ground and the sky without itching to tear down, by these very horrors women have learned to be socially useful and economically independent—as much so as men are. The basis of independence and of individuality is bread. As long as wives take bread from husbands because they are not capable of getting it in any other way, so long will the decree obtain: "Thy desire shall be to thy husband, and he shall rule over thee," so long will all talk about political "rights" be empty vagaries, hopeless crying against the wind.

There are those who contend that once the strain and the stress of commercialism are over, women will resume their ancient position, "natural," they call it, of child nurses and home-keepers, being ruled and protected. I say, NO: the broken chain will never be re-forged. No more "spheres," no more stops or lets or hindrances. I do not say that women will not be nurses and home-keepers at all; but I *do* say that they will not be such because they have to, because any priest so reads the ancient law—because any social prejudice checks them and forces them into it rather than allowing full, free development of natural bent. I say that the factory is laughing at the church; and the modern woman, who grasps her own self-hood, is laughing at the priest. I say that the greater half of the case of Orthodoxy *vs.* Woman is won—by woman; through pain, and misery, and sweat of brow and ache of hand, as all things worth winning are won. I don't mean that nothing remains to be done; there is as much in pursuing a victory as in winning it in the first place. But the citadel is taken—the right of self-maintenance—and all else must follow.

From the aforetime sterile ground the seeds are springing green. This is the season to pluck life from the tombs, the time of transfiguration when every scar upon the earth changes to glory, when before the eyes of man appears that miracle, of which all traditions of resurrection and of ascension are but faint, dim images, figures passing over the glass of the human mind, the projection of man's effort to identify himself with the All of Nature. This miracle, this blooming of the mold, this shooting of green peas where all was brown and barren, this resurrection of the sunken snow in tree-crowns, these workings, these responses to the knocking of the sunlight, these comings forth from burial, these rendings of shrouds, these ascensions from the graves, these flutterings, these swift, winged shadows passing, these tremolos high up in the atmosphere,—is it possible to feel all of this miracle and not to dream? Is it possible not to hope? The very fact that every religion has some kind of symbolic festival about the returning time of the green, proves that man, too, felt the upspringing in his breast—whether he rightly translates it or not, 'tis sure that he felt it, like all organic things. And whether it be the festival of a risen Christ, or of the passage of Judah from the bondage of Egypt, or the old Pagan worship of light, 'tis ever the same—the celebration of the breaking of bonds. We, too, may allow ourselves the poetic dream. Abroad in the April sunlight we behold in every freedom-going spark the risen dead—the flame which burned in the souls of Hypatia, Mary Wollstonecraft, Frances Wright, Ernestine L. Rose, Harriet Martineau, Lucretia Mott, that grand old negress, Sojourner Truth, our own brave old Lucy N. Coleman, and all of the beloved unknown whose lives ingrafted on the race what *their* tongues spoke. We, too, proclaim the Resurrection.

The Woman Question

This is an excerpt from a lecture given in Scotland, later reprinted in the *Herald of Revolt* in 1913. The "woman question" was the phrase then used to describe the issues that we would today call "feminism" or "women's rights." Her reference to "the section of anarchists" refers to the many anarchist men, radical in politics but not otherwise, who thought the only problem women faced was that some of their husbands made low wages.

The Woman Question

A section of Anarchists say there is no Women Question apart from our present industrial situation but the assertion is mostly made by men, and men are not the fittest to feel the slaveries of women. Scientists argue that the nutritive functions of society are best performed by the male, the reproductive by the female, the food finding is done away from, the rearing of children, at home; and if woman enters the industrial arena she will suffer in her distinctive powers. Amongst the working-classes this is not so, as the women work hard at home duties, and sometimes take in sewing, or go out washing for other people. Woman's domestic work is the most ill-paid labour in the world. Marriage is not in the interest of women. It is a pledge from the marrying man to the male half of society (women are not counted in the State), that he will not shirk his responsibilities upon them! Marriage is discredited, by its results as well as by its origins.

Men may not mean to be tyrants when they marry, but they frequently grow to be such. It is insufficient to dispense with the priest or registrar. The spirit of marriage makes for slavery. Women are becoming more and more engaged in industry. This means that other doors are open to her than the door of menial service. It also means that just as men have developed individuality, because of their being thrown into all sorts of employment and conditions, so likewise will women. And with the development of diversity will come the irrepressible desire for its expression, and by consequence the necessity of such material conditions as will permit that expression.

The unattainability of quietude in the ordinary home militates against such conditions, whilst the "abominably uneconomical" way in which the work is done—being on an infinitesimally small scale a laundry, bakery, lodging-house, restaurant and nursery rolled into one—also doom the home. With, however, the introduction of ideas bound to follow the introduction of female labour into industrialism, the home in its present form must go. ... Meanwhile I would strongly advise every woman contemplating sexual union of any kind, never to live together with the man you love, in the sense of renting a house or rooms, and becoming his housekeeper.

As to the children, seeing the number of infants who die, the alarm is rather hypocritical; but, ignoring this consideration, first of all it should be the business of women to study sex, and control parentage—never to have a child unless you want it, and never to want it (selfishly, for the pleasure of having a pretty plaything), unless you, yourself alone, are able to provide for it.

Sex Slavery

"That is adultery where woman submits herself sexually to man, without desire on her part.... And that is rape, where a man forces himself sexually upon a woman whether he licensed by the marriage law to do it or not." The occasion of the essay was the imprisonment for obscenity of Moses Harman, an individualist anarchist and "free love" publisher in Kansas, under the Comstock laws. Harman published feminist critiques of marriage in his magazine *Lucifer, the Light Bearer*, and served several prison terms for that crime, the final one breaking rocks at Joliet, Illinois starting in 1905 when he was in his seventies. The feminism Voltairine articulates was not original—such American precursors as Victoria Woodhull and Angela Heywood (as well as Harman) might be mentioned—but it is articulated here with characteristic clarity and passion.

August Bebel (1840–1913) was a German leftist leader.

Sex Slavery

Night in a prison cell! A chair, a bed, a small washstand, four blank walls, ghastly in the dim light from the corridor without, a narrow window, barred and sunken in the stone, a grated door! Beyond its hideous iron latticework, within the ghastly walls,—a man! An old man, gray-haired and wrinkled, lame and suffering. There he sits, in his great loneliness, shut in from all the earth. There he walks, to and fro, within his measured space, apart from all he loves! There, for every night in five long years to come, he will walk alone, while the white age-flakes drop upon his head, while the last years of the winter of life gather and pass, and his body draws near the ashes. Every night, for five long years to come, he will sit alone, this chattel slave, whose hard toil is taken by the State,—and without recompense save that the Southern planter gave his negroes,—every night he will sit there so within those four white walls. Every night, for five long years to come, a suffering woman will lie upon her bed, longing, longing for the end of those three thousand days; longing for the kind face, the patient hand, that in so many years had never failed her. Every night, for five long years to come, the proud spirit must rebel, the loving heart must bleed, the broken home must lie desecrated. As I am speaking now, as you are listening, there within the cell of that accursed penitentiary whose stones have soaked up the sufferings of so many victims, murdered, as truly as any outside their walls, by that slow rot which eats away existence inch-meal,—as I am speaking now, as you are listening, *there sits Moses Harman!*

Why? Why, when murder now is stalking in your streets, when dens of infamy are so thick within your city that competition has forced down the price of prostitution to the level of the wages of your starving shirt-makers; when robbers sit in State and national Senate and House, when the boasted "bulwark of our liberties," the elective franchise, has become a U.S. dice-box, wherewith great gamblers play away your liberties; when debauchees of the worst type hold all your public offices and dine off the food of fools who support them, why, then, sits Moses Harman there within his prison cell? If he is so *great* a criminal, why is he not with the rest of the spawn of crime, dining at Delmonico's or enjoying a trip to

Europe? If he is so bad a man, why in the name of wonder did he ever get in the penitentiary?

Ah, no; it is not because he has done any evil thing; but because he, a pure enthusiast, searching, searching always for the cause of misery of the kind which he loved with that broad love of which only the pure soul is capable, searched for the data of evil. And searching so he found the vestibule of life to be a prison cell; the holiest and purest part of the temple of the body, if indeed one part can be holier or purer than another, the altar where the most devotional love in truth should be laid, he found this altar ravished, despoiled, trampled upon. He found little babies, helpless, voiceless little things, generated in lust, cursed with impure moral natures, cursed, prenatally, with the germs of disease, forced into the world to struggle and to suffer, to hate themselves, to hate their mothers for bearing them, to hate society and to be hated by it in return,—a bane upon self and race, draining the lees of crime. And he said, this felon with the stripes upon his body, "Let the mothers of the race go free! Let the little children be pure love children, born of the mutual desire for parentage. Let the manacles be broken from the shackled slave, that no more slaves be born, no more tyrants conceived."

He looked, this obscenist, looked with clear eyes into this ill-got thing you call morality, sealed with the seal of marriage, and saw in it the consummation of *im*morality, impurity, and injustice. He beheld every married woman what she is, a bonded slave, who takes her master's name, her master's bread, her master's commands, and serves her master's passion; who passes through the ordeal of pregnancy and the throes of travail at *his* dictation,—not at her desire; who can control no property, not even her own body, without his consent, and from whose straining arms the children she bears may be torn at his pleasure, or willed away while they are yet unborn. It is said the English language has a sweeter word than any other,—*home*. But Moses Harman looked beneath the word and saw the fact,—a prison more horrible than that where he is sitting now, whose corridors radiate over all the earth, and with so many cells, that none may count them.

Yes, our Masters! The earth is a prison, the marriage-bed is a cell, women are the prisoners, and you are the keepers!

He saw, this corruptionist, how in those cells are perpetrated such outrages as are enough to make the cold sweat stand upon the forehead, and the nails clench, and the teeth set, and the lips grow white in agony and hatred. And he saw too how from those cells might none come forth to break her fetters, how no slave dare cry out, how all these murders are done quietly, beneath the shelter-shadow of home, and sanctified by the angelic benediction of a piece of paper, within the silence-shade of a marriage certificate, Adultery and Rape stalk freely and at ease.

Yes, for that is adultery where woman submits herself sexually to man, without desire on her part, for the sake of "keeping him virtuous," "keeping him at home," the women say. (Well, if a man did not love me and respect himself enough to be "virtuous" without prostituting me, he might go, and welcome. He has no virtue to keep.) And that is rape, where a man forces himself sexually upon a woman whether he is licensed by the marriage law to do it or not. And that is the vilest of all tyranny where a man compels the woman he says he loves, to endure the agony of bearing children that she does not want, and for whom, as is the rule rather than the exception, they cannot properly provide. It is worse than any other human oppression; it is fairly *God*-like! To the sexual tyrant there is no parallel upon earth; one must go to the skies to find a fiend who thrusts life upon his children only to starve and curse and outcast and damn them! And only through the marriage law is such tyranny possible. The man who deceives a woman outside of marriage (and mind you, such a man will deceive *in* marriage too) may deny his own child, if he is mean enough. He cannot tear it from her arms—he cannot touch it! The girl he wronged, thanks to your very pure and tender morality-standard, may die in the street for want of food. *He* cannot force his hated presence upon her again. But his wife, gentlemen, his wife, the woman he respects so much that he consents to let her merge her individuality into his, lose her identity and become his chattel, his wife he may not only force unwelcome children upon, outrage at his own good pleasure, and keep as a general cheap and convenient piece of furniture, but if she does not get a divorce (and she cannot for such cause) he can follow her wherever she goes, come into her house, eat her food, force her into the cell, *kill* her by virtue of his sexual authority! And she has no redress unless he is indiscreet enough to abuse her in some less brutal but unlicensed manner. I know a case in your city where a woman was followed so for ten years by her husband. I believe he finally developed grace enough to die; please applaud him for the only decent thing he ever did.

Oh, is it not rare, all this talk about the preservation of morality by marriage law! O splendid carefulness to preserve that which you have not got! O height and depth of purity, which fears so much that the children will not know who their fathers are, because, forsooth, they must rely upon their mother's word instead of the hired certification of some priest of the Church, or the Law! I wonder if the children would be improved to know what their fathers have done. I would rather, much rather, not know who my father was than know he had been a tyrant to my mother. I would rather, much rather, be illegitimate according to the statutes of men, than illegitimate according to the unchanging law of Nature. For what is it to be legitimate, born "according to law"? It is to be, nine cases out of ten, the

child of a man who acknowledges his fatherhood simply because he is
forced to do so, and whose conception of virtue is realized by the statement
that "a woman's duty is to keep her husband at home"; to be the child of a
woman who cares more for the benediction of Mrs. Grundy than the simple honor of her lover's word, and conceives prostitution to be purity and
duty when exacted of her by her husband. It is to have Tyranny as your
progenitor, and slavery as your prenatal cradle. It is to run the risk of
unwelcome birth, "legal" constitutional weakness, morals corrupted before
birth, possibly a murder instinct, the inheritance of excessive sexuality or
no sexuality, either of which is disease. It is to have the value of a piece of
paper, a rag from the tattered garments of the "Social Contract," set above
health, beauty, talent or goodness; for I never yet had difficulty in obtain-
ing the admission that illegitimate children are nearly always prettier and
brighter than others, even from conservative women. And how supremely
disgusting it is to see them look from their own puny, sickly, lust-born children, upon whom lie the chain-traces of their own terrible servitude, look
from these to some healthy, beautiful "natural" child, and say, "What a pity
its *mother* wasn't virtuous!" Never a word about *their* children's fathers'
virtue, they know too much! Virtue! Disease, stupidity, criminality! What
an *obscene* thing "virtue" is!

What is it to be illegitimate? To be despised, or pitied, by those whose
spite or whose pity isn't worth the breath it takes to return it. To be, possibly, the child of some man contemptible enough to deceive a woman; the
child of some woman whose chief crime was belief in the man she loved.
To be free from the prenatal curse of a slave mother, to come into the
world without the permission of any law-making set of tyrants who
assume to corner the earth, and say what terms the unborn must make for
the privilege of coming into existence. This is legitimacy and illegitimacy!
Choose.

The man who walks to and fro in his cell in Lansing penitentiary to-
night, this vicious man, said: "The mothers of the race are lifting their
dumb eyes to me, their sealed lips to me, their agonizing hearts to me.
They are seeking, seeking for a voice! The unborn in their helplessness, are
pleading from their prisons, pleading for a voice! The criminals, with the
unseen ban upon their souls, that has pushed them, pushed them to the
vortex, out of their whirling hells, are looking, waiting for a voice! *I will be
their voice.* I will unmask the outrages of the marriage-bed. I will make
known how criminals are born. I will make one outcry that shall be heard,
and let what will be, *be!*" He cried out through the letter of Dr. Markland,
that a young mother lacerated by unskilful surgery in the birth of her babe,
but recovering from a subsequent successful operation, had been stabbed,
remorselessly, cruelly, brutally stabbed, not with a knife, but with the

procreative organ of her husband, stabbed to the doors of death, and yet there was no redress!

And because he called a spade a spade, because he named that organ by its own name, so given in Webster's dictionary and in every medical journal in the country, because of this Moses Harman walks to and fro in his cell to-night. He gave a concrete example of the effect of sex slavery, and for it he is imprisoned. It remains for us now to carry on the battle, and lift the standard where they struck him down, to scatter broadcast the knowledge of this crime of society against a man and the reason for it; to inquire into this vast system of licensed crime, its cause and its effect, broadly upon the race. The Cause! Let woman ask herself, "Why am I the slave of Man? Why is my brain said not to be the equal of his brain? Why is my work not paid equally with his? Why must my body be controlled by my husband? Why may he take my labor in the household, giving me in exchange what he deems fit? Why may he take my children from me? Will them away while yet unborn?" Let every woman ask.

There are two reasons why, and these ultimately reducible to a single principle—the authoritarian, supreme-power, *God*-idea, and its two instruments, the Church—that is, the priests—and the State—that is, the legislators.

From the birth of the Church, out of the womb of Fear and the fatherhood of Ignorance, it has taught the inferiority of woman. In one form or another through the various mythical legends of the various myth- ical creeds, runs the undercurrent of the belief in the fall of man through the persuasion of woman, her subjective condition as punishment, her nat- ural vileness, total depravity, etc.; and from the days of Adam until now the Christian Church, with which we have specially to deal, has made *woman* the excuse, the scapegoat for the evil deeds of *man*. So thoroughly has this idea permeated Society that numbers of those who have utterly repudiated the Church, are nevertheless soaked in this stupefying narcotic to true morality. So pickled is the male creation with the vinegar of Authoritarianism, that even those who have gone further and repudiated the State still cling to the god, Society as it is, still hug the old theological idea that they are to be "heads of the family"—to that wonderful formula "of simple proportion" that "Man is the head of the Woman even as Christ is the head of the Church." No longer than a week since an Anarchist (?) said to me, "I will be boss in my own house"—a "Communist-Anarchist," if you please, who doesn't believe in "*my* house." About a year ago a noted libertarian speaker said, in my presence, that his sister, who possessed a fine voice and had joined a concert troupe, should "stay at home with her chil- dren; that is *her place*." The old Church idea! This man was a Socialist, and since an Anarchist; yet his highest idea for woman was serfhood to husband and children, in the present mockery called "home." Stay at home, ye malcontents! Be patient, obedient, submissive! Darn our socks, mend our shirts, wash our dishes, get our meals, wait on us and *mind the children!* Your fine voices are not to delight the public nor yourselves; your inventive genius is not to work, your fine art taste is not to be cultivated, your business faculties are not to be developed; you made the great mistake of being born with them, suffer for your folly! You are *women!* therefore housekeepers, servants, waiters, and child's nurses!

At Macon, in the sixth century, says August Bebel, the fathers of the Church met and proposed the decision of the question, "Has woman a soul?" Having ascertained that the permission to own a nonentity wasn't going to injure any of their parsnips, a small majority vote decided the momentous question in our favor. Now, holy fathers, it was a tolerably good scheme on your part to offer the reward of your pitiable "salvation or damnation" (odds in favor of the latter) as a bait for the hook of earthly submission; it wasn't a bad sop in those days of Faith and Ignorance. But fortunately fourteen hundred years have made it stale. You, tyrant radicals (?), have no heaven to offer,—you have no delightful chimeras in the form of "merit cards"; you have (save the mark) the respect, the good offices, the smiles—of a slave-holder! This in return for our chains! Thanks!

The question of souls is old—we demand our bodies, now. We are tired of promises, God is deaf, and his church is our worst enemy. Against it we bring the charge of being the moral (or immoral) force which lies behind the tyranny of the State. And the State has divided the loaves and fishes with the Church, the magistrates, like the priests take marriage fees; the two fetters of Authority have gone into partnership in the business of granting patent-rights to parents for the privilege of reproducing them-selves, and the State cries as the Church cried of old, and cries now: "See how we protect women!" The State has done more. It has often been said to me, by women with decent masters, who had no idea of the outrages practiced on their less fortunate sisters, "Why don't the wives leave?"

Why don't you run, when your feet are chained together? Why don't you cry out when a gag is on your lips? Why don't you raise your hands above your head when they are pinned fast to your sides? Why don't you spend thousands of dollars when you haven't a cent in your pocket? Why don't you go to the seashore or the mountains, you fools scorching with city heat? If there is one thing more than another in this whole accursed tissue of false society, which makes me angry, it is the asinine stupidity which with the true phlegm of impenetrable dullness says, "Why don't the women leave!" Will you tell me where they will go and what they shall do? When the State, the legislators, has given to itself, the politicians, the utter and absolute control of the opportunity to live; when, through this

precious monopoly, already the market of labor is so overstocked that workmen and workwomen are cutting each others' throats for the dear privilege
of serving their lords; when girls are shipped from Boston to the south and
north, shipped in carloads, like cattle, to fill the dives of New Orleans or the
lumber-camp hells of my own state (Michigan), when seeing and hearing
these things reported every day, the proper prudes exclaim, "Why don't the
women leave," they simply beggar the language of contempt.

When America passed the fugitive slave law compelling men to catch
their fellows more brutally than runaway dogs, Canada, aristocratic,
unrepublican Canada, still stretched her arms to those who might reach
her. But there is no refuge upon earth for the enslaved sex. Right where we
are, there we must dig our trenches, and win or die.

This, then, is the tyranny of the State; it denies, to both woman and
man, the right to earn a living, and grants it as a privilege to a favored few
who for that favor must pay ninety per cent toll to the granters of it. These
two things, the mind domination of the Church, and the body domination of the State are the causes of Sex Slavery.

First of all, it has introduced into the world the constructed crime of
obscenity: it has set up such a peculiar standard of morals that to speak the
names of the sexual organs is to commit the most brutal outrage. It reminds
me that in your city you have a street called "Callowhill." Once it was
called Gallows' Hill, for the elevation to which it leads, now known as
"Cherry Hill," has been the last touching place on earth for the feet of
many a victim murdered by the Law. But the sound of the word became
too harsh; so they softened it, though the murders are still done, and the
black shadow of the Gallows still hangs on the City of Brotherly Love.
Obscenity has done the same; it has placed virtue in the shell of an idea,
and labelled all "good" which dwells within the sanction of Law and
respectable (?) custom; and all bad which contravenes the usage of the
shell. It has lowered the dignity of the human body, below the level of all
other animals. Who thinks a dog is impure or obscene because its body is
not covered with suffocating and annoying clothes? What would you think
of the meanness of a man who would put a skirt upon his horse and compel it to walk or run with such a thing impeding its limbs? Why, the
"Society for the Prevention of Cruelty to Animals" would arrest him, take
the beast from him, and he would be sent to a lunatic asylum for treatment
on the score of an *impure* mind. And yet, gentlemen, you expect your
wives, the creatures you say you respect and love, to wear the longest skirts
and the highest necked clothing, in order to conceal the *obscene human
body*. There is no society for the prevention of cruelty to women. And you,
yourselves, though a little better, look at the heat you wear in this roasting
weather! How you curse your poor body with the wool you steal from the

sheep! How you punish yourselves to sit in a crowded house with coats and vests on, because dead Mme. Grundy is shocked at the "vulgarity" of shirt sleeves, or the naked arm!

Look how the ideal of beauty has been marred by this obscenity notion. Divest yourselves of prejudice for once. Look at some fashion-slaved woman, her waist surrounded by a high-board fence called a corset, her shoulders and hips angular from the pressure above and below, her feet narrowest where they should be widest, the body fettered by her ever-lasting prison skirt, her hair fastened tight enough to make her head ache and surmounted by a thing of neither sense nor beauty, called a hat, ten to one a hump upon her back like a dromedary,—look at her, and then imagine such a thing as that carved in marble! Fancy a statue in Fairmount Park with a corset and bustle on. Picture to yourselves the image of the equestrienne. We are permitted to ride, providing we sit in a position ruinous to the horse; providing we wear a riding-habit long enough to hide the obscene human foot, weighed down by ten pounds of gravel to cheat the Wind in its free blowing, so running the risk of disabling ourselves completely should accident throw us from the saddle. Think how we swim! We must even wear clothing in the water, and run the gauntlet of derision, if we dare battle in the surf minus stockings! Imagine a fish try-ing to make headway with a water-soaked flannel garment upon it. Nor are you yet content. The vile standard of obscenity even kills the little babies with clothes. The human race is murdered, horribly, "in the name of" Dress.

And in the name of Purity what lies are told! What queer morality it has engendered. For fear of it you dare not tell your own children the truth about their birth; the most sacred of all functions, the creation of a human being, is a subject for the most miserable falsehood. When they come to you with a simple, straightforward question, which they have a right to ask, you say, "Don't ask such questions," or tell some silly hollow-log story; or you explain the incomprehensibility by another—God! You say "God made you." You know you are lying when you say it. You know, or you ought to know, that the source of inquiry will not be dammed up so. You know that what you could explain purely, reverently, rightly (if you have any purity in you), will be learned through many blind gropings, and that around it will be cast the shadow-thought of wrong, embryo'd by your denial and nurtured by this social opinion everywhere prevalent. If you do not know this, then you are blind to facts and deaf to Experience.

Think of the double social standard the enslavement of our sex has evolved. Women considering themselves very pure and very moral, will sneer at the street-walker, yet admit to their homes the very men who vic-timized the street-walker. Men, at their best, will pity the prostitute, while they themselves are the worst kind of prostitutes. Pity yourselves, gentlemen—you need it!

How many times do you see where a man or woman has shot another through jealousy! The standard of purity has decided that it is right, "it shows spirit," "it is justifiable" to—murder a human being for doing exactly what you did yourself,—love the same woman or same man! Morality! Honor! Virtue!! Passing from the moral to the physical phase; take the statistics of any insane asylum, and you will find that, out of the different classes, unmarried women furnish the largest one. To preserve your cruel, vicious, indecent standard of purity (?) you drive your daughters insane, while your wives are killed with excess. Such is marriage. Don't take my word for it; go through the report of any asylum or the annals of any graveyard.

Look how your children grow up. Taught from their earliest infancy to curb their love natures—restrained at every turn! Your blasting lies would even blacken a child's kiss. Little girls must not be tomboyish, must not go barefoot, must not climb trees, must not learn to swim, must not do anything they desire to do which Madame Grundy has decreed "improper." Little boys are laughed at as effeminate, silly girl-boys if they want to make patchwork or play with a doll. Then when they grow up, "Oh! Men don't care for home or children as women do!" Why should they, when the deliberate effort of your life has been to crush that nature out of them. "Women can't rough it like men." Train any animal, or any plant, as you train your girls, and it won't be able to rough it either. Now *will* somebody tell me why either sex should hold a corner on athletic sports? Why any child should not have free use of its limbs?

These are the effects of your purity standard, your marriage law. This is your work—look at it! Half your children dying under five years of age, your girls insane, your married women walking corpses, your men so bad that they themselves often admit *Prostitution holds against* PURITY *a bond of indebtedness.* This is the beautiful effect of your god, Marriage, before which Natural Desire must abase and belie itself. Be proud of it!

Now for the remedy. It is in one word, the only word that ever brought equity anywhere—LIBERTY! Centuries upon centuries of liberty is the only thing that will cause the disintegration and decay of these pestiferous ideas. Liberty was all that calmed the blood-waves of religious persecution! You cannot cure serfhood by any other substitution. Not for you to say "in this way shall the race love." Let the race *alone.*

Will there not be atrocious crimes? Certainly. He is a fool who says there will not be. But you can't stop them by committing the arch-crime and setting a block between the spokes of Progress-wheels. You will never get right until you start right.

As for the final outcome, it matters not one iota. I have my ideal, and it is very pure, and very sacred to me. But yours, equally sacred, may be different and we may both be wrong. But certain am I that with free contract, that form of sexual association will survive which is best adapted to time and place, thus producing the highest evolution of the type. Whether that shall be monogamy, variety, or promiscuity matters naught to us; it is the business of the future, to which we dare not dictate.

For freedom spoke Moses Harman, and for this he received the felon's brand. For this he sits in his cell to-night. Whether it is possible that his sentence be shortened, we do not know. We can only try. Those who would help us try, let me ask to put your signatures to this simple request for pardon addressed to Benjamin Harrison. To those who desire more fully to inform themselves before signing; I say: Your conscientiousness is praiseworthy—come to me at the close of the meeting and I will quote the exact language of the Markland letter. To those extreme Anarchists who cannot bend their dignity to ask pardon for an offense not committed, and of an authority they cannot recognize, let me say: Moses Harman's back is bent, low bent, by the brute force of the Law, and though I would never ask anyone to bow for himself, I can ask it, and easily ask it, for him who fights the slave's battle. Your dignity is criminal; every hour behind the bars is a seal to your partnership with Comstock. No one can hate petitions worse than I; no one has less faith in them than I. But for *my* champion I am willing to try any means that invades no other's right, even though I have little hope in it.

If, beyond these, there are those here to-night who have ever forced sexual servitude from a wife, those who have prostituted themselves in the name of Virtue, those who have brought diseased, immoral or unwelcome children to the light, without the means of provision for them, and yet will go from this hall and say, "Moses Harman is an unclean man—a man rewarded by just punishment," then to *you* I say, and may the words ring deep within your ears UNTIL YOU DIE: Go on! Drive your sheep to the shambles! Crush that old, sick, crippled man beneath your Juggernaut! In the name of Virtue, Purity and Morality, do it! In the name of God, Home, and Heaven, do it! In the name of the Nazarene who preached the golden rule, do it! In the name of Justice, Principle, and Honor, do it! In the name of Bravery and Magnanimity put yourself on the side of the robber in the government halls, the murderer in the political convention, the libertine in public places, the whole brute force of the police, the constabulary, the court, and the penitentiary, to persecute one poor old man who stood alone against your licensed crime! Do it. And if Moses Harman dies within your "Kansas Hell," be satisfied *when you have murdered him!* Kill him! And you hasten the day when the Future shall bury you ten thousand fathoms deep beneath its curses. Kill him! And the stripes upon his prison clothes shall lash you like the knout! Kill him! And the insane shall glitter hate at you with their wild eyes, the unborn babes shall cry their blood upon you, and the graves that you have filled in the name of Marriage, shall yield food for a race that will pillory you, until the memory of your atrocity has become a nameless ghost, flitting with the shades of Torquemada, Calvin and Jehovah over the horizon of the World!

Would you smile to see him dead? Would you say, "We are rid of this obscenist"? Fools! The corpse would laugh at you from its cold eyelids! The motionless lips would mock, and the solemn hands, the pulseless, folded hands, in their quietness would write the last indictment, which neither Time nor you can efface. Kill him! And you write his glory and your shame! Moses Harman in his felon stripes stands far above you now, and Moses Harman *dead* will live on, immortal in the race he died to free! Kill him!

The Political Equality of
Women

This piece, first shown to be by Voltairine recently by Bob Helms, appeared in *The Conservator*, a Philadelphia paper, July 1894. It appeared above the initials "M.W." which stood for Mary Wollstonecraft, pioneering eighteenth century feminist and partner of ur-anarchist William Godwin. Voltairine explicitly rejects the concept of "natural rights" but argues that the rights of women must follow the change in their economic function in industrial capitalism.

Mount Pisgah: Biblical location in which Moses brought water for the Israelites from a rock. He was then condemned to remain there as the Jews took their final journey to the promised land.

The Political Equality of Woman

From the beginning the demand for the political equality of the sexes has been met by three determined opponents—the priest, the politician and the scientist. The first two have been, at least partially, convinced or silenced. Those who continue to vociferate fall back upon the scientist for arguments, which last continues to smile and smile and be a fossil still, for a most excellent reason—the leaders of the political equality movement, with a few exceptions, have failed to put their claims upon a modern scientific basis. They don the wornout armor of the past century, and endeavor to fight dynamite with a coat-of-mail. One is stuffed to satiety with the jargon of "natural rights," "inherent rights," "inalienable rights," "all are created equal," etc., formulas expressive of the metaphysical stage of thought which dominated the last century, and to disprove which is the easiest possible task for the stern devotee of "facts."

It may be venturesome for the writer to suggest the query whether this is a matter of ignorance or of policy on the part of the suffrage leaders. It is difficult to suppose the former, and might very reasonably be the latter, since it is an utmost piece of daring to attempt to carry a reform by breaking a nation's idols, and the American voter is most stupidly and stubbornly "wedded to the idol" of natural rights. Yet nothing is clearer than that, as is generally the case where policy compromises truth, we shall cut but a sorry figure before the tribunal of the wise if we continue to base our claims on that which is itself baseless.

Natural rights! They do not exist.

Created equal! Absurdity.

You have a "natural right to life, liberty and the pursuit of happiness." So has a sheep, or a potato, and you do most tyrannically deny it when you eat them. You smile at this, and complacently continue to eat, remarking, calmly, "Oh, it is a sheep." "Precisely," smiles back the iconoclast of "natural rights," "and you are a woman." The sheep has no rights which you are bound to respect, because it has no power to force you to respect them. Nature's ideals are not rights, but powers. According to her the master class alone has "rights," and the struggle for rights is a struggle for the division of

241

power; only when the power is obtained do the rights exist. To illustrate: A man has a "right" to live, it is said; but place this man without capital or opportunity to work, as thousands are placed to-day, and what becomes of his right to live? He has no *power* to live, and must therefore starve. The same inexorable logic applies to woman. The place which she has occupied in society at any given period in history has been the precise measure of her rights at that epoch. These have been constantly widened with the evolution of society, and it is the business of the claimants for political equality to show that the circle should now be extended to include that "right," because woman's position in society is so altered as to enable her to enforce that demand. And to satisfy the scientist it should be shown that this new position or power of woman in society is in accord with the historical progress of man. The whole question of rights and equality, political or otherwise, arose when, in the struggle for power, the individually weak races of the world pooled their strength to outwit the individually strong, and in so doing gave birth to society. In order to obtain the power of united effort, however, the individual effort had to be in some measure curtailed—how much and how far has been the eternal subject of dispute. Every epoch renders its own decision, and the examination of these decisions proves that those nations have attained nearest to nature's ideal of power, which, while consolidating their material and spiritual interests, have at the same time allowed the greatest amount of liberty to the individual, liberty being synonymous with equality.

Every new definition of right, every fresh leveling of powers, has been bought with the blood of the bravest and best; bought by the sacrifice of those who climbed Mount Pisgah but never entered the Promised Land. Changes in the material conditions of society have made these questions imperative. The system of vassalage whereby Europe gained its bread and butter crashed, like a top-heavy iceberg, and turned over monarchical institutions with it, when it had reached that point of development where the Titan beneath could no longer bear its weight. Out of this bitter travail the right of suffrage (to men) and representative government were born. The position of woman was not much altered thereby. But now the child of Feudalism. *Capitalism*, with its iron-shod feet, tramps the blood from the heart of the woman, who is no more the household goddess, but the tool which fashions profits. Woman must become self-supporting, whether she will or no; for wages fall, men cannot support families, and women must work or starve. Let it be so. She is no more the protected animal; she becomes an individual. She suffers, and dreams of "rights." She claims some other cause of consideration than that of wife, mother, sister, daughter; she stands alone, she becomes strong, and in recognition of her strength presses her claim of equality. She is buying it with the sweat of unpaid toil, with the flesh of her emaciated fingers, with the blood shed on her unsung battle-fields, in the weary journey through the wilderness. When she has sweat enough, starved enough, bled enough, she, too, may climb Mount Pisgah. And those who come after will inherit the victory.

—M. W.

Part VI

Not Another Brick in the Wall

Nonauthoritarian Education

Introduction

An anarchist activist by calling, Voltairine de Cleyre was, by occupation, an educator. She refused to accept monetary reward for her anarchist speeches and writings, instead eking out a sparse existence during her time in Philadelphia, teaching immigrants English, music, and other subjects. With characteristic zeal, she even learned Yiddish so she could help Jewish immigrants. In view of both her teaching activities and her own tortuous experience in a strict Catholic convent where she was never allowed to question, it is not surprising that she had strong and clear-cut views on educational reform.

Given Voltairine's place within the history of American thought and in the history of liberation movements, as an anarchist, freethinker and feminist, her radical views on education are also not surprising. One way to understand de Cleyre is as a transition figure between transcendentalism and pragmatism, between Emerson and Dewey—two of the most important American writers on the topic of education. Like Emerson, she emphasized the independence of the student and the idea that children should be taught to draw their own conclusions. This was a direct outcome of Emerson's radical advocacy of democracy; democracy requires a different sort of citizen than, for example, the European monarchies, and education is the process whereby such citizens are made. It is not enough to rehearse the catechisms of common wisdom; one must learn to learn; to develop one's own thought independently and critically, a sentiment compatible with anarchist ideals. Dewey's views on education emphasized practical, hands-on training, as opposed to mere abstractions, and the classroom as a social place where society takes shape. His views were also designed with a political upshot in mind, though Dewey's vision of democracy was more socialistic than Emerson's. The belief in the importance of hands-on learning was an idea that also appeared later in Francisco Ferrer's anarchist vision of the Modern School, as well as Voltairine's writings.

Voltairine, of course, was an advocate not of majority rule, but of an anarchism based on a deep respect for individual autonomy. Thus it is revealing that the only essay in this part, "Modern Educational Reform," starts its critique from the point of view of the student, who feels physically restrained in the classroom and subjected to rote memorization of irrelevant facts. Such a student-centered approach was unusual when it was written, but it is absolutely typical of de Cleyre: the political position emerges from a basic empathy. This empathy in turn emerges from her own experiences of feeling intolerably restrained in school. Anticipating late twentieth-century ideas about education, she also insisted that children be instructed in the practical aspects of life, including sex and child rearing, as well as reading and writing. But unlike current education, she insisted that students be prepared for independent learning and a lifetime of resistance to mere authority.

Educational reform was a natural outgrowth of anarchist philosophy, with its demand for freedom, skepticism about authority, and emphasis on independent thought. The execution of Spanish anarchist and freethinker Francisco Ferrer, founder of the Escuela Moderna, or Modern School, on trumped-up charges, but actually for daring to question the Spanish Church and its rigid pedagogy, sparked a reaction in radical communities around the world as well as in the United States. Voltairine translated Ferrer's essay, "The Modern School," publishing it in *Mother Earth* in November 1909, only weeks after his death on October 13, 1909. She also translated his book, *The Modern School* and wrote an essay on Ferrer which was later published in her *Selected Works*.

Building on nearly a century's worth of libertarian and anarchist criticism of standard educational practices that included the influence of Bakunin, Kropotkin, Malatesta, Reclus and notably, Jean Grave, Ferrer organized a school based on overtly anti-authoritarian ideas. The Modern School emphasized "learning in a natural environment … recognition of the rights and dignity of the child, give and take between pupil and teacher …," says anarchist historian Paul Avrich in his book on the Modern School movement. "Against the dogmas of conventional education," continues Avrich, "Ferrer set a system based on reason, science and observation."[1]

The anarchist community readily embraced the anti-authoritarian concept of the Modern School. A Francisco Ferrer Association immediately formed, prospering over the next five years, while several schools based on the Modern School concept sprang up in the years following his death. Voltairine participated in this activity, giving speeches and briefly teaching at the Chicago Modern School. Since she shared with Ferrer a hatred of the Catholic Church and its authoritarian methods, Voltairine's initial positive reaction to Ferrer's ideas was understandable. In fact, at one of the most successful of the Modern Schools, the Stelton Colony in New Jersey, the main thoroughfare was called Voltairine de Cleyre Street.

She had already expressed her concern with encouraging children to think for themselves in her earlier writings on education, including the essay, for example, "Secular Education," found elsewhere in this volume. Nonetheless, she was later to become disillusioned with the American Modern Schools, considering them to offer "[T]oo much liberty and too little orderly work." Avrich, however, suspects that her own ill health and returning malaise may have contributed to her disenchantment.

The lessons of the Modern School and the ideas promulgated by Voltairine in her writings such as "Modern Educational Reform," are, sadly, no less relevant today than in her time. Though public education is not as overtly rigid now, beneath the veneer of modernity, it is still easy to find in many schools the lurking desire to teach children to be good little boys and girls who docilely obey and become "good citizens." The idea of children thinking for themselves is, in spite of occasionally fancy words to the contrary, scarcely found in the average grade and high school curriculum. By the time many students get to college and encounter critical thinking courses or the occasional class where they are actually required to think instead of learn by rote memory, they have been cognitively crippled. Though Voltairine's essay is nearly a hundred years old, it is still strikingly radical and ahead of its time, with valuable lessons to teach and inspire educators.

—Crispin Sartwell and Sharon Presley

Notes

1. Paul Avrich. *The Modern School Movement: Anarchism and Education in the United States.* Princeton, NJ: Princeton University Press, 1980, p. 20.

Modern Educational Reform

A defense of freedom in education, "Modern Educational Reform" is almost as relevant now as it was when it was delivered as a lecture on a tour of upstate New York in October 1910. It urges respect for children as free people, for allowing them to shape their own education, and for making that education humane and practical.

Francisco Ferrer was imprisoned after one of his former followers was arrested in a plot to assassinate the Royal Family of Spain in 1906. In the aftermath of disturbances in 1909, Ferrer was again arrested, then executed ("the world-shocking execution of a great educator").

Luther Burbank (1849–1926) was an eminent American horticulturalist.

Modern Educational Reform

Questions of genuine importance to large masses of people, are not posed by a single questioner, nor even by a limited number. They are put with more or less precision, with more or less consciousness of their scope and demand by all classes involved. This is a fair test of its being a genuine question, rather than a temporary fad. Such is the test we are to apply to the present inquiry, What is wrong with our present method of Child Education? What is to be done in the way of altering or abolishing it?

The posing of the question acquired a sudden prominence, through the world-shocking execution of a great educator for alleged complicity in the revolutionary events of Spain during the Moroccan war. People were not satisfied with the Spanish government's declarations as to this official murder; they were not convinced that they were being told the truth. They inquired why the Government should be so anxious for that man's death. And they learned that as a teacher he had founded schools wherein ideas hostile to governmental programs for learning, were put in practice. And they have gone on asking to know what these ideas were, how they were taught, and how can those same ideas be applied to the practical questions of education confronting them in the persons of their own children.

But it would be a very great mistake to suppose that the question was raised out of nothingness, or out of the brilliancy of his own mind, by Francisco Ferrer. If it were, if he were the creator of the question instead of the response to it, his martyr's death could have given it but an ephemeral prominence which would speedily have subsided.

On the contrary, the inquiry stimulated by that tragic death was but the first loud articulation of what has been asked in thousands of school-rooms, millions of homes, all over the civilized world. It has been put, by each of the three classes concerned, each in its own peculiar way, from its own peculiar viewpoint,—by the Educator, by the Parent, and by the Child itself.

There is a fourth personage who has had a great deal to say, and still has; but to my mind he is a pseudo-factor, to be eliminated as speedily as possible. I mean the "Statesman." He considers himself profoundly important, as representing the interests of society in general. He is anxious for the formation of good citizens to support the State, and directs education in such channels as he thinks will produce these.

I prefer to leave the discussion of his peculiar functions for a later part of this address, here observing only that if he is a legitimate factor, if by chance he is a genuine educator strayed into statesmanship, *as* a statesman he is interested only from a secondary motive; i.e., he is not interested in the actual work of schools, in the children as persons, but in the producing of a certain type of character to serve certain subsequent ends.

The criticism offered by the child itself upon the prevailing system of instruction, is the most simple,—direct; and at the same time, the critic is utterly unconscious of its force. Who has not heard a child say, in that fretted whine characteristic of a creature who knows its protest will be ineffective: "But what do I have to learn that for?"—"Oh, I don't see what I have to know that for; I can't remember it anyway." "I hate to go to school; I'd just as lief take a whipping!" "My teacher's a mean old thing; she expects you to sit quiet the whole morning, and if you just make the least little noise, she keeps you in at recess. Why do we have to keep still so long? What good does it do?"

I remember well the remark made to me once by one of my teachers— and a very good teacher, too, who nevertheless did not see what her own observation ought to have suggested. "School-children," she said, "regard teachers as their natural enemies." The thought which it would have been logical to suppose would have followed this observation is, that if children in general are possessed of that notion, it is because there is a great deal in the teacher's treatment of them which runs counter to the child's nature: that possibly this is so, not because of natural cussedness on the part of the child, but because of inapplicability of the knowledge taught, or the manner of teaching it, or both, to the mental and physical needs of the child. I am quite sure no such thought entered my teacher's mind,—at least regarding the system of knowledge to be imposed; being a sensible woman, she perhaps occasionally admitted to herself that she might make mistakes in applying the rules, but that the body of knowledge to be taught was indispensable, and must somehow be injected into children's heads, under threat of punishment, if necessary, I am sure she never questioned. It did not occur to her any more than to most teachers, that the first business of an educator should be to find out what are the needs, aptitudes, and tendencies of children, before he or she attempts to outline a body of knowledge to be taught, or rules for teaching it. It does not occur to them that the child's question, "What do I have to learn that for?" is a perfectly legitimate question; and if the teacher cannot answer it to the child's satisfaction, something is wrong either with the thing taught, or with the teaching; either the thing taught is out of rapport with the child's age, or his natural tendencies, or his condition of development; or the method by which it is taught repels him, disgusts him, or at best fails to interest him.

When a child says, "I don't see why I have to know that; I can't remember it anyway," he is voicing a very reasonable protest. Of course, there are plenty of instances of willful shirking, where a little effort can overcome the slackness of memory; but every teacher who is honest enough to reckon with himself knows he cannot give a sensible reason why things are to be taught which have so little to do with the child's life that to-morrow, or the day after examination, they will be forgotten; things which he himself could not remember were he not repeating them year in and year out, as a matter of his trade. And every teacher who has thought at all for himself about the essential nature of the young humanity he is dealing with, knows that six hours of daily herding and in-penning of young, active bodies and limbs, accompanied by the additional injunction that no feet are to be shuffled, no whispers exchanged, and no paper wads thrown, is a frightful violation of all the laws of young life. Any gardener who should attempt to raise healthy, beautiful, and fruitful plants by outraging all those plants' instinctive wants and searchings, would meet as his reward—sickly plants, ugly plants, sterile plants, dead plants. He will not do it; he will watch very carefully to see whether they like much sunlight, or considerable shade, whether they thrive on much water or get drowned in it, whether they like sandy soil, or fat mucky soil; the plant itself will indicate to him when he is doing the right thing. And every gardener will watch for indications with great anxiety. If he finds the plant revolts against his experiments, he will desist at once, and try something else; if he finds it thrives, he will emphasize the particular treatment so long as it seems beneficial. But what he will surely not do, will be to prepare a certain area of ground all just alike, with equal chances of sun and amount of moisture in every part, and then plant everything together without discrimination,—mighty close together!—saying beforehand, "If plants don't want to thrive on this, they ought to want to; and if they are stubborn about it, they must be made to."

Or if a raiser of animals were to start in feeding them on a regimen adapted not to their tastes but to his; if he were to insist on stuffing the young ones with food only fitted for the older ones; if he were to shut them up and compel them somehow to be silent, stiff, and motionless for hours together,—he would—well, he would very likely be arrested for cruelty to animals.

Of course there is this difference between the grower of plants or animals and the grower of children; the former is dealing with his subject as a superior power with a force which will always remain subject to his, while the latter is dealing with a force which is bound to become his equal, and taking it in the long and large sense, bound ultimately to supersede him.

The fear of "the footfalls of the young generation" is in his ears, whether he is aware of it or not, and he instinctively does what every living thing seeks to do; viz., to preserve his power. Since he cannot remain forever the superior, the dictator, he endeavors to put a definite mould upon that power which he must share—to have the child learn what he has learned, *as* he has learned it, and to the same end that he has learned it.

The grower of flowers, or fruits, or vegetables, or the raiser of animals, secure in his forever indisputable superiority, has nothing to fear when he inquires into the ways of his subjects; he will never think: "But if I heed such and such manifestation of the flower's or the animal's desire or repulsion, it will develop certain tendencies as a result, which will eventually overturn me and mine, and all that I believe in and labor to preserve." The grower of children is perpetually beset by this fear. He must not listen to a child's complaint against the school: it breaks down the mutual relation of authority and obedience; it destroys the faith of the child that his olders know better than he; it sets up little centers of future rebellion in the brain of every child affected by the example. No: complaint as to the wisdom of the system must be discouraged, ignored, frowned down, crushed by superior dignity; if necessary, punished. The very best answer a child ever gets to its legitimate inquiry, "Why do I have to learn such and such a thing?" is, "Wait till you get older, and you will understand it all. Just now you are a little too young to understand the reasons."—(In ninety-nine cases out of a hundred the answerer got the same reply to his own question twenty years before; and he has never found out since, either). "Do as we tell you to, now," say the teachers, "and be sure that we are instructing you for your good. The explanations will become clear to you some time." And the child smothers his complaint, cramps his poor little body to the best of his ability, and continues to repeat definitions which mean nothing to him but strings of long words, and rules which to him are simply torture—apparatus invented by his "natural enemies" to plague children.—I recall quite distinctly the bitter resentment I felt toward the inverted divisor. The formula was easy enough to remember: "Invert the terms of the divisor and proceed as in multiplication of fractions." I memorized it in less than a minute, and followed the prescription, and got my examples, correct. But Oh, how, how was the miracle accomplished? Why should a fraction be made to stand on its head? and how did that change a division suddenly into a multiplication?"—And I never found out till I undertook to teach some one else, years afterward. Yet the thing could have been made plain then; perhaps would have been, but for the fact that as a respectful pupil I was so trained to think that my teachers' methods must not be questioned or their explanations reflected upon, that I sat mute, mystified, puzzled, and silently indignant. In the end I swallowed it as I did a lot of other "pre-digested" knowledge (?) and consented to use its miraculous nature, very much as my Christian friends use the body and blood of Christ to "wash their sins away" without very well understanding the modus operandi.

Another advantage which the botanical or zoölogical cultivator has over the child-grower, by which incidentally the plants and animals profit, is that since he is not seeking to produce a universal type, but rather to develop as many new and interesting types as he can, he is very studious to notice the inclinations of his subjects, observing possible beginnings of differentiation, and adapting his treatment to the development of such beginnings. Of course he also does what no child-cultivator could possibly do,—he ruthlessly destroys weaklings; and as the superior intermeddling divinity, he fosters those special types which are more serviceable to himself, irrespective of whether they are more serviceable to plant or animal life apart from man.

But is the fact that children are of the same race as ourselves, the fact that their development should be regarded from the point of how best shall they serve themselves, their own race and generation, not that of a discriminating overlord, assuming the power of life and death over them,—a reason for us to disregard their tendencies, aptitudes, likes and dislikes, altogether?—a reason for us to treat their natural manifestations of non-adaptation to our methods of treatment with less consideration than we give to a fern or a hare? I should, on the contrary, suppose it was a reason to consider them all the more.

I think the difficulty lies in the immeasurable vanity of the human adult, particularly the pedagogical adult, (I presume I may say it with less offense since I am a teacher myself), which does not permit him to recognize as good any tendency in children to fly in the face of his conceptions of a correct human being; to recognize that may be here is something highly desirable, to be encouraged, rather than destroyed as pernicious. A flower-gardener doesn't expect to make another voter or householder out of his fern, so he lets it show what it wants to be, without being at all horrified at anything it does; but your teacher has usually well-defined conceptions of what men and women have to be. And if a boy is too lively, too noisy, too restless, too curious, to suit the concept, he must be trimmed and subdued. And if he is lazy, he has to be spurred with all sorts of whips, which are offensive both to the handler and the handled. The weapons of shaming and arousing the spirit of rivalry are two which are much used,— the former with sometimes fatal results, as in the case of the nine year old boy who recently committed suicide because his teacher drew attention to his torn coat, or young girls who have worried themselves into fevers from a scornful word respecting their failures in scholarship, and arousing rivalry brings an evil train behind it of spites and jealousies. I do not say, as some enthusiasts do, "there are no bad children," or "there are no lazy children"; but I am quite sure that both badness and laziness often result from lack of understanding and lack of adaptation; and that these can only be attained by teachers comprehending that they must seek to understand as well as to be understood. Badness is sometimes only dammed up energy, which can no more help flooding over than dammed up water. Laziness is often the result of forcing a child to a task for which it has no natural liking, while it would be energetic enough, given the thing it liked to do.

At any rate, it is worth while to try to find out what is the matter, in the spirit of a searcher after truth. Which is the first point I want to establish: That the general complaints of children are true criticisms of the school system; and Superintendents of Public Instruction, Boards of Education, and Teachers have as their first duty to heed and consider these complaints.

Let us now consider the complaints of parents. It must be admitted that the parents of young children, particularly their mothers, and especially these latter when they are the wives of workingmen with good-sized families, regard the school rather as a convenience for getting rid of the children during a certain period of the day than anything else. They are not to be blamed for this. They have obeyed the imperative mandate of nature in having families, with no very adequate conception of what they were doing; they find themselves burdened with responsibilities often greatly beyond their capacity. They have all they can do, sometimes more than they can do, to manage the financial end of things, to see to their children's material wants and to get through the work of a house; very often they are themselves deficient in even the elementary knowledge of the schools; they feel that their children need to know a great deal that they have never known, but they are utterly without the ability to say whether what they learn is useful and important or not. With the helplessness of ignorance towards wisdom, they receive the system provided by the State on trust, presuming it is good; and with the pardonable relief of busy and overburdened people, they look at the clock as school hour approaches, and breathe a sigh of relief when the last child is out of the house. They would be shocked at the idea that they regard their children as nuisances; they would vigorously defend themselves by saying that they feel that the children are in better hands than their own, safe and well treated. But before long even these ignorant ones observe that their children have learned a number of things which are not good. They have mixed with a crowd of others, and somewhere among them they have learned bad language, bad ideas, and bad habits. These are complaints which may be heard from intelligent, educated, and conservative parents also,—parents who may be presumed to be satisfied with the spirit and general purpose of the knowledge imparted in the class-room. Also the children suffer in health through their schools; and later on, when the cramming and crowding of their brains goes on in earnest, as it does in the higher grades, and particularly the High Schools, Oh then springs up a terrible crop of headache, nervous prostration, hysterics, over-delicacy, anaemia, heart-palpitation (especially among the girls), and a harvest of other physical disorders which were very probably planted back in the primary departments, and fostered in the higher rooms. The students are so overtrained that they often "become good for nothing in the house," the parents say, and too late the mothers discover that they themselves become servants to the whimsical little ladies and gentlemen they have raised up, who are more interested in text-books than in practical household matters.

Such are the ordinary complaints heard on every side, uttered by those who really have no fault to find with the substance of the instruction itself,—some because they do not know, and some because it fairly represents their own ideas.

The complaint becomes much more vital and definite when it proceeds from a parent who is an informed person, with a conception of life at variance with that commonly accepted. I will instance that of a Philadelphia physician, who recently said to me: "In my opinion many of the most horrid effects of malformations which I have to deal with, are the results of the long hours of sitting imposed on children in the schools. It is impossible for a healthy active creature to sit stiffly straight so many hours; no one can do it. They will inevitably twist and squirm themselves down into one position or another which throws the internal organs out of position, and which by iteration and reiteration results in a continuously accentuating deformity. Motherhood often becomes extremely painful and dangerous through the narrowing of the pelvis produced in early years of so much uncomfortable sitting. I believe that the sort of schooling which necessitates it should not begin till a child is fourteen years of age."

He added also that the substance of our education should be such as would fit the person for the conditions and responsibilities he or she may reasonably be expected to encounter in life. Since the majority of boys and girls will most likely become fathers and mothers in the future, why does not our system of education take account of it, and instruct the children not in the Latin names of bones and muscles so much, as in the practical functioning and hygiene of the body? Every teacher knows, and most of our parents know, that no subject is more carefully ignored by our text-books on physiology than the reproductive system.

A like book on zoölogy has far more to say about the reproduction of animals than is thought fit to be said by human beings to human beings about themselves. And yet upon such ignorance often depends the ruin of lives. Such is the criticism of an intelligent physician, himself the father of five children. It is a typical complaint of those who have to deal with the physical results of our school system.

A still more forcible complaint is rising up from a class of parents who object not only negatively, but positively, to the instruction of the schools. These are saying: I do not want to have my children taught things which are positively untrue, nor truths which have been distorted to fit some one's political or religious conception. I do not want any sort of religion or politics to be put into his head. I want the accepted facts of natural science and discovery to be taught him, in so far as they are within the grasp of his intellect. I do not want them colored with the prejudice of any system. I want a school system which will be suited to his physical well-being. I want what he learns to become his, by virtue of its appealing to his taste, his aptitude for experiment and proof; I do not want it to be a foreign stream pouring over his lips like a brook over its bed, leaving nothing behind. I do not want him to be tortured with formal examinations, nor worried by credit marks with averages and per cents and tenths of per cents, which haunt him waking and sleeping, as if they were the object of his efforts. And more than that, and above all, I do not want him made an automaton. I do not want him to become abjectly obedient. I do not want his free initiative destroyed. I want him, by virtue of his education, to be well-equipped bodily and mentally to face life and its problems.

This is my second point: That parents, conservatives and radicals, criticise the school

1st, As the producer of unhealthy bodies;

2d, As teaching matter inappropriate to life; or rather, perhaps, as not teaching what is appropriate to life;

3d, As perverting truth to serve a political and religious system; and as putting an iron mould upon the will of youth, destroying all spontaneity and freedom of expression.

The third critic is the teacher. Owing to his peculiarly dependent position, it is very, very seldom that any really vital criticism comes out of the mouth of an ordinary employé in the public school service: first, if he has any subversive ideas, he dares not voice them for fear of his job; second, it is extremely unlikely that any one with subversive ideas either will apply for the job, or having applied, will get it; and third, if through some fortuitous combination of circumstances, a rebellious personage has smuggled himself into the camp, with the naive notion that he is going to work reforms in the system, he finds before long that the system is rather remoulding him; he falls into the routine prescribed, and before long ceases to struggle against it.

Still, however conservative and system-logged teachers may be, they will all agree upon one criticism; viz., that they have too much to do; that it is utterly impossible for them to do justice to every pupil; that with from thirty to fifty pupils all depending upon one teacher for instruction, it is out of the question to give any single one sufficient attention, to say nothing of any special attention which his peculiar backwardness might require. He could do so only at the expense of injustice to the rest.

And, indeed, the best teacher in the world could not attend properly to the mental needs of fifty children, nor even of thirty. Furthermore, this overcrowding makes necessary the stiff regulation, the formal discipline, in the maintenance of which so much of the teacher's energy is wasted. The everlasting roll-call, the record of tardiness and absence, the eye forever on the watch to see who is whispering, the ear forever on the alert to catch the scraper of feet, the mischievous disturber, the irrepressible noisemaker; with such a divided and subdivided attention, how is it possible to teach?

Here and there we find a teacher with original ideas, not of subjects to be taught, but of the means of teaching. Sometimes there is one who inwardly revolts at what he has to teach, and takes such means as he can to counteract the glorifications of political aggrandizement, with which our geographies and histories are redolent.

In general, however, public school teachers, like government clerks, believe very much in the system whereby they live.

What they do find fault with, and what they have very much reason to find fault with, is not the school system, but the counteracting influences of bad homes. Teachers are often heard to say that they think they could do far better with the children, if they had entire control of them, or, as they more commonly express themselves, "if only their parents had some common sense!" Lessons of order, neatness, cleanliness, and hygiene, are often entirely thrown away, because the children regard them as statements to be memorized, not things to be practised. Those children whose mothers know nothing of ventilation, the necessity for exercise, the chemistry of food, and the functioning of the organs of the body, will forget instructions because they are never made part of their lives. (Which criticism is a sort of confirmation of that sage observation: "If you want to reform a man, begin with his grandmother.")

So much for criticism.

What, now, can we offer in the way of suggestions for reform? Speaking abstractly, I should say that the purpose of education should be to furnish a child with such fundamental knowledge and habits as will preserve and strengthen his body, and make him a self-reliant social being, having an all-around acquaintance with the life which is to surround him and an adaptability to circumstances which will render him able to meet varying conditions.

But we are immediately confronted by certain practical queries, when we attempt to conceive such a school system.

The fact is that the training of the body should be begun in very early childhood; and can never be rightly done in a city. No other animal than man ever conceived such a frightful apparatus for depriving its young of the primary rights of physical existence as the human city. The mass of our city children know very little of nature. What they have learned of it through occasional picnics, excursions, visits in the country, etc., they have learned as a foreign thing, having little relation to themselves; their "natural" habitat is one of lifeless brick and mortar, wire and iron, poles, pavements, and noise. Yet all this ought to be utterly foreign to children. *This* ought to be the thing visited once in a while, not lived in.

There is no pure air in a city; it is *all* poisoned. Yet the first necessity of lunged animals—especially little ones—is pure air. Moreover, every child ought to know the names and ways of life of the things it eats; how to grow them, etc. How are gardens possible in a city? Every child should know trees, not as things he has read about, but as familiar presences in his life, which he recognizes as quickly as his eyes greet them. He should know his oneness with nature, not through the medium of a theory, but through feeling it daily and hourly. He should know the birds by their songs, and by the quick glimpse of them among the foliage; the insect in its home, the wild flower on its stalk, the fruit where it hangs. Can this be done in a city?

It is the city that is wrong, and its creations can never be right; they may be improved; they can never be what they should.

Let me quote Luther Burbank here: he expressed so well, and just in the tumultuous disorder and un-coordination dear to a child's soul, the early rights of children. "Every child should have mud-pies, grasshoppers, water-bugs, tadpoles, frogs, mud-turtles, elderberries, wild strawberries, acorns, chestnuts, trees to climb, brooks to wade in, water-lilies, woodchucks, bats, bees, butterflies, various animals to pet, hay-fields, pine-cones, rocks to roll, sand, snakes, huckleberries, and hornets; and any child who has been deprived of these has been deprived of the best part of his education." He is of opinion that until ten years of age, these things should be the real educators of children,—not books. I agree with him. But neither city homes nor city schools can give children these things. Furthermore, I believe that education should be integral; that the true school must combine physical and intellectual education from the beginning to the end. But I am confronted by the fact that this is impossible to the mass of the people, because of the economic condition in which we are all floundering.

What is possible can be only a compromise. Physical education will go on in the home principally, and intellectual education in the school. Something might be done to organize the teaching of parents; lectures and demonstrations at the public schools might be given weekly, in the evenings, for parents, by competent nurses or hygienists. But they would remain largely ineffective. Until the whole atrocious system of herding working people in close-built cities, by way of making them serviceable cogwheels in the capitalistic machine for grinding out rent and profit, comes to an end, the physical education of children will remain at best a pathetic compromise.

We have left to consider what may be done in the way of improving intellectual education. What is really necessary for a child to know which he is not taught now? and what is taught that is unnecessary?

As to reading and writing there is no dispute, though there is much dispute about the way of doing it. But beyond that children should know— *things*; from their earlier school days they should know the geography of their own locality, not rehearsing it from a book, but by going over the ground, having the relations of places explained to them, and by being shown how to model relief maps themselves. They should know the indications of the weather, being taught the use of instruments for measuring air-pressures, temperatures, amount of sunshine, etc.; they should know the special geology of their own locality, the nature of the soil and its products, through practical exhibition; they should be allowed to construct, from clay, stone, or brick, such little buildings as they usually like to make, and from them the simple principles of geometry taught. You see, every school needs a big yard, and play-rooms with tools in them,—the use of which tools they should be taught.

Arithmetic, to be sure, they need to know—but arithmetic connected with things. Let them learn fractions by cutting up things and putting them together, and not be bothered by abstractions running into the hundreds of thousands, the millions, which never in time will they use. And drop all that tiresome years' work in interest and per cent; if decimals are understood, every one who has need will be amply able to work out systems of interest when necessary.

Children should know the industrial life through which they live, into which they are probably going. They should see how cloth is woven, thread is spun, shoes are made, iron forged and wrought; again not alone by written description, but by eye-witness. They should, as they grow older, learn the history of the arts of peace.

What they do not need to know, is so much of the details of the history of destruction; the general facts and results of wars are sufficient. They do not need to be impressed with the details of killings, which they sensibly forget, and inevitably also.

Moreover, the revolting patriotism which is being inculcated, whereby children learn to be proud of their country, not for its contributions to the general enlightenment of humanity, but for its crimes against humanity; whereby they are taught to consider themselves, their country, their flag, their institutions, as things to be upheld and maintained, right or wrong; whereby the stupid and criminal life of the soldier is exalted as honorable, should be wholly omitted from the educational system.

However, it is utterly impossible to expect that it will be, by anything short of general public sentiment against it; and at present such sentiment is for it. I have alluded before to the function of the statesman in directing education. So long as schools are maintained by governments, the Statesman, not the true educator, will determine what sort of history is to be taught; and it will be what it is now, only continually growing worse. Political institutions must justify themselves to the young generation. They begin by training childish minds to believe that what they do is to be accepted, not criticised. A history becomes little better than a catechism of patriotic formulas in glorification of the State.

Now there is no way of escaping this, for those who disapprove it, short of eliminating the statesman, establishing voluntarily supported schools, wherein wholly different notions shall be taught; in which the spirit of teaching history shall be one of honest statement and fearless criticism; wherein the true image of war and the army and all that it means shall be honestly given.

The really Ideal School, which would not be a compromise, would be a boarding school built in the country, having a farm attached, and workshops where useful crafts might be learned, in daily connection with intellectual training. It presupposes teachers able to train little children to habits of health, order, and neatness, in the utmost detail, and yet not tyrants or rigid disciplinarians. In free contact with nature, the children would learn to use their limbs as nature meant, feel their intimate relationship with the growing life of other sorts, form a profound respect for work and an estimate of the value of it; wish to become real doers in the world, and not mere gatherers in of other men's products; and with the respect for work, the appreciation of work, the desire to work, will come the pride of the true workman who will know how to maintain his dignity and the dignity of what he does.

At present the major portion of our working people are sorry they are working people (as they have good reason to be). They take little joy or pride in what they do; they consider themselves as less gifted and less valuable persons in society than those who have amassed wealth and, by virtue of that amassment, live upon their employees; or those who by attaining book knowledge have gotten out of the field of manual production, and lead an easier life. They educate their children in the hope that these, at least, may attain that easier existence, without work, which has been beyond them. Even when such parents themselves have dreams of a reorganization of society, wherein all shall labor and all have leisure due, they impress upon the children that no one should be a common workingman if he can help it. Workingmen are slaves, and it is not well to be a slave.

Our radicals fail to realize that to accomplish the reorganization of work, it is necessary to have *workers*,—and workers with the free spirit, the rebellious spirit, which will consider its own worth and refuse to accept the slavish conditions of capitalism. These must be bred in schools where work is done, and done proudly, and in full consciousness of its value; where the dubious services of the capitalist will likewise be rated at their true worth; and no man reckoned as above another, unless he has done a greater social service. Where political institutions and the politicians who operate them— judges, lawmakers, or executives—will be candidly criticised, and repudiated when justice dictates so, whether in the teaching of their past history, or their present actions in current events.

Whether the workers, upon whom so many drains are already made, will be able to establish and maintain such schools, is a question to be solved upon trial through their organizations.

The question is, Will you breed men for the service of the Cannon, to be aimed at you in the hour of Strikes and Revolts, men to uphold the machine which is crushing you, or will you train them in the knowledge of the true worth of Labor and a determination to reorganize it as it should be?

Part VII

Breaking the Chains

Changing Society through Direct Action

Introduction

In the late nineteenth and early twentieth centuries "direct action" was a euphemism for violence, and in particular assassination, as a mode of political agitation. Voltairine, following Tucker and others, had long considered herself a pacifist, but by 1910 at the latest, she had endorsed violent revolutionary action in some cases, and in particular, the anarchist revolutionaries of Mexico. However, she also insisted on a wider interpretation of the phrase, considering "direct" action any action outside mainstream electoral politics. In the initial essay of this section, for example, she discusses the underground railroad as an example of direct action. And even at her most radical, Voltairine carefully dissociated herself from what we would today call "terrorism," though for example in her discussion of the McKinley assassination she also implicitly defends Czolgosz by pointing to the conditions that lead to violence.

Nevertheless, Voltairine's endorsement of direct action would certainly have been read at the time as a radicalization of her position and also as a part of her continuing movement to the left. American individualist anarchism had typically tried to achieve its ends by peaceful secession. In fact, the American ur-Anarchist Josiah Warren (1798–1874) had participated in the founding of several utopian communities, as had his follower Stephen Pearl Andrews (1812–1886). Both explicitly repudiated violence as a means of achieving their goals. The communist anarchists of Europe, however, engaged in terrorism as well as more widespread and systematic forms of violent action as strategies of agitation. The great Russian anarchist Mikhail Bakunin (1814–1876), for example, seemingly formed a secret violent cell every few weeks, and indeed seemed at times more enthusiastic about conspiracy than violence itself. According to Christine Stansell, the Greenwich Village raconteur Mabel Dodge said of Emma Goldman and her friends: "I felt they had Plans. ... I knew they continually plotted and planned and discussed times and places. Their obvious activity seems to be publishing the anarchist magazine *Mother Earth*, but beneath this there was a great busy humming complex of Planning; and many times they referred to the day when blood would flow in the streets of New York."[1] And of course Emma and her friend (and Voltairine's) Alexander Berkman actually did plot the shooting of Henry Clay Frick, so these "Plans" must be taken with some seriousness. Still, though, there is, as Dodge saw, something just a bit absurd about the whole scene. And also counter-productive: it is fair to say that anarchist participation in bombings and assassinations widely discredited the entire movement. There is no reason to think that Voltairine engaged in conspiracies of this kind, but also no reason to think that, by the end of her life, she would not have, if she had believed that such actions were likely to be effective.

—Crispin Sartwell

NOTES

1. Christine Stansell, *American Moderns: Bohemian New York and the Creation of a New Century* (New York: Henry Holt, 2000), p. 144.

Direct Action

This lecture, delivered in Chicago on 21 January 1912, and issued by *Mother Earth* as a pamphlet, was later translated into Yiddish. "Direct Action" is among Voltai's last works (she died on 20 June of that year), and expresses more clearly than any other text her late conversion to violent social change. She connects her own advocacy to the revolutionary heritage of America, including violent agitation for the abolition of slavery such as John Brown's. For Voltairine, "direct" is opposed to "political" action, and does not necessarily entail violence. Rather, direct action is action outside the political system.

"The McNamaras": James and John, brothers who confessed to bombing the *Los Angeles Times* building in 1910. *Times* publisher Harrison Gray Otis was anti-union. The McNamaras were defended by Clarence Darrow.

Bacon's Rebellion took place at Jamestown, Virginia in 1676, led by Nathaniel Bacon. The issues were taxes and defense against the Indians.

"Whittier" is James Greenleaf Whittier (1807–92), American poet and Quaker.

"The stars in their courses fought against Sisera" is a quotation from the biblical Book of Judges.

Gerrit Smith (1797–1874) was an abolitionist and financial supporter of John Brown. He was a friend of Frederick Douglass and a cousin of the feminist Elizabeth Cady Stanton.

"Wm. D. Haywood" is William Dudley ("Big Bill") Haywood (1869–1928), radical American labor leader who helped organize the Industrial Workers of the World.

Frank Bohn was a radical labor leader active in the Socialist Labor Party and the American Federation of Labor.

Oscar Ameringer was a labor organizer and member of the Knights of Labor, later a humorist.

"Madero" is Francisco Ignacio Madero (1873–1913), leader of Mexican resistance to despotic president Porfirio Diaz, who later distanced himself from more radical Mexican revolutionaries. Voltairine was very active late in her life supporting the Mexican Revolution.

"Briand" is Aristide Briand (1862–1932), a French moderate socialist politician and European unionist, winner of the 1926 Nobel Peace Prize.

Direct Action

From the standpoint of one who thinks himself capable of discerning an undeviating route for human progress to pursue, if it is to be progress at all, who, having such a route on his mind's map, has endeavored to point it out to others; to make them see it as he sees it; who in so doing has chosen what appeared to him clear and simple expressions to convey his thoughts to others,—to such a one it appears matter for regret and confusion of spirit that the phrase "Direct Action" has suddenly acquired in the general mind a circumscribed meaning, not at all implied in the words themselves, and certainly never attached to it by himself or his co-thinkers.

However, this is one of the common jests which Progress plays on those who think themselves able to set metes and bounds for it. Over and over again, names, phrases, mottoes, watchwords, have been turned inside out, and upside down, and hindside before, and sideways, by occurrences out of the control of those who used the expressions in their proper sense; and still, those who sturdily held their ground, and insisted on being heard, have in the end found that the period of misunderstanding and prejudice has been but the prelude to wider inquiry and understanding.

I rather think this will be the case with the present misconception of the term Direct Action, which through the misapprehension, or else the deliberate misrepresentation, of certain journalists in Los Angeles, at the time the McNamaras pleaded guilty, suddenly acquired in the popular mind the interpretation, "Forcible Attacks on Life and Property." This was either very ignorant or very dishonest of the journalists; but it has had the effect of making a good many people curious to know all about Direct Action.

As a matter of fact, those who are so lustily and so inordinately condemning it, will find on examination that they themselves have on many occasion practised direct action, and will do so again.

Every person who ever thought he had a right to assert, and went boldly and asserted it, himself, or jointly with others that shared his convictions, was a direct actionist. Some thirty years ago I recall that the Salvation Army was vigorously practising direct action in the maintenance of the freedom of its members to speak, assemble, and pray. Over and over they were arrested, fined, and imprisoned; but they kept right on singing, praying, and marching, till they finally compelled their persecutors to let them alone. The Industrial Workers are now conducting the same fight, and have, in a number of cases, compelled the officials to let them alone by the same direct tactics. Every person who ever had a plan to do anything, and went and did it, or who laid his plan before others, and won their co-operation to do it with him, without going to external authorities to please do the thing for them, was a direct actionist. All co-operative experiments are essentially direct action.

Every person who ever in his life had a difference with anyone to settle, and went straight to the other persons involved to settle it, either by a peaceable plan or otherwise, was a direct actionist. Examples of such action are strikes and boycotts; many persons will recall the action of the housewives of New York who boycotted the butchers, and lowered the price of meat; at the present moment a butter boycott seems looming up, as a direct reply to the price-makers for butter.

These actions are generally not due to any one's reasoning overmuch on the respective merits of directness or indirectness, but are the spontaneous retorts of those who feel oppressed by a situation. In other words, all people are, most of the time, believers in the principle of direct action, and practicers of it. However, most people are also indirect or political actionists. And they are both these things at the same time, without making much of an analysis of either. There are only a limited number of persons who eschew political action under any and all circumstances; but there is nobody, nobody at all, who has ever been so "impossible" as to eschew direct action altogether. The majority of thinking people are really opportunist, leaning, some perhaps more to directness, some more to indirectness as a general thing, but ready to use either means when opportunity calls for it. That is to say, there are those who hold that balloting governors into power is essentially a wrong and foolish thing; but who nevertheless under stress of special circumstances, might consider it the wisest thing to do, to vote some individual into office at that particular time. Or there are those who believe that in general the wisest way for people to get what they want is by the indirect method of voting into power some one who will make what they want legal; yet who all the same will occasionally under exceptional conditions advise a strike; and a strike, as I have said, is direct action. Or they may do as the Socialist Party agitators (who are mostly declaiming now against direct action) did last summer, when the police were holding up their meetings. They went in force to the meeting-places, prepared to speak whether-or-no, and they made the police back down. And while that was not logical on their part, thus to oppose the legal executors of the majority's will, it was a fine, successful piece of direct action.

Those who, by the essence of their belief, are committed to Direct Action only are—just who? Why, the non-resistants; precisely those who do not believe in violence at all! Now do not make the mistake of inferring that I say direct action means non-resistance; not by any means. Direct action may be the extreme of violence, or it may be as peaceful as the waters of the Brook of Siloa that go softly. What I say is, that the real non-resistants can believe in direct action only, never in political action. For the basis of all political action is coercion; even when the State does good things, it finally rests on a club, a gun, or a prison, for its power to carry them through.

Now every school child in the United States has had the direct action of certain non-resistants brought to his notice by his school history. The case which everyone instantly recalls is that of the early Quakers who came to Massachusetts. The Puritans had accused the Quakers of "troubling the world by preaching peace to it." They refused to pay church taxes; they refused to bear arms; they refused to swear allegiance to any government. (In so doing they were direct actionists, what we may call negative direct actionists.) So the Puritans, being political actionists, passed laws to keep them out, to deport, to fine, to imprison, to mutilate, and finally, to hang them. And the Quakers just kept on coming (which was positive direct action); and history records that after the hanging of four Quakers, and the flogging of Margaret Brewster at the cart's tail through the streets of Boston, "the Puritans gave up trying to silence the new missionaries"; that "Quaker persistence and Quaker non-resistance had won the day."

Another example of direct action in early colonial history, but this time by no means of the peaceable sort, was the affair known as Bacon's Rebellion. All our historians certainly defend the action of the rebels in that matter, for they were right. And yet it was a case of violent direct action against lawfully constituted authority. For the benefit of those who have forgotten the details, let me briefly remind them that the Virginia planters were in fear of a general attack by the Indians; with reason. Being political actionists, they asked, or Bacon as their leader asked, that the governor grant him a commission to raise volunteers in their own defense. The governor feared that such a company of armed men would be a threat to him; also with reason. He refused the commission. Whereupon the planters resorted to direct action. They raised volunteers without the commission, and successfully fought off the Indians. Bacon was pronounced a traitor by the governor; but the people being with him, the governor was afraid to proceed against him. In the end, however, it came so far that the rebels burned Jamestown; and but for the untimely death of Bacon, much more might have been done. Of course the reaction was very dreadful, as it usually is where a rebellion collapses or is crushed. Yet even during the brief period of success, it had corrected a good many abuses. I am quite sure that the political-action-at-all-costs advocates of those times, after the reaction came back into power, must have said: "See to what evils direct action brings us! Behold, the progress of the colony has been set back twenty-five years;" forgetting that if the colonists had not resorted to direct action, their scalps would have been taken by the Indians a year sooner, instead of a number of them being hanged by the governor a year later.

In the period of agitation and excitement preceding the revolution, there were all sorts and kinds of direct action from the most peaceable to the most violent; and I believe that almost everybody who studies United States history finds the account of these performances the most interesting part of the story, the part which dents into the memory most easily.

Among the peaceable moves made, were the non-importation agreements, the leagues for wearing homespun clothing and the "committees of correspondence." As the inevitable growth of hostility progressed, violent direct action developed; e.g., in the matter of destroying the revenue stamps, or the action concerning the tea-ships, either by not permitting the tea to be landed, or by putting it in damp storage, or by throwing it into the harbor, as in Boston, or by compelling a tea-ship owner to set fire to his own ship, as at Annapolis. These are all actions which our commonest textbooks record, certainly not in a condemnatory way, not even in an apologetic way, though they are all cases of direct action against legally constituted authority and property rights. If I draw attention to them, and others of like nature, it is to prove to unreflecting repeaters of words that *direct action has always been used, and has the historical sanction of the very people now reprobating it.*

George Washington is said to have been the leader of the Virginia planters' non-importation league; he would now be "enjoined," probably by a court, from forming any such league; and if he persisted, he would be fined for contempt.

When the great quarrel between the North and the South was waxing hot and hotter, it was again direct action which preceded and precipitated political action. And I may remark here that political action is never taken, nor even contemplated, until slumbering minds have first been aroused by direct acts of protest against existing conditions.

The history of the anti-slavery movement and the Civil War is one of the greatest of paradoxes, although history is a chain of paradoxes. Politically speaking, it was the slave-holding States that stood for greater political freedom, for the autonomy of the single State against the interference of the United States; politically speaking, it was the non-slave-holding States that stood for a strong centralized government, which, Secessionists said and said truly, was bound progressively to develop into more and more tyrannical forms. Which happened. From the close of the Civil War on, there has been continual encroachment of the federal power upon what was formerly the concern of the States individually. The wage-slaves, in their struggles of today, are continually thrown into conflict with that centralized power against which the slave-holder protested (with liberty on his lips but tyranny in his heart). Ethically speaking, it was the non-slave-holding States that in a general way stood for greater human liberty, while the Secessionists stood for race-slavery. In a general way only; that is, the majority of northerners, not being accustomed to the actual presence of negro slavery about them, thought it was probably a mistake; yet they were in no great ferment of anxiety to have it abolished. The Abolitionists only, and they were relatively few, were the genuine ethicals, to whom slavery itself—not secession or union—was the main question. In fact, so paramount was it with them, that a considerable number of them were themselves for the dissolution of the union, advocating that the North take the initiative in the matter of dissolving, in order that the northern people might shake off the blame of holding negroes in chains.

Of course, there were all sorts of people with all sorts of temperaments among those who advocated the abolition of slavery. There were Quakers like Whittier (indeed it was the peace-at-all-costs Quakers who had advocated abolition even in early colonial days); there were moderate political actionists, who were for buying off the slaves, as the cheapest way; and there were extremely violent people, who believed and did all sorts of violent things.

As to what the politicians did, it is one long record of "how-not-to-do-it," a record of thirty years of compromising, and dickering, and trying to keep what was as it was, and to hand sops to both sides when new conditions demanded that something be done, or be pretended to be done. But "the stars in their courses fought against Sisera"; the system was breaking down from within, and the direct actionists from without as well were widening the cracks remorselessly.

Among the various expressions of direct rebellion was the organization of the "underground railroad." Most of the people who belonged to it believed in both sorts of action; but however much they theoretically subscribed to the right of the majority to enact and enforce laws, they didn't believe in it on that point. My grandfather was a member of the "underground;" many a fugitive slave he helped on his way to Canada. He was a very patient, law-abiding man in most respects, though I have often thought that he respected it because he didn't have much to do with it; always leading a pioneer life, law was generally far from him, and direct action imperative. Be that as it may, and law-respecting as he was, he had no respect whatever for slave laws, no matter if made by ten times of a majority; and he conscientiously broke every one that came in his way to be broken.

There were times when in the operation of the "underground" that violence was required, and was used. I recollect one old friend relating to me how she and her mother kept watch all night at the door, while a slave for whom a posse was searching hid in the cellar; and though they were of Quaker descent and sympathies, there was a shotgun on the table. Fortunately it did not have to be used that night.

When the fugitive slave law was passed with the help of the political actionists of the North who wanted to offer a new sop to the slave-holders, the direct actionists took to rescuing recaptured fugitives. There was the "rescue of Shadrach," and the "rescue of Jerry," the latter rescuers being led by the famous Gerrit Smith; and a good many more successful and unsuccessful attempts. Still the politicals kept on pottering and trying to smooth things over, and the Abolitionists were denounced and decried by the ultra-law-abiding pacificators, pretty much as Wm. D. Haywood and Frank Bohn are being denounced by their own party now.

The other day I read a communication in the Chicago *Daily Socialist* from the secretary of the Louisville local Socialist Party to the national secretary, requesting that some safe and sane speaker be substituted for Bohn, who had been announced to speak there. In explaining why, Mr. Dobbs makes this quotation from Bohn's lecture: "Had the McNamaras been successful in defending the interests of the working class, they would have been right, just as John Brown would have been right, had he been successful in freeing the slaves. Ignorance was the only crime of John Brown, and ignorance was the only crime of the McNamaras."

Upon this Mr. Dobbs comments as follows: "We dispute emphatically the statements here made. The attempt to draw a parallel between the open—if mistaken—revolt of John Brown on the one hand, and the secret and murderous methods of the McNamaras on the other, is not only indicative of shallow reasoning, but highly mischievous in the logical conclusions which may be drawn from such statements."

Evidently Mr. Dobbs is very ignorant of the life and work of John Brown. John Brown was a man of violence; he would have scorned anybody's attempt to make him out anything else. And once a person is a believer in violence, it is with him only a question of the most effective way of applying it, which can be determined only by a knowledge of conditions and means at his disposal. John Brown did not shrink at all from conspiratorial methods. Those who have read the autobiography of Frederick Douglass and the Reminiscences of Lucy Coleman, will recall that one of the plans laid by John Brown was to organize a chain of armed camps in the mountains of West Virginia, North Carolina, and Tennessee, send secret emissaries among the slaves inciting them to flee to these camps, and there concert such measures as times and conditions made possible for further arousing revolt among the negroes. That this plan failed was due to the weakness of the desire for liberty among the slaves themselves, more than anything else.

Later on, when the politicians in their infinite deviousness contrived a fresh proposition of how-not-to-do-it, known as the Kansas-Nebraska Act, which left the question of slavery to be determined by the settlers, the direct actionists on both sides sent bogus settlers into the territory, who proceeded to fight it out. The pro-slavery men, who got in first, made a constitution recognizing slavery and a law punishing with death any one who aided a slave to escape; but the Free Soilers, who were a little longer in arriving since they came from more distant States, made a second constitution, and refused to recognize the other party's laws at all. And John Brown was there, mixing in all the violence, conspiratorial or open; he was "a horse-thief and a murderer," in the eyes of decent, peaceable, political actionists. And there is no doubt that he stole horses, sending no notice in advance of his intention to steal them, and that he killed pro-slavery men. He struck and got away a good many times before his final attempt on Harper's Ferry. If he did not use dynamite, it was because dynamite had not yet appeared as a practical weapon. He made a great many more intentional attacks on life than the two brothers Secretary Dobbs condemns for their "murderous methods." And yet history has not failed to understand John Brown. Mankind knows that though he was a violent man, with human blood upon his hands, who was guilty of high treason and hanged for it, yet his soul was a great, strong, unselfish soul, unable to bear the frightful crime which kept 4,000,000 people like dumb beasts, and thought that making war against it was a sacred, a God-called duty, (for John Brown was a very religious man—a Presbyterian).

It is by and because of the direct acts of the forerunners of social change, whether they be of peaceful or warlike nature, that the Human Conscience, the conscience of the mass, becomes aroused to the need for change. It would be very stupid to say that no good results are ever brought about by political action; sometimes good things do come about that way. But never until individual rebellion, followed by mass rebellion, has forced it. Direct action is always the clamorer, the initiator, through which the great sum of indifferentists become aware that oppression is getting intolerable.

We have now an oppression in the land—and not only in this land, but throughout all those parts of the world which enjoy the very mixed blessings of Civilization. And just as in the question of chattel slavery, so this form of slavery has been begetting both direct action and political action. A certain percent of our population (probably a much smaller percent than politicians are in the habit of assigning at mass meetings) is producing the material wealth upon which all the rest of us live; just as it was 4,000,000 chattel Blacks who supported all the crowd of parasites above them. These are the *land workers* and the *industrial workers*.

Through the unprophesied and unprophesiable operation of institutions which no individual of us created, but found in existence when he came here, these workers, the most absolutely necessary part of the whole social structure, without whose services none can either eat, or clothe, or shelter himself, are just the ones who get the least to eat, to wear, and to be housed withal—to say nothing of their share of the other social benefits which the rest of us are supposed to furnish, such as education and artistic gratification.

These workers have, in one form or another, mutually joined their forces to see what betterment of their condition they could get; primarily by direct action, secondarily by political action. We have had the Grange, the Farmer's Alliance, Co-operative Associations, Colonization Experiments, Knights of Labor, Trade Unions, and Industrial Workers of the World. All of them have been organized for the purpose of wringing from the masters in the economic field a little better price, a little better conditions, a little shorter hours; or on the other hand to resist a reduction in price, worse conditions, or longer hours. None of them has attempted a final solution of the social war. None of them, except the Industrial Workers, has recognized that there is a social war, inevitable so long as present legal-social conditions endure. They accepted property institutions as they found them. They were made up of average men, with average desires, and they undertook to do what appeared to them possible and very reasonable things. They were not committed to any particular political policy when they were organized, but were associated for direct action of their own initiation, either positive or defensive.

Undoubtedly there were and are among all these organizations, members who looked beyond immediate demands; who did see that the continuous development of forces now in operation was bound to bring about conditions to which it is impossible that life continue to submit, and against which, therefore, it will protest, and violently protest; that it will have no choice but to do so; that it must do so or tamely die; and since it is not the nature of life to surrender without struggle, it will not tamely die. Twenty-two years ago I met Farmer's Alliance people who said so, Knights of Labor who said so, Trade Unionists who said so. They wanted larger aims than those to which their organizations were looking; but they had to accept their fellow members as they were, and try to stir them to work for such things as it was possible to make them see. And what they could see was better prices, better wages, less dangerous or tyrannical conditions, shorter hours. At the stage of development when these movements were initiated, the land workers could not see that their struggle had anything to do with the struggle of those engaged in the manufacturing or transporting service; nor could these latter see that theirs had anything to do with the movement of the farmers. For that matter very few of them see it yet. They have yet to learn that there is one common struggle against those who have appropriated the earth, the money, and the machines. Unfortunately the great organizations of the farmers frittered itself away in a stupid chase after political power. It was quite successful in getting the power in certain States; but the courts pronounced its laws unconstitutional, and there was the burial hole of all its political conquests. Its original program was to build its own elevators, and store the products therein, holding these from the market till they could escape the speculator. Also, to organize labor exchanges, issuing credit notes upon products deposited for exchange. Had it adhered to this program of direct mutual aid, it would, to some extent, for a time at least, have afforded an illustration of how mankind may free itself from the parasitism of the bankers and the middlemen. Of course, it would have been overthrown in the end, unless it had so revolutionized men's minds by the example as to force the overthrow of the legal monopoly of land and money; but at least it would have served a great educational purpose. As it was, it "went after the red herring" and disintegrated merely from its futility.

The Knights of Labor subsided into comparative insignificance, not because of failure to use direct action, nor because of its tampering with politics, which was small, but chiefly because it was a heterogenous mass of workers who could not associate their efforts effectively.

The Trade Unions grew strong as the Knights of Labor subsided, and have continued slowly but persistently to increase in power. It is true the increase has fluctuated; that there have been set-backs; that great single organizations have been formed and again dispersed. But on the whole trade unions have been a growing power. They have been so because, poor as they are, they have been a means whereby a certain section of the workers have been able to bring their united force to bear directly upon their masters, and so get for themselves some portion of what they wanted—of what their conditions dictated to them they must try to get. The strike is their natural weapon, that which they themselves have forged. It is the direct blow of the strike which nine times out of ten the boss is afraid of. (Of course there are occasions when he is glad of one, but that's unusual.) And the reason he dreads a strike is not so much because he thinks he cannot win out against it, but simply and solely because he does not want an interruption of his business. The ordinary boss isn't in much dread of a "class-conscious vote"; there are plenty of shops where you can talk Socialism or any other political program all day long; but if you begin to talk Unionism you may forthwith expect to be discharged or at best warned to shut up. Why? Not because the boss is so wise as to know that political action is a swamp in which the workingman gets mired, or because he understands that political Socialism is fast becoming a middle-class movement; not at all. He thinks Socialism is a very bad thing; but it's a good way off! But he knows that if his shop is unionized, he will have trouble right away.

His hands will be rebellious, he will be put to expense to improve his factory conditions, he will have to keep workingmen that he doesn't like, and in case of strike he may expect injury to his machinery or his buildings.

It is often said, and parrot-like repeated, that the bosses are "class-conscious," that they stick together for their class interest, and are willing to undergo any sort of personal loss rather than be false to those interests. It isn't so at all. The majority of business people are just like the majority of workingmen; they care a whole lot more about their individual loss or gain than about the gain or loss of their class. And it is his individual loss the boss sees, when threatened by a union.

Now everybody knows that a strike of any size means violence. No matter what any one's ethical preference for peace may be, he knows it will not be peaceful. If it's a telegraph strike, it means cutting wires and poles, and getting fake scabs in to spoil the instruments. If it is a steel rolling mill strike, it means beating up the scabs, breaking the windows, setting the gauges wrong, and ruining the expensive rollers together with tons and tons of material. If it's a miners' strike, it means destroying tracks and bridges, and blowing up mills. If it is a garment workers' strike, it means having an unaccountable fire, getting a volley of stones through an apparently inaccessible window, or possibly a brickbat on the manufacturer's own head. If it's a street-car strike, it means tracks torn up or barricaded with the contents of ash-carts and slop-carts, with overturned wagons or stolen fences, it means smashed or incinerated cars and turned switches. If it is a system federation strike, it means "dead" engines, wild engines, derailed freights, and stalled trains. If it is a building trades strike, it means dynamited structures. And always, everywhere, all the time, fights between strike-breakers and scabs against strikers and strike-sympathizers, between People and Police.

On the side of the bosses, it means search-lights, electric wires, stockades, bull-pens, detectives and provocative agents, violent kidnapping and deportation, and every device they can conceive for direct protection, besides the ultimate invocation of police, militia, State constabulary, and federal troops.

Everybody knows this; everybody smiles when union officials protest their organizations to be peaceable and law-abiding, because everybody knows they are lying. They know that violence is used, both secretly and openly; and they know it is used because the strikers cannot do any other way, without giving up the fight at once. Nor to they mistake those who thus resort to violence under stress for destructive miscreants who do what they do out of innate cussedness. The people in general understand that they do these things through the harsh logic of a situation which they did not create, but which forces them to these attacks in order to make good in their struggle to live or else go down the bottomless descent into poverty, that lets Death find them in the poorhouse hospital, the city street, or the river-slime. This is the awful alternative that the workers are facing; and this is what makes the most kindly disposed human beings—men who would go out of their way to help a wounded dog, or bring home a stray kitten and nurse it, or step aside to avoid walking on a worm—resort to violence against their fellow men. They know, for the facts have taught them, that this is the only way to win, if they can win at all. And it has always appeared to me one of the most utterly ludicrous, absolutely irrelevant things that a person can do or say, when approached for relief or assistance by a striker who is dealing with an immediate situation, to respond with "Vote yourself into power!" when the next election is six months, a year, or two years away.

Unfortunately the people who know best how violence is used in union warfare cannot come forward and say: "On such a day, at such a place, such and such specific action was done, and as a result such and such concession was made, or such and such boss capitulated." To do so would imperil their liberty and their power to go on fighting. Therefore those that know best must keep silent and sneer in their sleeves, while those that know little prate. Events, not tongues, must make their position clear.

And there has been a very great deal of prating these last few weeks. Speakers and writers, honestly convinced, I believe, that political action and political action only can win the workers' battle, have been denouncing what they are pleased to call "direct action" (what they really mean is conspiratorial violence) as the author of mischief incalculable. One Oscar Ameringer, as an example, recently said at a meeting in Chicago that the Haymarket bomb of '86 had set back the eight-hour movement twenty-five years, arguing that the movement would have succeeded but for the bomb. It's a great mistake. No one can exactly measure in years or months the effect of a forward push or a reaction. No one can demonstrate that the eight-hour movement could have been won twenty-five years ago. We know that the eight-hour day was put on the statute books of Illinois in 1871 by political action, and has remained a dead letter. That the direct action of the workers could have won it, then, cannot be proved; but it can be shown that many more potent factors than the Haymarket bomb worked against it. On the other hand, if the reactive influence of the bomb was really so powerful, we should naturally expect labor and union conditions to be worse in Chicago than in the cities where no such thing happened. On the contrary, bad as they are, the general conditions of labor are better in Chicago than in most other large cities, and the power of the unions is more developed there than in any other American city except San Francisco. So if we are to conclude anything for the influence of the Haymarket bomb, keep these facts in mind. Personally I do not think its influence on the labor movement, as such, was so very great.

It will be the same with the present furore about violence. Nothing fundamental has been altered. Two men have been imprisoned for what they did (twenty-four years ago they were hanged for what they did not do); some few more may yet be imprisoned. But the forces of life will continue to revolt against their economic chains. There will be no cessation in that revolt, no matter what ticket men vote or fail to vote, until the chains are broken.

How will the chains be broken?

Political actionists tell us it will be only by means of working-class party action at the polls; by voting themselves into possession of the sources of life and the tools; by voting that those who now command forests, mines, ranches, waterways, mills, and factories, and likewise command the military power to defend them, shall hand over their dominion to the people.

And meanwhile?

Meanwhile, be peaceable, industrious, law-abiding, patient, and frugal (as Madero told the Mexican peons to be, after he sold them to Wall Street)! Even if some of you are disenfranchised, don't rise up even against that, for it might "set back the party."

Well, I have already stated that some good is occasionally accomplished by political action—not necessarily working-class party action either. But I am abundantly convinced that the occasional good accomplished is more than counterbalanced by the evil; just as I am convinced that though there are occasional evils resulting through direct action, they are more than counterbalanced by the good.

Nearly all the laws which were originally framed with the intention of benefitting the workers, have either turned into weapons in their enemies' hands, or become dead letters unless the workers through their organizations have directly enforced their observance. So that in the end, it is direct action that has to be relied on anyway. As an example of getting the tarred end of a law, glance at the anti-trust law, which was supposed to benefit the people in general and the working class in particular. About two weeks since, some 250 union leaders were cited to answer to the charge of being trust formers, as the answer of the Illinois Central to its strikers.

But the evil of pinning faith to indirect action is far greater than any such minor results. The main evil is that it destroys initiative, quenches the individual rebellious spirit, teaches people to rely on someone else to do for them what they should do for themselves; finally renders organic the anomalous idea that by massing supineness together until a majority is acquired, then through the peculiar magic of that majority, this supineness is to be transformed into energy. That is, people who have lost the habit of striking for themselves as individuals, who have submitted to every injustice while waiting for the majority to grow, are going to become metamorphosed into human high-explosives by a mere process of packing!

I quite agree that the sources of life, and all the natural wealth of the earth, and the tools necessary to co-operative production, must become freely accessible to all. It is a positive certainty to me that unionism must widen and deepen its purposes, or it will go under; and I feel sure that the logic of the situation will gradually force them to see it. They must learn that the workers' problem can never be solved by beating up scabs, so long as their own policy of limiting their membership by high initiation fees and other restrictions helps to make scabs.

They must learn that the course of growth is not so much along the line of higher wages, but shorter hours, which will enable them to increase membership, to take in everybody who is willing to come into the union. They must learn that if they want to win battles, all allied workers must act together, act quickly (serving no notice on bosses), and retain their freedom to do so at all times. And finally they must learn that even then (when they have a complete organization) they can win nothing permanent unless they strike for everything—not for a wage, not for a minor improvement, but for the whole natural wealth of the earth. And proceed to the direct expropriation of it all! They must learn that their power does not lie in their voting strength, that their power lies in their ability to stop production. It is a great mistake to suppose that the wage-earners constitute a majority of the voters. Wage-earners are here today and there tomorrow, and that hinders a large number from voting; a great percentage of them in this country are foreigners without a voting right. The most patent proof that Socialist leaders know this is so, is that they are compromising their propaganda at every point to win the support of the business class, the small investor. Their campaign papers proclaimed that their interviewers had been assured by Wall Street bond purchasers that they would be just as ready to buy Los Angeles bonds from a socialist as a capitalist administrator; that the present Milwaukee administration has been a boon to the small investor; their reading notices assure their readers in this city that we need not go to the great department stores to buy—buy rather of So-and-so on Milwaukee Avenue, who will satisfy us quite as well as a "big business" institution. In short, they are making every desperate effort to win the support and to prolong the life of that middle-class which socialist economy says must be ground to pieces, because they know they cannot get a majority without them.

The most that a working-class party could do, even if its politicians remained honest, would be to form a strong faction in the legislatures which might, by combining its vote with one side or another, win certain political or economic palliatives.

But what the working-class can do, when once they grow into a solidified organization, is to show the possessing class, through a sudden cessation of all work, that the whole social structure rests on them; that the possessions of the others are absolutely worthless to them without the workers' activity; that such protests, such strikes, are inherent in the system of property and will continually recur until the whole thing is abolished— and having shown that effectively, proceed to expropriate.

"But the military power," says the political actionist; "we must get political power, or the military will be used against us!"

Against a real General Strike, the military can do nothing. Oh, true, if you have a Socialist Briand in power, he may declare the workers "public officials" and try to make them serve against themselves! But against the solid wall of an immobile working-mass, even a Briand would be broken.

Meanwhile, until this international awakening, the war will go on as it had been going, in spite of all the hysteria which well-meaning people who do not understand life and its necessities may manifest; in spite of all the shivering that timid leaders have done; in spite of all the reactionary revenges that may be taken; in spite of all the capital that politicians make out of the situation. It will go on because Life cries to live, and Property denies its freedom to live; and Life will not submit.

And should not submit.

It will go on until that day when a self-freed Humanity is able to chant Swinburne's Hymn of Man:

Glory to Man in the highest,
For Man is the master of Things.

The Eleventh of November, 1887

This Haymarket address was delivered in Chicago, the scene of the Haymarket affair, on 11 November 1901 and published in *Free Society* on 24 November. Here she confesses something forgivable to us but not to her: that when she first heard of the Haymarket riot, she exclaimed that the anarchists should be hanged. She herself read much of her life's work as an attempt to transcend that moment of brutal emotion. The address also contains one of her most direct defenses of her anarchism.

"The recent outburst of savagery" refers to the repression that followed the McKinley assassination.

"Winkelried" is Arnold von Winkelried, fourteenth-century Swiss hero who advanced alone against the forces of Austria.

The Eleventh of November, 1887

Let me begin my address with a confession. I make it sorrowfully and with self-disgust; but in the presence of great sacrifice we learn humility, and if my comrades could give their lives for their belief, why, let me give my pride. Yet I would not give it, for personal utterance is of trifling importance, were it not that I think at this particular season it will encourage those of our sympathizers whom the recent outburst of savagery may have disheartened, and perhaps lead some who are standing where I once stood to do as I did later.

This is my confession: Fifteen years ago last May when the echoes of the Haymarket bomb rolled through the little Michigan village where I then lived, I, like the rest of the credulous and brutal, read one lying newspaper headline, "Anarchists throw a bomb in a crowd in the Haymarket in Chicago," and immediately cried out, "They ought to be hung."—This, though I had never believed in capital punishment for ordinary criminals. For that ignorant, outrageous, blood-thirsty sentence I shall never forgive myself, though I know the dead men would have forgiven me, though I know those who loved them forgive me. But my own voice, as it sounded that night, will sound so in my ears till I die,—a bitter reproach and shame. What had I done? Credited the first wild rumor of an event of which I knew nothing, and, in my mind, sent men to the gallows without asking one word of defense! In one wild, unbalanced moment threw away the sympathies of a lifetime, and became an executioner at heart. And what I did that night millions did, and what I said millions said. I have only one word of extenuation for myself and all those people—ignorance. I did not know what Anarchism was. I had never seen it used save in histories, and there it was always synonymous with social confusion and murder. I believed the newspapers. I thought these men had thrown that bomb, unprovoked, into a mass of men and women, from a wicked delight in killing. And so thought all those millions of others. But out of those millions there were some few thousand— I am glad I was one of them—who did not let the matter rest there.

I know not what resurrection of human decency first stirred within me after that,—whether it was an intellectual suspicion that may be I did not

289

know all the truth of the case and could not believe the newspapers, or whether it was the old strong undercurrent of sympathy which often prompts the heart to go out to the accused, without a reason; but this I do know that though I was no Anarchist at the time of the execution, it was long and long before that, that I came to the conclusion that the accusation was false, the trial a farce, that there was no warrant either in justice or in law for their conviction; and that the hanging, if hanging there should be, would be the act of a society composed of people who had said what I said on the first night, and who had kept their eyes and ears fast shut ever since, determined to see nothing and to know nothing but rage and vengeance. Till the very end I hoped that mercy might intervene, though justice did not; and from the hour I knew neither would nor ever could again, I distrusted law and lawyers, judges and governors alike. And my whole being cried out to know what it was these men had stood for, and why they were hanged, seeing it was not proven they knew anything about the throwing of the bomb.

Little by little, here and there, I came to know that what they had stood for was a very high and noble ideal of human life, and what they were hanged for was preaching it to the common people,—the common people who were as ready to hang them, in their ignorance, as the court and the prosecutor were in their malice! Little by little I came to know that these were men who had a clearer vision of human right than most of their fellows; and who, being moved by deep social sympathies, wished to share their vision with their fellows, and so proclaimed it in the market-place. Little by little I realized that the misery, the pathetic submission, the awful degradation of the workers, which from the time I was old enough to begin to think had borne heavily upon my heart, (as they must bear upon all who have hearts to feel at all), had smitten theirs more deeply still,—so deeply that they knew no rest save in seeking a way out,—and that was more than I had ever had the sense to conceive. For me there had never been a hope there should be no more rich and poor; but a vague idea that there might not be so rich and so poor, if the workingmen by combining could exact a little better wages, and make their hours a little shorter. It was the message of these men, (and their death swept that message far out into cars that would never have heard their living voices), that all such little dreams are folly. That not in demanding little, not in striking for an hour less, not in mountain labor to bring forth mice, can any lasting alleviation come; but in demanding, much,—all,—in a bold self-assertion of the worker to toil any hours he finds sufficient, not that another finds for him,—here is where the way out lies. That message, and the message of others, whose works, associated with theirs, their death drew to my notice, took me up, as it were, upon a mighty hill, wherefrom I saw the roofs of the workshops of the little world. I saw the machines, the things that men had made to ease their burden, the wonderful things, the iron genii, I saw them set their iron teeth in the living flesh of the men who made them; I saw the maimed and crippled stumps of men go limping away into the night that engulfs the poor, perhaps to be thrown up in the flotsam and jetsam of beggary for a time, perhaps to suicide in some dim corner where the black surge throws its slime.

I saw the rose fire of the furnace shining on the blanched face of the man who tended it, and knew surely as I knew anything in life, that never would a free man feed his blood to the fire like that.

I saw swart bodies, all mangled and crushed, borne from the mouths of the mines to be stowed away in a grave hardly less narrow and dark than that in which the living form had crouched ten, twelve, fourteen hours a day; and I knew that in order that I might be warm—I, and you, and those others who never do any dirty work—those men had slaved away in those black graves, and been crushed to death at last.

I saw beside city streets great heaps of horrible colored earth, and down at the bottom of the trench from which it was thrown, so far down that nothing else was visible, bright gleaming eyes, like a wild animal's hunted into its hole. And I knew that free men never chose to labor there, with pick and shovel in that foul, sewage-soaked earth, in that narrow trench, in that deadly sewer gas ten, eight, even six hours a day. Only slaves would do it.

I saw deep down in the hull of the ocean liner the men who shoveled the coal—burned and seared like paper before the grate; and I knew that "the record" of the beautiful monster, and the pleasure of the ladies who laughed on the deck, were paid for with these withered bodies and souls.

I saw the scavenger carts go up and down, drawn by sad brutes driven by sadder ones; for never a man, a man in full possession of his self-hood, would freely choose to spend all his days in the nauseating stench that forces him to swill alcohol to neutralize it.

And I saw in the lead works how men were poisoned, and in the sugar refineries how they went insane; and in the factories how they lost their decency; and in the stores how they learned to lie; and I knew it was slavery made them do all this. I knew the Anarchists were right,—the whole thing must be changed, the whole thing was wrong,—the whole system of production and distribution, the whole ideal of life.

And I questioned the government then; they had taught me to question it. What have you done—you the keepers of the Declaration and the Constitution—what have you done about all this? What have you done to preserve the conditions of freedom to the people?

Lied, deceived, fooled, tricked, bought and sold and got gain! You have sold away the land, that you had no right to sell. You have murdered the aboriginal people, that you might seize the land in the name of the white race, and then steal it away from them again, to be again sold by a second and a third robber. And that buying and selling of the land has driven the people off the healthy earth and away from the clean air into these rot-heaps of humanity called cities, where every filthy thing is done, and filthy labor breeds filthy bodies and filthy souls. Our boys are decayed with vice before they come to manhood; our girls—ah, well might John Harvey write:

> "Another begetteth a daughter white and gold,
>   She looks into the meadow land water, and the world
> Knows her no more; they have sought her field and fold
>   But the City, the City hath bought her,
> It hath sold
>   Her piecemeal, to students, rats, and reek of the graveyard mould."

You have done this thing, gentlemen who engineer the government; and not only have you caused this ruin to come upon others; you your-selves are rotten with this debauchery. You exist for the purpose of grant-ing privileges to whoever can pay most for you, and so limiting the freedom of men to employ themselves that they must sell themselves into this fright-ful slavery or become tramps, beggars, thieves, prostitutes, and murderers. And when you have done all this, what then do you do to them, these crea-tures of your own making? You, who have set them the example in every villainy? Do you then relent, and remembering the words of the great reli-gious teacher to whom most of you offer lip service on the officially reli-gious day, do you go to these poor, broken, wretched creatures and love them? Love them and help them, to teach them to be better? No: you build prisons high and strong, and there you beat, and starve, and hang, finding by the working of your system human beings so unutterably degraded that they are willing to kill whomsoever they are told to kill at so much monthly salary.

This is what the government is, has always been, the creator and defender of privilege; the organization of oppression and revenge. To hope that it can ever become anything else is the vainest of delusions. They tell you that Anarchy, the dream of social order without government, is a wild fancy. The wildest dream that ever entered the heart of man is the dream that mankind can ever help itself through an appeal to law, or to come to any order that will not result in slavery wherein there is any excuse for government.

It was for telling the people this that these five men were killed. For telling the people that the only way to get out of their misery was first to learn what their rights upon this earth were;—freedom to use the land and all within it and all the tools of production—and then to stand all together and take them, themselves, and not to appeal to the jugglers of the law. Abolish the law—that is abolish privilege,—and crime will abolish itself.

They will tell you these men were hanged for advocating force. What! These creatures who drill men in the science of killing, who put guns and clubs in hands they train to shoot and strike, who hail with delight the latest inventions in explosives, who exult in the machine that can kill the most with the least expenditure of energy, who declare a war of extermination upon people who do not want their civilization, who ravish, and burn, and garotte and guillotine, and hang, and electrocute, they have the impertinence to talk about the unrighteousness of force! True, these men did advocate the right to resist invasion by force. You will find scarcely one in a thousand who does not believe in that right. The one will be either a real Christian or a non-resistant Anarchist. It will not be a believer in the State. No, no; it was not for advocating forcible resistance on principle, but for advocating forcible resistance to their tyrannies, and for advocating a society which would forever make an end of riches and poverty, of governors and governed.

The spirit of revenge, which is always stupid, accomplished its brutal act. Had it lifted its eyes from its work, it might have seen in the background of the scaffold that bleak November morning the dawn-light of Anarchy whiten across the world.

So it came first,—a gleam of hope to the proletaire, a summons to rise and shake off his material bondage. But steadily, steadily the light has grown, as year by year the scientist, the literary genius, the artist, and the moral teacher, have brought to it the tribute of their best work, their unpaid work, the work they did for love. To-day it means not only material emancipation, too; it comes as the summing up of all those lines of thought and action which for three hundred years have been making towards freedom; it means fullness of being, the free life.

And I say it boldly, notwithstanding the recent outburst of condemnation, notwithstanding the cry of lynch, burn, shoot, imprison, deport, and the Scarlet Letter A to be branded low down upon the forehead, and the latest excuse for that fond esthetic decoration "the button," that for two thousand years no idea has so stirred the world as this,—none which had such living power to break down barriers of race and degree, to attract prince and proletaire, poet and mechanic, Quaker and Revolutionist. No other ideal but the free life is strong enough to touch the man whose infinite pity and understanding goes alike to the hypocrite priest and the victim of Siberian whips; the loving rebel who stepped from his title and his wealth to labor with all the laboring earth; the sweet strong singer who sang

"No Master, high or low";

the lover who does not measure his love nor reckon on return; the self-centered one who "will not rule, but also will not ruled be"; the philosopher who chanted the Over-man; the devoted woman of the people; ay, and these too,—these rebellious flashes from the vast cloud-hung ominous obscurity of the anonymous, these souls whom governmental and capitalistic brutality has whipped and goaded and stung to blind rage and bitterness, these mad young lions of revolt, these Winkelrieds who offer their hearts to the spears.

Our Present Attitude

This brief essay from *Mother Earth* (April 1908) shows Voltairine's late movement toward more radical solutions and toward communist anarchism. The view of property and poverty that she articulates here is the classical anarchist one of Proudhon, who held that a person has a natural right to the product of her own labor, but that property considered as ownership beyond that point is "theft."

Our Present Attitude

The present organization of society, working logically and inexorably, has brought about a situation which both Socialists and Anarchists have all along foreseen and foretold. It was no more to be avoided than the leap of Niagara is to be avoided, when once the headwaters start on their outward course to the sea.

Those who imagine that industrial conditions can be made or unmade by this or that inadequate legal patchwork, find themselves in the midst of a frightful boiling of irreconcilable elements, which they weakly and child-ishly try to explain by some trivial reason, such as the attitude of this or that politician, or this or that capitalist, or by some single political move (such as protection without restriction of immigration), or by the wicked-ness of human nature, or by blaming the "calamity press," or by the will of God, and so on. The condition is so terrible that somehow they are com-pelled to "sit up and take notice"; but they do not perceive that it is the inevitable result of the whole politico-economic lie that man can be free and the institution of property continue to exist.

I wish a sharp distinction made between the legal institution of prop-erty, and property in the sense that what a man definitely produces by his own labor is his own. It is the legal institution of property which has pro-duced this condition, in which the elemental cries of humanity are swelling up in a frightful discordant chorus, because the elemental needs of human-ity are being denied,—and denied to masses of men.

Now, what has happened and what must continue to happen? The people in whom Christian ethical instincts predominate are starving and dying in corners; the people in whom natural instincts predominate over ordinary rules of action are stealing in preference to starving; the jails, the courts, the prisons, are full of these victims of social injustice, who, under free conditions, would be active, energetic, useful people. And still the streets are full of beggars for the means of life.

Now, in times like these, wild outbursts of desperation must be expected. It is not the business of Anarchists to preach wild and foolish acts,—acts of violence. For, truly, Anarchism has nothing in common with violence, and can never come about save through the conquest of men's minds. But when some desperate and life-denied victim of the present system does strike back at it, by violence, it is not our business to heap infamies upon his name, but to explain him as we explain others, whether our enemies or our friends, as the fated fruit of the existing "order."

We must expect that such people will be called Anarchists, in advance. No matter what they themselves say, no matter what we say, the majority of people will believe they acted not as desperate *men*, but as theoretical *Anarchists*. Such has been the fate of every new idea which sought to penetrate the human mind and to uplift it; the sins of the existing order were blamed at its door, and every calumny that rage and fear could invent was heaped upon it. This is an old, old story.

Well, what of it? If this is the price to be paid for an idea, then let us pay. There is no need of being troubled about it, afraid, or ashamed. This is the time to stand boldly and say, "Yes, I believe in the displacement of this system of injustice by a just one; I believe in the end of starvation, exposure, and the crimes caused by them; I believe in the human soul regnant over all laws which man has made or will make; I believe there is no peace now, and there never will be peace, so long as man rules over man; I believe in the total disintegration and dissolution of the principle and practice of authority; *I am an Anarchist*, and if for this you condemn me, I stand ready to receive your condemnation."

It has been my experience that when you face an enemy and look him in the eyes, he will accord you far more respect than when you shuffle and shirk. And, moreover, you stand far more chance of convincing him, or the indifferent man at the side, by an open-eyed declaration than by any indirection. I say these things because I have been pained to see that in the present period of repression many of our comrades think and act otherwise. I am sure that most who thus act Peter and deny their Master, do it out of reasoned conviction, and not cowardice; but I am also sure that it is a very mistaken policy, and can have only wretched results.

Face and outface—for these are times when "valor is discretion."

McKinley's Assassination from the Anarchist Standpoint

Published in *Mother Earth* in October 1907, six years after McKinley was killed by the anarchist Leon Czolgosz, this essay embodies a defense of anarchism from the charge that it entails or simply is mindless violence. "There have been Christian assassins," writes Voltairine, "Republican assassins, Socialist assassins, and Anarchist assassins; *in no case was the act of assassination an expression of any of those religious or political creeds*, but of temperamental reaction against the injustice created by the prevailing system of the time."

McKinley's Assassination
From the Anarchist Standpoint

Six years have passed since William McKinley met his doom at Buffalo and the return stroke of justice took the life of his slayer, Leon Czolgosz. The wild rage that stormed through the brains of the people, following that revolver shot, turning them into temporary madmen, incapable of seeing, hearing, or thinking correctly, has spent itself. Figures are beginning to appear in their true relative proportions, and there is some likelihood that sane words will be sanely listened to. Instead of the wild and savage threats, "Brand the anarchists with hot iron," "Boil in oil," "Hang to the first lamp-post," "Scourge and shackle," "Deport to a desert island," which were the stock phrases during the first few weeks following the tragedy, and were but the froth of the upheaved primitive barbarity of civilized men, torn loose and raging like an unreasoning beast, we now hear an occasional serious inquiry: "But what have the anarchists to say about it? Was Czolgosz really an anarchist? Did he say he was? And what has Anarchism to do with assassination altogether?"

To those who wish to know what the anarchists have to say this leaflet is addressed. We have to say that *not Anarchism, but the state of society which creates men of power and greed and the victims of power and greed*, is responsible for the death of both McKinley and Czolgosz. Anarchism has this much to do with assassination, that as it teaches the possibility of a society in which the needs of life may be fully supplied for all, and in which the opportunities for complete development of mind and body shall be the heritage of all; as it teaches that the present unjust organization of the production and distribution of wealth must finally be completely destroyed, and replaced by a system which will insure to each the liberty to work, without first seeking a master to whom he must surrender a tithe of his product, which will guarantee his liberty of access to the sources and means of production; as it teaches that all this is possible without the exhaustion of body and mind which is hourly wrecking the brain and brawn of the nations in the present struggle of the workers to achieve a competence, it follows that Anarchism does create rebels. Out of the blindly submissive, it makes the discontented, out of the unconsciously dissatisfied, it makes the consciously dissatisfied. Every movement for the social betterment of the peoples, from time immemorial, has done the same. And since among the ranks of dissatisfied people are to be found all manner of temperaments and degrees of mental development—just as are found among the satisfied also—it follows that there are occasionally those who translate their dissatisfaction into a definite act of reprisal against the society which is crushing them and their fellows. Assassination of persons representing the ruling power is such an act of reprisal. There have been Christian assassins, Republican assassins, Socialist assassins, and Anarchist assassins; *in no case was the act of assassination an expression of any of these religious or political creeds*, but of temperamental reaction against the injustice created by the prevailing system of the time (excluding, of course, such acts as were merely the result of personal ambition or derangement). Moreover, Anarchism less than any of these can have anything to do in determining any specific action, since, in the nature of its teaching, every anarchist must act purely on his own initiative and responsibility; there are no secret societies nor executive boards of any description among anarchists. But that among a mass of people who realize fully what a slaughterhouse capitalism has made of the world, how even little children are daily and hourly crippled, starved, doomed to the slow death of poisoned air, to ruined eyesight, wasted limbs, and polluted blood; how through the sapping of the present generation's strength, the unborn are doomed to a rotten birthright, all that riches may be heaped where they are not needed; who realize that all this is as unnecessary and stupid as it is wicked and revolting; that among these there should be some who rise up and strike back, whether wisely or unwisely, effectively or ineffectively, is no matter for wonder; the wonder is there are not more. *The hells of capitalism create the desperate; the desperate act,—desperately!*

And in so far as Anarchism seeks to arouse the consciousness of oppression, the desire for a better society, and a sense of the necessity for unceasing warfare against Capitalism and the State, the authors of all this unrecognized but Nemesis-bearing crime, in so far it is responsible and does not shirk its responsibility: "For it is impossible but that offences come; but woe unto them through whom they come."

Many offences had come through the acts of William McKinley. Upon his hand was the "damned spot" of official murder, the blood of the Filipinos, whom he, in pursuance of the capitalist policy of Imperialism, had sentenced to death. Upon his head falls the curse of all the workers against whom, time and time again, he threw the strength of his official power. Without doubt he was in private life a good and kindly man; it is even probable he saw no wrong in the terrible deeds he had commanded done. Perhaps he was able to reconcile his Christian belief, "Do good to them that hate you" with the slaughters he ordered; perhaps he slaughtered the Filipinos "to do them good"; the capitalist mind is capable of such contortions. But whatever his private life, he was the representative of wealth and greed and power; in accepting the position he accepted the rewards and the dangers, just as a miner who goes down in the mine for $2.50 a day or less, accepts the danger of the firedamp. McKinley's rewards were greater and his risks less; moreover, he didn't need the job to keep bread in his mouth; but he too met an explosive force—the force of a desperate man's will. And he died; *not as a martyr, but as a gambler who had won a high stake and was struck down by the man who had lost the game*: for that is what capitalism has made of human well-being—a gambler's stake, no more.

Who was this man? No one knows. A child of the great darkness, a spectre out of the abyss! Was he an anarchist? We do not know. None of the anarchists knew him, save as a man with whom some few of them had exchanged a few minutes' conversation, in which he said that he had been a Socialist, but was then dissatisfied with the socialist movement. The police said he was an anarchist; the police said he attributed his act to the influence of a lecture of Emma Goldman's. But the police have lied before, and, like the celebrated Orchard, they need "corroborative evidence." All that we really know of Czolgosz is his revolver shot and his dying words: "I killed the President because he was the enemy of the people, the good, working people." All between is blank. What he really said, if he said anything, remains in the secret papers of the Buffalo Police Department and the Auburn prison. If we are to judge inferentially, considering his absolutely indifferent behavior at his "trial," he never said anything at all. He was utterly at their mercy, and had they been able to twist or torture any word of his into a "conspiracy," they would have done it. Hence it is most probable he said nothing.

Was he a normal or an abnormal being? In full possession of his senses, or of a disturbed or weak mentality? Again we do not know. All manner of fables arose immediately after his act as to his boyhood's career; people knew him in his childhood as evil, stupid, cruel; even some knew him who had heard him talk about assassinating the President years before; other legends contradicted these; all were equally unreliable. His indifference at the "trial" may have been that of a strong man enduring a farce, or of a clouded and non-realizing mind. His last words were the words of a naïve and devoted soul, a soul quite young, quite unselfish, and quite forlorn. If martyrdom was insisted upon, which was the martyr, the man who had the good of life, who was past middle years, who had received reward and distinction to satiety, who had ordered others killed without once jeopardizing his own life, and to whom death came more easily than to millions who die of long want and slow tortures of disease, or this young strong soul which struck its own blow and paid with its own life, so capable of the utterest devotion, so embittered and ruined in its youth, so hopeless, so wasted, so cast out of the heart of pity, so altogether alone in its last agony? This was the greater tragedy—a tragedy bound to be repeated over and over, until "the good working people" (in truth they are not so good) learn that the earth is theirs and the fullness thereof, and that there is no need for any one to enslave himself to another. This Anarchism teaches, and this the future will realize, though many martyrdoms lie between

Part VIII

The Political Is the Personal

Anarchist Esthetics

Introduction

Art was central to anarchism in the period of Voltairine's life, and anarchism to art. The idea was that one could become the artist of one's own life: that freedom was a necessity of art and that art gave rise to freedom. Thus, the artist became a model for what people would be like when a real liberation had been achieved. In fact, art was for much of the political left (including Marx) a model of non-alienated labor. Art was held to be work that engaged a person fully, that was done for its own sake, and that led toward self-realization. Not only were anarchists such as Emma Goldman and Voltairine centrally concerned with art and literature, then; they regarded this interest as part and parcel of their political commitments. In fact, much of Emma Goldman's most original work concerned contemporary drama.

Several recent authors have emphasized the central role that anarchist theory and anarchist figures played in the development of modern art.[1] Indeed, the artistic milieu surrounding such figures as Picasso was teeming with anarchist theory, and the liberation from traditions and academic niceties that such figures embodied was political as well as aesthetic. Indeed, much literature of the nineteenth and twentieth centuries was written with explicitly political content. That is particularly true of Russian authors such as Dostoevsky and Tolstoy—who were deeply admired by many anarchists—but also of various European and American authors. Voltairine probably regarded herself primarily as a poet, and also played and taught music and wrote short stories.

—Crispin Sartwell

NOTES

1. See, e.g., Christine Stansell, *American Moderns: Bohemian New York and the Creation of a New Century* (New York: Henry Holt, 2000). Alan Antliff, *Anarchist Moderns: Art, Politics, and the First American Avant-Garde* (Chicago: University of Chicago Press, 2001).

Literature the Mirror of Man

A defense of popular as opposed to respectable literature, and of ordinary as opposed to refined language, this essay has great prescience and good humor. As she says, one gets to love the "quaint illogical tangle" that is the English language.

Playwrights: Henrik Ibsen (Norwegian, 1828–1906), Bjornstjerne Bjornson (Norwegian, 1832–1910), Maurice Maeterlinck (Belgian, 1862–1949), Gerhart Hauptmann (German, 1862–1946), George Bernard Shaw (English, 1856–1950).

Literature the Mirror of Man

PERHAPS I had better say the Mirror-reflection,—the reflection of all that he has been and is, the hinting fore-flashing of something of what he may become. In so considering it, let it be understood that I speak of no particular form of literature, but the entire body of a people's expressed thought, preserved either traditionally, in writing, or in print.

The majority of lightly thinking, fairly read people, who make use of the word "literature" rather easily, do so with a very indistinct idea of its content. To them it usually means a certain limited form of human expression, chiefly works of the imagination—poetry, drama, the various forms of the novel. History, philosophy, science are rather frowning names,—stern second cousins, as it were, to the beguiling companions of their pleasant leisure hours,—not legitimately "literature." Biography,—well, it depends on who writes it! If it can be made so much like a work of fiction that the subject sketched serves the purposes of a fictive hero, why then—maybe.

To such talkers about literature, evidence of familiarity with it, and title to have one's opinions thereon asked and respected, are witnessed by the ability to run glibly off the names of the personages in the dramas of Ibsen, Björnson, Maeterlinck, Hauptmann or Shaw; or in the novels of Gorki, Andreyev, Tolstoy, Zola, Maupassant, Hardy, and the dozen or so of lesser lights who revolve with these through the cycle of the magazine issues.

Not only do these same people thus limit the field of literature, (at least in their ordinary conversation,—if you press them they will dubiously admit that the field may be extended) but they are also possessed of the notion that only one particular mode even of fiction, is in fact the genuine thing. That this mode has not always been in vogue they are aware; and they allow other modes to have been literature in the past, as a sort of kindly concession to the past—a blanket-indulgence to its unevolved state. At present, however, no indulgences are allowed; whatever is not the mode, is anathema; it is not literature at all. When confronted by the *very* great names of the Past, which they can neither consign to oblivion, nor patronize by toleration for their undeveloped condition, names which are names for all ages, which they need to use as conjuration words in their comparisons and criticisms, names such as Shakespeare or Hugo, they complacently close their eyes to contradictions and swear that fundamentally these men's works *are in the modern mode, the accepted mode, the one and only enduring mode*, the mode that they approve.

"Which is?"—I hear you ask. *Which is* what they are pleased to call "Realism."

If you wish to know how far they are obsessed by this notion, go pick yourself a quiet corner in some café where light literature readers meet to make comparisons, and listen to the comments. Before very long, voices will be getting loud about some character at present stalking across the pages of the magazines, or bestirring itself among the latest ton of novel; and the dispute will be, "Does such a type exist?"—"Of course he exists,"—"He does not exist,"—"He must exist,"—"He cannot exist,"—"Under such conditions,"—"There are no such conditions,"—"But be reasonable: you have not been in all places, and you cannot say there may not be such conditions; supposing—" "All right: I will give you the conditions; all the same, no man would act so under any conditions." "I swear I have seen such men—" "Impossible—" "What is there impossible about it?—"

And the voices get louder and louder, as the disputants proceed to pick the character to pieces, speech by speech, and action by action, till, nothing being left, each finally subsides somehow, each confirmed in his own opinion, each convinced that the main purpose of literature—Realism—has either been served, or not served, by the author under discussion. To such disputants "Literature the Mirror of Man," means that only such literature as gives so-called absolutely faithful representations of life as it is demonstrably lived, is a genuine Mirror. No author is to be considered worthy of a place, unless his works can be at least twisted to fit this conception. With some slight refinement of idea, in so far as it recognizes the obscurer recesses of the mind as entitled to representation as well as the externals, it corresponds to the one-time development of portrait painting, which esteemed it necessary to paint the exact number of hairs in the wart on Oliver Cromwell's nose, in order to have a true likeness of him.

As before suggested, I do not, when I speak of Literature as the Mirror of Man, have any such 12 × 18 mirror in view; nor the limitation of literature to any one form of it, to any one age of it, to any set of standard names; nor the limitation of Man to any preconceived notion of just what he may logically be allowed to be. The composite image we are seeking to find is an image wrought as much of his dreams of what he would like to be, as of his actual being; that is no true picture of Man, which does not include his cravings for the impossible, as well as his daily performance of the possible. Indeed, the logical, calculable man, the man who under certain circumstances may be figured out to turn murderer and under others saint, is hardly so interesting as the illogical being who upsets the calculation by becoming neither, but something not at all predictable.

The objects of my lecture then are these:

1. To insist on a wider view of literature itself than that generally accepted.
2. To suggest to readers a more satisfactory way of considering what they read than that usually received.
3. To point to certain phases of the human appearance reflected in the mirror which are not generally noticed, but which I find interesting and suggestive.

You would think it very unreasonable, would you not, for any one to insist that because your highly polished glass backed by quicksilver, gives back so clear and excellent an image, *therefore* the watery vision you catch of yourself in the shifting, glancing ripples of a clear stream is not an image at all! With all the curious elongating and drifting and shortening back and breaking up into wavering circles, done by that unresting image, you know very certainly that is you; and if you look into the still waters of some summer pool, or mountain rain-cup, the image there is almost as sharp-lined as that in your polished glass, except for the vague tremor that seems to move under the water rather than on its surface, and suggest an ethereal something missing in your drawing-room shadow. Yet that vision conjured in the water-depth is you—surely you. Nay, even more,—that *first* image of you, you perceived when as a child you danced in the firelight and saw a misshapen darkness rising and falling along the wall in teasing mockery,—that too was surely an image of you—an image of interception, not of reflection; a blur, a vacancy, a horror, from which you fled shrieking to your mother's arms;—and yet it was the distorted outline of you.

You grew familiar with it later, amused yourself with it, twisted your hands into strange positions to see what curious shapes they would form upon the wall, and made whole stories with the shadows. Long afterward you went back to them with deliberate and careful curiosity, to see how the figures stumbled on by accident could be definitely produced, at will, according to the laws of interception.

Even so the first *Man-Images*, cast back from the blank wall of Language, are uncouth, ungraspable, vague, vacant, menacing—to the men who saw them, frightful. Mankind produced this paradox: the early *lights* of literature were *darkness*!

Later these darknesses grew less fearsome; the child-man began to jest with them; to multiply figures and send them chasing past each other up and down the wall, with fresh glee at each newly created shadow-sport. The wall at last became luminous, the shadows shining. And out of the old monosyllabic horror of the primitive legend, out of Man's fright at the projection of his own soul, out of his wide stare at those terrific giants on the wall who suddenly with shadow-like shifting became grotesque dwarfs, and mocking little beasts that danced and floated, ever most fearful because of their elusive emptiness; out of this, bit by bit, grew the steady contemplation, the gradual effacement of fright, the feeling of power and amusement, and the sense of Creative Mastery, which, understanding the shadows, began to command them, till there arose all the beauty of fairy tales and shining myths and singing legends.

Now any one who desires to see in Literature the most that there is in it; who desires to read not merely for the absorption of the moment but for the sake of permanent impression; who wishes to have an idea of Man not only as he is now, but through the whole articulate record of his existence; who would know the thoughts of his infancy and the connected course of his development,—and no one has any adequate conception of the glory of literature, unless he includes this much in it—any such a reader, I say, must find among its most attractive pages, the stories of early superstitions, the fictions of Fear, the struggles of the Race-Child's intelligence with over-looming problems. Think of the Ages and Ages that men saw the Demon Electricity riding the air; think that even now they do not know what he is; and yet he played mightily with their daily lives for all those ages. Think how this staring savage was put face to face with world-games which were spun and tossed around him, and compelled by the nature of his own activity to try to find an explanation to them; think that most of us, if we were not the heritors of the ages that have passed since then, should be staggered and out-breathed even now by all these lights and forms through which we move; and then turn to the record of those pathetic strivings of the frightened child with some little tenderness and sympathy, some solemn curiosity to know *what* men were able to think and feel when they led their lives as in a threatening Wonder-house, where everything was an Unknown, invested with crouching hostility. And never be too sure you know just how men will act, or try to act, under any conditions, if you have not read the record of what they have thought and fancied and done; and after you have read it, Oh, then you will never be sure you know! For then you will realize that every man is a burial-house, full of dead men's ghosts,—and the ghosts of very, very ancient days are there, forever whispering in an ancient, ancient tongue of ancient passions and desires, and prompting many actions which the doer thereof can give himself no accounting for.

There are two ways of reading these old stories; and as one who has gotten pleasure and profit, too, from both, I would recommend them both to be used. The first way is to read yourself backward into it as much as possible. Do not be a critic, on first reading; put the critic asleep. Let yourself *seem to believe it*, as did he who wrote it. Read it aloud, if you are where you will not annoy anybody; let the words sing themselves over your lips, as they sung themselves over the lips of the people who were dead so long ago,—in their strange faraway homes with their vanished surroundings; sung themselves, just as the wind sung through the echoing forests, and murmured back from the rocks; just as the songs slipped out of the birds' throats. You will find that half the beauty and the farce of old-time legend lies in the bare sound of it. Far, far more is it dependent on the voice, than any modern writings are. And surely, the reason is simple enough: for *it* was not *writing* in its creation; ancient literature addressed itself to the ear, always, while modern literature speaks to the eye.

If once you can get your ears washing with the sounds of the old language, as with the washing of the seas when you sit on the beach, or the lapping of the rivers when the bank-grass caresses you some idle summer afternoon, it will be much easier for you to forget that you are the child of another age and thought. You will begin to luxuriate in fancies and prefigure impossibilities; then you will know how it feels to be fancy free, loosed from the chain of the possible; and once having felt, you will also understand better, when you re-read with other intent.

When you are ready for such re-reading, then be as critical as you please,—which does not necessarily mean be condemnatory. It means rather take notice of all generals and particulars, and question them.

You will naturally pose yourself the question, Why is it that the bare sounds of these old stories are so much more vibrating, drum-like, shrilling, at times, than any modern song or poem? You will find that the mitigating influence of civilization,—knowledge, moderation,—creeping into expression, produces flat, neutral, diluted sounds,—watery words, so to speak, long-drawn out and glidingly inoffensive. In any modern writing remarkable for strength, will be found a preponderance of "barbaric yawp"—as Whitman called it.

Fear creates sharp cries; the rebound of Fear, which is Bravado, produces drum-tones, roars, and growls; unrestrained Passions howl in wind-notes, irregular, breaking short off. God carries a hammer, and Love a spear. The hymn clangs, and the love-song clashes. Through those fierce sounds one feels again hot hearts.

Those who perceive colors accompanying sounds, sense clean cut lights streaking the night-ground of these early word-pictures; sharp, hard, reds and yellows. It is our later world which has produced green tintings not to be told from gray, nor gray from blue, nor anything from anything. In our fondness for smoothness and gradation we have attained practical colorlessness.

If it appears to you that I am talking nonsense, permit me to tell you it is because you have dulled your own powers of perception; in seeking to become too intellectually appreciative, you have lost the power to feel primitive things. Try to recover it.

Another source of interesting observation, especially in English literature of early writing: this time the eye.

It is admitted by everybody that as a serviceable instrument for expressing definite sounds in an expeditious and comprehensible manner, English written language is a woeful failure. If any inventor of a theory of symbols should, would, or could have devised such a ridiculous conception of spelling, such a hodge-podge of contradictory jumbles, he would properly have been adjudged to an insane asylum; and that, every man who ever contrived an English spelling-book, and every teacher who is obliged to worry this incongruous mess through the steadily revolting reason-and-memory process of children, is ably convinced. But Man, English-speaking Man, has actually—*executed* such conception; (he probably executed it first and conceived it afterward, as most of our poor victims do when they start on that terrible blind road through the spelling-book). Whether or no, the thing is here, and we've all to accept it, and deal with it as best we may, sadly hoping that possibly the tenth generation from now may at least be rid of a few unnecessary "e's."

And since the thing is here, and is a mighty creation, and very indicative of how the human brain in large sections works; since we've got to put up with it anyway, we may as well, in revenge for its many inconveniences, get what little satisfaction we can out of it. And I find it one of the most delightful little side amusements of wandering through the field of old literature, while in the critical vein, to stray around among the old stumps and crooked cowpaths of English spelling. Much pleasure is to be derived from seeing what old words grew together and made new ones; what syllables or letters got lopped off or twisted, how silent letters became silent and why; from what older language planted, and what its relatives are. It is much the same pleasure that one gets from trailing around through the narrow crooked streets and senseless meanderings of London City. Everybody knows it's a foolish way to build a city; that all streets should be straight and wide and well-distributed. But since they are not, and London is too big for one's individual exertion to reform, one consents to take interest in explaining the crookedness—in mentally dissolving the great city into the hundred little villages which coalesced to make it; in marking this point as the place where St. Somebody-or-Other knelt and prayed once and therefore there had to be a cross-street here; and this other point as the place where the road swept round because martyrs were wont to be burnt there, etc., etc. The trouble is that after a while one gets to love all that quaint illogical tangle, seeing always the thousand years of history in it; and so one's senses actually become vitiated enough to permit him to love the outrages of English spelling, because of the features of men's souls that are imaged therein. When I look at the word "laugh," I fancy I hear the joyous deep guttural "gha-gha-gha" of the old Saxon who died long before the foreign graft on the English stock softened the "gh" to an "f"!

Really one must become more patient with the "un-system," knowing how it grew, and feeling that this is the way of Man,—the way he always grows,—not as he ought, but as he can.

I have spoken of forms: word-sounds, word-symbols; as to the spirit of those early writings, full of inarticulate religious sentiment, emotions so strong they burst from the utterer's throat one might almost say in barks; gloomy and foreboding; these gradually changing to more lightsome fancies,—beauty, delicacy, airiness taking their place, as in the fairy tales and folk-songs of the people, wherein the deeds of supernaturals are sported with, and it becomes evident that love and winsomeness are usurping the kingdom of Power and Fear,—through all we are compelled to observe one constant tendency of the human mind,—the desire to free itself from its own conditions, to be what it is not, to represent itself as something beyond its powers of accomplishment. In their minds, men had wings, and breathed in water, and swam on land, and ate air, and thrived in deserts, and walked through seas, and gathered roses off ice-bergs, and collected frozen dew off the tails of sunbeams, dispersed mountains with mustard seeds of faith, and climbed into solid caves under the rainbow; did everything which it was impossible for them to do.

It is in fact this imaginative faculty which has forerun the accomplishments of science and while, under the influence of practical experiment and the extension of knowledge such dreams have passed away, this much remains and will long, long remain in humankind, covered over and shamefacedly concealed as much as may be—that men perpetually conceive themselves as chrysalid heroes and wonder workers; and, under strain of occasion, this element crops out in their actions, making them do all manner of curious things which the standard-setters of realism will declare utterly illogical and impossible. Often it is the commonest men who do them.

I have a fondness for realism myself; at least I have a very wicked feeling towards what is called "symbolism," and various other things which I don't understand; but as the "Unrealists," the "Exaggeratists," the whatever-you-call-them express what I believe to be a very permanent characteristic of humankind, as evidenced in all the traces of its work, I think they probably give quite as true reflections of Man's Soul as the present favorites.

These early literatures, most of which have of course been lost, were the embryos of our more imposing creations; and it is a pleasant and an instructive thing to follow the unfolding of Monster Tales into Great Religious Literatures; to compare them and see how the same few simple figures, either transplanted or spontaneously produced at different points, evolved into all manner of Creators, Redeemers and miracles in their various altered habitats. No one can so thoroughly appreciate what is in the face of a man turned upward in prayer, as he who has followed the evolution of the black Monster up to that impersonal conception of God prettily called by Quakers "the Inner Light."

Fairy Tales on the other hand have evolved into allegories and Dramas,—first the dramas of the sky, now the dramas of earth.

Tales of Sexual exploits have become novels, novelettes, short stories, sketches,—a many-expressioned countenance of Man. But the old Heroic Legend,—and the Hero is always the next born after the Monster in the far-back dawn-days, is the lineal progenitor of History,—History which was first the glorification of a warrior and his aids; then the story of Kings, courts, and intrigues; now mostly the report of the deeds of nations in their ugly moods; and *to become* the record of what people have done in their more amiable moments,—the record of the conquests of peace; how men have lived and labored; dug and built, hewn and cleared, gardened and reforested, organized and coöperated, manufactured and used, educated and amused themselves. Those of us who aspire to be more or less suggesters of social change, are greatly at a loss, if we do not know the face of Man as reflected in history; and I mean as much the reflection of the minds of historians as seen in their histories as the reflection of the minds of others they sought to give; not so much in the direct expression of their opinions either, as in the choice of what they thought it worth while to try to stamp perpetuity upon.

When we read in the Anglo-Saxon Chronicle these items which are characteristic of the whole:

"A.D. 611. This year Cynegils succeeded to the government in Wessex, and held it 31 winters. Cynegils was the son of Ceol, Ceol of Cutha, Cutha of Cymric."

And then,

"614. This year Cynegils and Cuiehelm fought at Bampton and slew 2046 of the Welsh."

And then

"678. This year appeared the comet star in August, and shone every morning during three months like a sunbeam. Bishop Wilfred being driven from his bishopric by King Everth, two bishops were consecrated in his stead."

—when we read these we have not any very adequate conception of what the Anglo-Saxon people were doing; but we have a very striking and lasting impression of what the only men who tried to write history at all in that period of English existence, thought it was worth while to record.

"Cynegils was the son of Ceol, and he of Cutha, and Cutha of Cymric." It reads considerably like a stock-raiser's pedigree book. The trouble is, we have no particular notion of Cymric. Probably if we went back we should find he was the son of Somebody. But at any rate, he had a grandson, and the grandson was a king, and the chronicler therefore recorded him. Nothing happened for three years; and then the chronicle records that two kings fought and slew 2046 men. Then comes the momentous year 678 when a comet appeared and a bishop lost his job. No doubt the comet foretold the loss. There are no records of when shoemakers lost their jobs that I know of, nor how many shoemakers were put in their places; and I imagine it would have been at least as interesting for us to know as the little matter of Bishop Wilfred. But the chronicler did not think so; he preserved the Bishop's troubles—no doubt he did just what the shoemakers of the time would also have done, providing they had been also chroniclers. It is a fair sample of what was in men's minds as important.—If any one fancies that this disposition has quite vanished, let him pick up any ordinary history, and see how many pages, relatively, are devoted to the doings of persons intent on slaying, and those intent on peaceful occupation; and how many times we are told that certain politicians lost their jobs, and how we are not told anything about the ordinary people losing their jobs; and then reflect whether the old face of Man-the-Historian is quite another face yet.

Biography, as a sort of second offspring of the Hero legend, is another revelation, when we read it, not only to know its subject, but to know its writer,—the standpoint from which he values another man's life. Ordinarily there is a great deal of "Cynegils the son of Cutha the son of Cymric" in it; and a great deal of emphasis upon the man as an individual phenomenon; when really he would be more interesting and more comprehensible left in connection with the series of phenomena of which he was part. As an example of what to me is a perfect biography, I instance Conway's Life of Thomas Paine, itself a valuable history. But it is not so correct a mirror of the general attitude of biographers and readers of biography as Bosworth's Life of Johnson, except in so far as it indicates that the great face in the glass is changing. It is rather the type of what biography is *becoming*, than what it has been, or is.

There are two divisions of literature which are generally named in one breath, and are certainly closely connected; and yet the one came to highly perfected forms long, long ago, while the other is properly speaking very young; and for all that, the older is the handmaid of the younger. I mean the literatures of philosophy and science.

Philosophy is simply the coördination of the sciences; the formulation of the general, and related principles deduced from the collection and orderly arrangement of the facts of existence. Yet Man had rich literatures of philosophy, while his knowledge of facts was yet so extremely limited as hardly to be worth while writing books about. None of the appearances of Man's Soul is more interesting than that reflected in the continuous succession of philosophies he has poured out. Let him who reads them, read them always twice; first, simply to know and grasp what is said, to become familiar with the idea as it formed itself in the minds of those who conceived it; second, for the sake of figuring the restless activity of brain, the positive need of the mind under all conditions to formulate what knowledge it has, or thinks it has, into some sort of connected whole. This is one of the most pronounced and permanent features seen in the mirror: the positive refusal of the mind to accept the isolation of existences; no matter how far apart they lie, Man proceeds to spin connecting threads somehow. The woven texture is often comical enough, but the weaver is just as positively revealed in the cobwebs of ancient philosophy as in the reasoning of Herbert Spencer.

Concerning the literature of Science itself, in strict terms, I should be very presumptuous to speak of it, because I know extremely little about it; but of those general popularizations of it, which we have in some of the works of Haeckel, Darwin, and their similars, I should say that beyond the important information they contain in themselves (which surely no one can afford to be in ignorance of) they present the most transformed reflection of Man which any literature gives. Their words are cold, colorless, burdened with the labor of exactness, machine like, sustained, uncompromising, careless of effect. The spirit they embody is like unto them. They offer the image of Man's Soul in the time while imagination is in abeyance, reason ascendent.

This coldness and quietness sound the doom of poetry. A people which shall be fully permeated with the spirit and word of Science will never conceive great poems. They will never be overcome long enough at a time by their wonder and admiration, by their primitive impulses, by their power of simple impression, to think or to speak poetically. They will never see trees as impaled giants any more; they will see them as evolved descendants of phytoplasm. Dewdrops are no more the jewels of the fairies; they are the produce of condensation under given atmospheric conditions. Singing stones are not the prisons of punished spirits, but problems in acoustics. The basins of fjords are not the track of the anger of Thor, but the pathways of glaciation. The roar and blaze and vomit of

Etna, are not the rebellion of the Titan, but the explosion of so and so many million cubic feet of gas. The comet shall no more be the herald of the wrath of heaven, it is a nebulous body revolving in an elliptical orbit of great elongation. Love—love will not be the wound of Cupid, but the manifestation of universal reproductive instincts.

No, the great poems of the world *have been* produced; they have sung their song and gone their way. Imagination remains to us, but weakened, mixed, tamed, calmed. Verses we shall have,—and *many* fragments,—fragments of beauty and power; but never again the thunder-roll of the mighty early song. We have the benefits of science; we must have its derogations also. The powerful fragments will be such as deal with the still unexplored regions of Man's own internity—if I may coin the word. Science is still balking here. But not for long. We shall soon have madmen turned inside out, and their madness painstakingly reduced to so-and-so many excessive or deficient nerve-vibrations per second. Then no more of Poe's "Raven" and Ibsen's "Brand."

I have said that I intended to indicate a wider concept of literature than that generally allowed. So far I have not done it; at least all that I have dealt with is usually mentioned in works on literature. But I wish now to maintain that some very lowly forms of written expression must be included in literature,—always remembering that I am seeking the complete composite of Man's Soul.

Here then: I include in literature, beside what I have spoken on, not only standard novels, stories, sketches, travels, and magazine essays of all sorts, but the poorest, paltriest dime novel, detective story, daily newspaper report, baseball game account, and splash advertisement.

Oh, what a charming picture of ourselves we see therein! And a faithful one, mind you! Think what a speaking likeness of ourselves was the report of national, international, racial importance—the Jeffries-Johnson fight! Nay, I am not laughing. The people of the future are going to look back at the record a thousand years from now; and say, "This is what interested men in the year 1910." I wonder which will appear most ludicrous then, Bishop Wilfred in juxtaposition with the comet star, or the destiny of the white race put in jeopardy by a pugilistic contest between one white and one black man! O the bated breath, the expectant eyes, the inbitten lip, the taut muscles, the riveted attention, of hundreds of thousands of people watching the great "scientific" combat. I wonder whether the year 3000 will admire it more or less than the Song of Beowulf and the Battle of Brunanburh.

Consider the soul reflected on the sporting page. Oh, how mercilessly correct it is! Consider the soul reflected on the advertising page. Oh, the consummate liar that strides across it! Oh, the gull, the simpleton, the would-be getter of something for nothing whose existence it argues! Yea, commercial man has set his image therein; let him regard himself when he gets time.

And the body of our reform literature, which really reflects the very best social aspirations of men, how prodigal in words it is,—how indefinite in ideas! How generous of brotherhood—and sisterhood—in the large; how chary in the practice! Do we not appear therein as curious little dwarfs who have somehow gotten "big heads"? Mites gesticulating at the stars and imagining they are afraid because they twinkle. I would not discourage any comrade of mine in the social struggle, but sometimes it is a wholesome thing to reconsider our size.

A word in defense of the silly story. Let us not forget that lowly minds have lowly needs; and the mass of minds are lowly, and have a right to such gratification as is not beyond their comprehension. So long as I do not *have to read* those stories, I feel quite glad for the sake of those who are not able to want better that such gratification is not denied them. I would not wish to frown the silly story out of existence so long as it is a veritable expression of many people's need. There are those who have only learned the art of reading at all because of the foolish story. And quite in a side way I learned the other day through the grave assertion of a physician that the ability to read even these, whereby some little refinement of conception is introduced into the idea of love, is one of the restraining influences upon sexual degradation common among poor and ignorant young women. The face of man revealed in them is therefore not altogether without charm, though it may look foolish to us. I said there were some appearances in the Mirror not generally remarked, but which to me are suggestive. One of these is the evident delight of the human soul in *smut*. In the older literature these things are either badly set down, as law and cursing, as occasionally in the Bible; or they are clothed and mixed with sprightly imaginations as in the tales of Boccaccio and Chaucer; or they are thinly veiled with a possible modest meaning as in the puns of the Shakespearian period; but in our day, they compose a subterranean literature of themselves, like segregated harlots among books. Should I say that I blush for this face of Man? I ought to, perhaps, but I do not: all I say is, the thing is there, a very real, a very persistent image in the glass; no one who looks straight into it can avoid seeing it. Mixed with the humorous, as it often— rather usually—is, it seems to be one of the normal expressions of normal men. We deceive ourselves greatly if we fancy that Man has become purified of such imaginations because they are not used openly in modern dramas and stories, as they were in the older ones.

It may be dangerous to say it, but I believe from the evidence of literature as a whole, that a moderate amount of amusement in smut is a saving balance in the psychology of nearly every man and woman,—a sign of anchorage in a robust sanity, which takes things as they are—and laughs at them. I believe it is a much more wholesome appearance, than that betrayed in our fever-bred stories and sketches which deal with the abnormalities of men, and which are growing more and more in vogue, in spite of our cry about realism.

Personally, I am more interested in the abnormalities, which I find very fascinating. And I am very eager to know whether they will prove to be the result of the abnormal conditions of life which Modern Man has created for himself in his tampering with the forces of nature,—his strenuous industrial existence, his turning of night into day, his whirling himself over the world at a pace not at all in conformity with his native powers of locomotion, and other matters in accordance. Or will they prove to be the revenge of the dammed up, cribbed, cabined, and confined imagination, which can no longer exert itself upon externals,—since the Investigating Man has explained and mastered these or is doing so—and now turns in to wreak frightful wreck upon the mind itself?

At any rate, the fact is that we have some very curious appearances in the Mirror just now; madmen explaining their own madness, diseased men picking apart their own diseases, perverted men analyzing their own perversions, anything, everything but sane and normal men. Does it mean that in our day there is nothing interesting in good health, in well-ordered lives? Or does it mean that the rarest thing in all the world is the so-called normal man, whom tacit consent assumes to be the commonest? That everybody, while outwardly wearing a mask of reputable common sense, is within a raging conglomeration of psychic elements that hurl themselves on one another like hissing flames? Or does it mean simply that the most powerful writers are themselves diseased, and can only paint disease?

I put these questions and do not presume to answer them. I point to the mirror,—the Ibsen Drama, the Andreyev Story, the Maeterlinck Poem, the Artzibashev novel,—and I say the image is there. Explain it as you can.

For the rest, let me recall to you what I told you was my intent:

First: To insist on a more inclusive view of Literature; you see I would have it extended both up and down,—*down* even to the advertisement, the sporting page, and the surreptitious anecdote,—*up* to the fullest and most comprehensive statements of the works of reason.

Second: To suggest that readers acquire the habit of reading twice, or at least with a double intent. When serious literature is to be considered, I would insist on actually reading twice; but of course it would be both impractical and undesirable to apply such a method to most of the print we look at.

Those who are confirmed in the habits of would-be critics will have the greatest trouble in learning to read a book from the simple man's standpoint,—and yet no one can ever form a genuine appreciation of a work who has not first forgotten that he is a critic, and allowed himself to be carried away into the events and personalities depicted therein. In that first reading, also, one should train himself to feel and hear the music of language,—this great instrument which Men have jointly built, and out of which come great organ tones, and trumpet calls, and thin flute notes, sweeping and wailing, an articulate storm—a conjuring key whereby all the passions of the dead, the millions of the dead, have given to the living the power to call their ghosts out of the grave and make them walk. Yea, every word is the mystic embodiment of a thousand years of vanished passion, hope, desire, thought—all that battled through the living figures turned to dust and ashes long ago. Train your ears to hear the song of it; it helps to feel what the writer felt.

And after that read critically, with one eye on the page, so to speak, and the other on the reflection in the mirror, looking for the mind behind the work, the things which interested the author and those he wrote for.

Third: To suggest inquiry into the curious paradox of the people of the most highly evolved scientific and mechanical age taking especial delight in psychic abnormalities and morbidities,—whereby the most utterly unreasonable fictive creation becomes the greatest center of curiosity and attraction to the children of Reason.

A Mirror Maze is literature, wherein Man sees all faces of himself, lengthened here, widened there, distorted in another place, restored again to due proportion, with every possible expression on his face, from abjectness to heroic daring, from starting terror to icy courage, from love to hate and back again to worship, from the almost sublime down to the altogether grotesque,—now giant, now dwarf,—but always with one persistent character,—his *superb curiosity to see himself.*

Index

Note on use of Index: Some concepts, such as anarchism, are broad and interwoven through-out the entire work. They are listed here only in more specific or explicitly stated occurrences.